LANGUAGE AND WRITING: APPLICATIONS OF LINGUISTICS TO RHETORIC AND COMPOSITION

LANGUAGE AND WRITING: APPLICATIONS OF LINGUISTICS TO RHETORIC AND COMPOSITION

Victor Raskin and Irwin Weiser

Purdue University

ABLEX Publishing Corporation
Norwood, New Jersey 07648

Library of Congress Cataloging-in-Publication Data
Raskin, Victor, 1944–
Language and writing: applications of linguistics to rhetoric and composition/Victor Raskin and Irwin Weiser.
p. cm.
Bibliography: p.
Includes indexes
ISBN 0-89391-405-3
1. English language—Rhetoric—Study and teaching. 2. Linguistics. 3. English language—Composition and exercises—Study and teaching. I. Weiser, Irwin. II. Title.
PE1404.R37 1987 86-17753
808'.042'07—dc19 CIP

Ablex Publishing Corporation
355 Chestnut Street
Norwood, New Jersey 07648

8-1-90

Table of Contents

Acknowledgments

The authors have profited greatly from the intellectually stimulating environment in the Department of English at Purdue University created by the active cooperation between the graduate programs in English Linguistics and in Rhetoric and Composition. The interdepartmental graduate seminar in rhetoric and composition offered every semester for a number of years has been a most useful forum for exchanging ideas and broadening one's perspectives.

Victor Raskin's thinking on the limits and methods of linguistic applications to rhetoric and composition has been affected by systematic complaints from his colleagues and students in that field about the narrowmindedness and dogmaticity of linguists. He learned a great deal about the mysterious way the rhetorician's mind works from numerous friendly debates with graduate students in rhetoric and composition in his linguistics seminars. Frequent discussions with colleagues in rhetoric and composition in the various dissertation committees, the usual meeting place for linguists and rhetoricians, also helped considerably. Conversations with Janice Lauer, Kathleen Yancey, Katherine Rowan, and Julie Farrar were particularly useful. Working with Julie Farrar in a couple of his seminars also contributed a great deal to his understanding of communication techniques which work best in a dialogue with a rhetorician.

Irwin Weiser would like to thank the Department of English at Purdue University, especially Professor Leon Gottfried, Head of the Department, for granting him released time in the fall of 1985 to complete the first draft of this book.

Inappropriate as it may sound, the authors would like to thank each other. We both learned much, not only about one another's discipline, but, through our efforts to answer one another's questions, about our own, especially as it was seen by the other. Our collaboration has been mutually rewarding, and we encourage others in our fields to engage in such interactions.

We wish to thank John Battenburg for his speedy and efficient compilation of the Subject Index. We would also like to thank Ann Moore and Maydene Crosby, word-processing secretaries in the Department of English, who helped us through the intricacies of printing the final draft of this text.

Acknowledgments

Preface

In recent years, rhetoric has enjoyed renewed scholarly attention based in part upon the concerns of writing teachers and researchers. In many American universities, graduate programs have begun which emphasize the relationship between rhetoric and composition studies, programs which because of the complex nature of human communication are often interdisciplinary. Rhetoricians and writing researchers read the theories and study the methods of fields such as psychology, sociology, and anthropology in their efforts to learn how people use language to learn, to express feelings, to convey information, to persuade. Each of these disciplines has contributed to our understanding of how cognitive, social, and cultural factors interplay in writing specifically and in language use generally. Rhetoric and composition has also turned to linguistics as an obvious, perhaps the most obvious, discipline which can provide information about the way we use language to make meaning. It has always been assumed that linguistics, because it is the formal study of language, has much to offer those interested in writing, but there has not been, until now, a thorough study of the specific problems in rhetoric and composition which linguistics can shed light upon or of the ways in which linguistics can, and should, go about doing that. This book is such a study.

We begin by presenting, in Chapters 1–3, problems which writing teachers and researchers confront and which seem to us to be clearly language-related. We discuss word-, sentence-, and discourse-related problems which can be identified in the language the writer uses. We begin by identifying these problems since we believe, as will be made explicit in Chapter 15, that interdisciplinary applications must occur because there exist problems in one field which the theories and methods of another can address. We do not think that it is legitimate or fruitful to arm oneself with a theory or method from one discipline and go hunting for places to use it. Thus the topics discussed in the first three chapters provide the problems in rhetoric and composition which we will address through linguistics. These three chapters are written largely in a style typical for writings in rhetoric and composition, and they are relatively free of linguistic terminology. In fact, some linguistic terms are used there as they normally are in rhetoric and composition, which may be unacceptable in linguistics. Thus, for instance, we discuss the 'subject—verb—object' structure of the sentence, a common phrase in the composition literature but unacceptable in linguistics because 'subject' and 'object' are relational terms while 'verb' is a part of speech—the correct linguistic usage would be 'subject—predicate—object' (linguistics itself is not quite sinless in this respect: in typology, it is customary to talk about SVO and SOV languages).

Chapters 4–9 are a concise, self-contained introduction to linguistics, intended to provide rhetoricians and writing researchers with a basis for current linguistic theory and practice. Numerous examples demonstrate how linguistic theories are translated into linguistic analysis, not only to illustrate the theory but also to provide readers with background to understand the applications which follow as well as with guidance for self-instruction in any particular problem or aspect of linguistics, if necessary and/or desirable. The exposition in these chapters is geared specifically for people in rhetoric and composition, and while all the basics are addressed, much more "coverage" is given to those areas of linguistics which are likely to be of more immediate use to the intended audience. The exposition also focuses on the positive content of the concepts, ideas, and methods, while staying away as much as possible from the numerous controversies. The resulting short cuts, brutal simplifications, and crude approximations will upset some fellow linguists, especially those with partisan views, and still serve our purpose here well. Those colleagues may be assuaged if they think of these chapters as a kind of the "common-denominator" introduction. It should be born in mind, however, that in spite of this veiled disclaimer, this introduction does provide the foundation of modern linguistics and the starting point for all current issues and controversies. It cannot be mistaken for a state-of-the-art overview, which would require much more space even if it were possible to write it. Such an overview would include "heresies" which deny the existence of the phoneme in phonology and revise the concept of transformation in syntax. It is possible that in the process of applying linguistics to rhetoric and composition a scholar might want to go into some such particular linguistic approach. It is impossible, however, to do that without having absorbed the material of Chapters 4–9 first.

It is fair to say that this is one of those books that need a double introduction or two inputs, as it were. Most interdisciplinary works are like that. The first three chapters introduce readers unfamiliar with writing research, e.g., linguists, to problems in rhetoric and composition. The following six chapters introduce readers familiar with rhetoric and composition to linguistic theories and methods.

Chapter 10, immediately following the linguistic introduction, is geared even more towards rhetoric and composition. It provides a brief overview of up-to-date linguistic ideas, methods, and theories, most notably the given-new contract and script-based semantics, which might bear significantly on writing. While the number of bibliographic references in the introduction is deliberately reduced to a minimum, Chapter 10 is much more generous in this respect.

In general, Chapters 10–14 demonstrate how linguistics can be applied to some of the problems discussed in Chapters 1–3, thus illuminating the origins of those problems. Chapters 11–13 examine selected problems in more detail. Characteristically, while Chapters 1–3 are written in a style and with a terminology largely unaffected by linguistics, Chapters 11–13 draw heavily upon the ideas and terminology of Chapters 4–10. Our intention in the analysis of selected problems is to demonstrate that linguistics can often help rhetoricians and composition instructors understand why some problems occur, though it will become clear that we do not believe that every language-related problem in composition can be solved, at least completely, by a linguistic application.

In Chapter 14 we discuss how linguistic knowledge can help writing teachers to develop pedagogical strategies and address problems in the context of a process-oriented writing course. We turn from a discussion of language problems in isolation to an extensive analysis of the problems of student writers as they compose whole texts, and we identify both those problems which linguistics can illuminate and those which are non-linguistic. Chapter 15 continues to discuss this distinction. In it, we outline the limits of legitimate applications of one field to another, and, for the first time, suggest a distinction between appropriate and non-appropriate metaphorical extensions of linguistics. Neither linguistics nor any other field can address all of the issues which are relevant to understanding why some texts succeed and others fail, why some are adequate and others excellent. As we point out, there are issues in rhetoric and composition which are clearly extra-linguistic, just as there are areas within linguistics which do not correlate to problems in rhetoric and composition. The two fields are, indeed, distinct, but there is much the rhetorician and the writing teacher can gain from a knowledge of linguistics.

The book attempts to outline the goal, format, direction, and principles of execution for legitimate and fruitful applications of linguistics to rhetoric and composition. Together, these form elements of an applied linguistic theory for rhetoric and composition, a *sine qua non* for any useful effort in this area. The book cannot, and does not, contain all linguistic applications to writing—it suggests some of them; our readers, we trust, will discover others. We do believe that their findings will conform by necessity to the theoretical framework we have developed for all applications of linguistics to rhetoric and composition.

* * *

Besides the usual bibliographic references, the book contains a large number of internal crossreferences. Material in other chapters is referred to in two possible ways. A reference to the text is made as follows, "Chapter X, Section Y(.Z)," e.g., "see Chapter 4, Section 3" or "see Chapter 8, Section 3.2.1"). A reference to an example follows this format "(#) in Chapter X," e.g., "cf. (23) in Chapter 5." References within the same chapter were made by section or example number only, e.g., "see Section 3.2.1" or "cf. (23)."

A note on non-sexist usage also seems to be necessary. It is one of the ironies of this book that the limits of our language affect our own writing. English does not easily yield to social consciousness in the matter of personal pronoun use. Although we have tried, whenever possible, to avoid the generic use of the masculine pronoun, often our discussion by necessity focuses on the situation of a single writer. In such cases, we have weighed the linguistic awkwardness of the repeated use of *he or she* or *his or her* against the total rejection of the generic *he* or *his* by some readers. The balance sometimes tilted one way and sometimes to the other. Our explanation, not totally satisfactory perhaps, is that, as we point out in Chapter 9, language conventions change slowly, often more slowly than social conventions, and as language users, we must conform to the conventions which enable us to communicate most effectively. Even when we do use the masculine pronouns generically, the usage is not intentionally sexist. We truly anticipate that even the most feminist readers will discover more serious and interesting problems in the substance of the book.

This preface is the only part of the book which we wrote together. Otherwise, every chapter or section was written by one of us. Thus, Weiser authored Chapters 1–3, 11–14, and Chapter 15, Section 4. Complementarily, Raskin authored Chapters 4–10 and Chapter 15, Sections 1–3. Every sentence of the book was read, discussed and, therefore, fully coauthored by both of us but the primary responsibility still lies with the author of each part.

Victor Raskin

Irwin Weiser

West Lafayette, Indiana
June 1986

CHAPTER 1

The Word

SECTION 1. DICTION

We begin our discussion of diction with a consideration of factors that influence a writer's choice of words as he or she struggles to convey ideas. Certainly, a writer's choice of a particular word involves his knowledge of words. His vocabulary is much smaller than the more than 150,000 entries contained in current college-edition dictionaries. And each writer's vocabulary runs the spectrum from those words he knows well and uses correctly through those words he is familiar with but does not use, and includes those words the writer misuses because he does not really understand them. Student writers in particular often misuse words because they wish to sound learned. They attempt to use a word they have read or heard, but because they do not understand it, they use it inappropriately. A second factor influencing a writer's lexical choices involves his ability to recognize nuances, connotations, multiple meanings, and levels of formality. Inexperienced writers may not be able to recognize that *house* and *home,* though partially synonymous, differ in both meaning and connotation since *home* carries with it associations of warmth, affection, safety, and so on, which *house* does not. Similarly, inexperienced writers often undeliberately mix slang with more formal language, either because they are not aware of the conventions that guide a particular type of discourse, or because their vocabularies are limited and they do not know the appropriate word for the context, or because, as suggested earlier, they are trying to conform to an unfamiliar style. Rhetorical awareness affects diction, too, since consciousness of audience, purpose, and subject enables writers to make lexical decisions appropriate for their goals. Finally, word choices involve a writer's ability to distinguish between abstract and concrete words and to use specific rather than ambiguous words. Effective writers consciously *use* their vocabularies to communicate their ideas with precision and, often, originality.

Shaughnessy (1977:189) points out that "errors in vocabulary already attest to the student's knowledge, at some level, of the words he is using (or misusing)." Her point here is worth consideration. Writers can choose only from those words they have heard or read in context or that they already have in their active vocabularies. Their mistakes arise from incomplete knowledge of words, particularly from incomplete knowledge of the elements of connotation, formality, and rhetorical appropriateness mentioned earlier. Those words that are totally unfamiliar to students do not lead them to error simply because they do not, indeed cannot, attempt to use them. Certainly many students have meager vocabularies, and some kinds of diction problems—for example, using common nouns and verbs such as *thing* and *do* instead of more specific words, or mixing formal and informal words—may be attributed to a writer's small repertoire of words from which to choose. Studies of vocabulary growth offer the writing teacher guidance in such cases, but these studies do not address the kinds of **errors in diction** that the next section describes.

1.1. Categories of Diction Errors

Diction errors may include both the coining of words because of their phonological or visual similarity to other words or the misuse of legitimate words because the writer is only partially familiar with the meaning(s) of the words he uses.

1.1.1. Non-words and Word Blends. In her analysis of the errors of basic writers, Shaughnessy (1977:190) provides the following examples of sentences containing non-words:

(1) (i) I wish my life to be *forfilling* with happiness.
(ii) I would like to *coulternate* childrens [*sic*] mind [*sic*].
(iii) With my capacities of learning brought forth by my education, I can be *subcepticle* to learn a variety of things.

In each of these sentences, the author has invented a word with a phonological similarity to the word he wishes to use (*fulfilling, cultivate, susceptible*). The approximate spelling of such words suggests that the writer's familiarity is aural, that he probably has not seen the word in print—or if he has, that he has not associated it with the word he has heard. And although the writer has probably heard the word being used, he has not heard it correctly or often enough to distinguish its pronunciation.

Whereas the non-words in the previous examples are a writer's approximation of a single specific, identifiable existing word, word blends are the result of the writer's confusion of two words. The following sentence serves as an example:

(2) An individual may find that placing capital letters in the right place is an easy task, while word division is *notrocious*.

Notrocious is apparently a blend of *notorious* and *atrocious*. Although one might argue that neither word is really appropriate, it is possible to see how a writer with incomplete knowledge of each word might be led to such an error. In this case, the student wants to suggest that correctly dividing words between syllables at the end of a line is a common problem for writers. She knows that she needs a word with a negative meaning, and as she thinks about her choices, two words that she imperfectly knows blend. The student apparently has the idea that *notorious* can mean "well-known," and that it carries a negative connotation. In addition, the student has knowledge of the negative meaning of *atrocious*. But since the student is not completely familiar with either word, her consciousness of her need to finish her sentence with a negative word, coupled with the similar sound and spelling of the two words, causes her to combine them. Thus two words with semantic and phonetic similarities become blended into one nonexistent word.

1.1.2. Incorrect Words. Word blends are created when writers combine words that are semantically and phonetically similar. Another kind of diction error can occur when a writer chooses a word phonetically similar to but semantically different from the appropriate word. Sometimes the words are quite different semantically, as when a writer uses *pacific* instead of *specific* or confuses *loose* and *lose*. In the latter example, the confusion can be explained by the atypical pronunciation of the *o* in *lose* as *oo* and by the inconsistencies of English spelling which make *lose* rhyme with *choose* while *loose* and *moose* rhyme with each other but not with *lose* or *choose*. In other cases, such as in the substitution of *ideal* for *idea* in (3), there may be a distant etymological connection between the words, although the student is probably not aware of it. Nor is the student who confuses *stagnant* and *stagnate* aware that he is confusing an adjective with a verb. These errors occur because students are more attuned to phonological similarities than to semantic or orthographic differences.

(3) I have a good ideal about that.

1.1.3. Incorrect Derivations. In her study of the errors that basic writers make, Shaughnessy (1977:75, 190, 213) emphasizes that errors with derivational suffixes appear frequently in the writing of these very poorly prepared students. She provides examples of sentences like (4.i–ii) to demonstrate the kinds of difficulties a student may have if he "does not know the forms (in the sense that he does not habitually produce them in speech) or [if] in his concentration on getting all the letters of words down on the page he forgets the grammatical constraints of his sentence and simply writes the form that comes most easily" (75).

(4) (i) People are judged by what they *product* on the job.
(ii) He works without *supervise*.

Such problems are compounded by the large number of derivational suffixes used to indicate a single part of speech, particularly nouns (*-ment, -tion,*

-ance, -ence, -ism, -ness, -ty, -ship, and many more). Not only does this variety of suffixes confuse some writers, it also leads to spelling errors and, for readers, to difficulty in following the syntax of a sentence.

1.1.4. Unidiomatic Prepositions. Students who write *to dispense of* or *regardless to* are grappling with a problem which, like the problem of incorrect derivations, is complicated by the apparent lack of rules to govern what is correct. These same students have no difficulty in using prepositions correctly to convey a specific location, for example, in a phrase like *out the window* or *to the left*. But when prepositions are used idiomatically, as in phrases like *to dispense with* and *in regard to,* students are hard-pressed to understand why only a specific preposition is correct. And teachers are hard-pressed to explain the idiom.

1.1.5. Redundancy. Redundancy occurs when writers unintentionally repeat semantic elements. In some cases, redundancy is the result of the writer's failure to recognize that a prefix conveys a specific meaning which renders the use of a second word unnecessary. Such is the case in phrases like *return back*. The word *back* is redundant since the prefix *re-* means *back* or *again*. Another form of redundancy occurs when writers ignore the denotation of a word and follow it when a prepositional phrase which repeats a quality inherent in the original word itself. *Blue in color, heavy in weight, soft to touch* are examples of such phrases. Since blue is a color, heavy is a quality of weight, and soft is a quality of texture, such phrases are redundant. However, not all such phrases are necessarily redundant. Although *light in weight* follows the same pattern of the phrases listed above, in some contexts it may be employed to distinguish between something which is not heavy and something which is not dark. The two possible meanings of *light* may otherwise lead to ambiguity. Redundancy may also be the result of unnecessary modifiers, as in *mix together, past memories,* or *advanced planning* (Axelrod and Cooper, 1985:612). *Mix* means *to combine* or *to put together, memories* are about the past, and *planning* is done in advance of an activity. Thus, in each of the redundant phrases, the modifier repeats meaning already contained in the word it modifies. Redundancy may also occur when words with similar meanings are paired with one another, such as *full and complete, precise and accurate,* and *each and every*. These pairs are often used to create emphasis or to enhance the rhythm of a sentence, but more frequently they are employed automatically by writers who have not considered their redundancy. Though redundancy rarely prevents a reader from understanding and is not a serious diction error, it nevertheless leads to flabby prose.

1.1.6. Inappropriate Context. The student who writes about a *maladjusted environment* is likely to make his point, but his readers will also recognize that *maladjusted* is not an appropriate modifier for *environment*. Such errors occur when writers do not recognize the contextual limits determining whether or not a particular word can be used. In this example, the writer has failed to realize that *maladjusted* describes a person's inability to adjust to an environment or situation and must therefore modify a word with human qualities (or at the very least with qualities of life, since one might legitimately, if metaphorically, refer to a maladjusted pet). The correct use of count and noncount adjectives is also a contextual matter. People who write *There was a large amount of cars in the parking lot* or *We saw less pigeons as we left the city behind* are missing the contextual cue which should tell them to choose the words *number* and *fewer* if they are writing about countable, quantifiable nouns. And of course the same error occurs when one uses *number* and *fewer* to refer to what cannot be counted.

SECTION 2. USAGE ERRORS

An examination of several handbooks of grammar and usage quickly demonstrates that the term 'usage' means different things to different writers about language. For some, usage refers to the use of the correct word or form of a word—those matters we have identified as having to do with diction. For others, usage errors include fragments, fused sentences, and comma splices—errors we will discuss in chapter 2. Shaughnessy offers one of the more useful definitions of what we mean by usage errors; she refers to "errors that do not seriously impair meaning" (1977:90). Though our categories of usage errors do not correspond exactly with her "common errors," we find it helpful to employ her definition as we survey the wide range of serious and not-so-serious usage problems.

2.1. Categories of Usage Errors

The two categories of usage errors discussed below illustrate why such errors do not usually prevent communication from occurring. Both agreement errors and double negatives are typical in many dialects of English, and thus both are familiar to most native speakers. In standard English, however, both are considered to be usage errors.

2.1.1. Agreement Errors. The complex relationships of words that are based on number, person, and gender often cause problems for inexperienced writers. Not only must subjects and verbs agree in number, but pronouns must agree with their antecedents in number, person, and gender. Undoubtedly, sentences such as 5.i–iii) are incorrect, but the agreement errors in these sentences do not render them incomprehensible.

(5) (i) They *was* the first people to arrive.
(ii) A person who wishes to succeed should realize that *they* will have to work hard.

(iii) If *they* make *their* career choices carefully, *one* can find satisfaction in *his* work.

Indeed, some pronoun-antecedent agreement errors go unrecognized by the majority of readers. Many would overlook the inconsistency between the singular subject *person* and the plural pronoun *they* in (5.ii). The indefinite pronouns *one, anyone, everyone, everybody,* and so on are the source of many agreement errors. Their ambiguity seems to invite the use of plural pronouns or shifts between singular and plural pronouns, as in sentences such as (5.iii). And a few textbook writers have suggested that the use of plural pronouns to refer to these indefinite pronouns might be an acceptable way to avoid what some consider the sexist use of third person singular masculine pronouns in cases in which the sex of the person referred to is either unmentioned or unknown. Thus (6.i) would be preferred to (6.ii).

(6) (i) Everyone should bring *their* books.
(ii) Everyone should bring *his* books.

Though shifts in person are more often recognized by readers, Shaughnessy points out that writers frequently do not notice them. She also points out that such shifts "are almost invariably movements from first- or third-person pronouns to the second person, *you*," and cites as an example "A lot of people have been told if *they* want a good job *you* have to stay in school" (1977:113).

Subject-verb structures such as (7.i–ii) are common to some dialects of American English and often appear in the writing of those whose dialect varies from formal edited English.

(7) (i) They was always late.
(ii) He don't usually come on time.
(iii) The decisions of the president was unpopular.
(iv) There is several reasons that you should be on time.
(v) Jack and Jill is going up the hill.
(vi) The dogs and the cat plays together nicely.

More frequently, subject-verb agreement errors occur when a phrase or clause separates the subject and verb of a sentence. In (7.iii), the writer's selection of a singular verb results from the proximity of the singular head of the prepositional phrase, *president*. The writer mistakes this singular noun for the subject of the sentence, apparently forgetting or ignoring the real subject of the sentence, *decisions,* which is plural and therefore requires a plural verb. A third common subject-verb agreement error occurs in sentences beginning with the expletive *there*. Often writers automatically follow *there* with the singular noun *is* and ignore the number of the actual subject which follows the verb. The result is a sentence such as (7.iv). Here the error seems to occur because the writer does not anticipate the plural subject *reasons*. Other common subject-verb agreement errors occur with compound subjects. Though occasionally errors appear when the compound subjects are the same number (7.v), more often the mistake occurs when the second of the pair is singular and the first is plural (7.vi). In these cases, the writer does not recognize that the compound subject is to be treated as plural, even if the individual nouns are singular. And writers who learn this rule may have difficulty understanding the difference of a compound subject joined by the conjunction *or: Jack or Jill is going up the hill.* This structure appears quite similar to the compound subject joined by *and;* yet *or,* like *neither . . . nor* and *either . . . or,* indicates a singular subject and verb if the nouns are singular. Collective nouns also present subject-verb agreement problems since they are usually considered singular (8.i) but can be treated as plural when individual members of the group are acting separately (8.ii).

(8) (i) The committee is ready to make its report.
 (ii) The committee were unable to agree on a plan.

In (8.i) the word *committee* is used as a unit, but in (8.ii) *committee* refers to individual members of the committee.

2.1.2. Double Negatives. The double negative, like some types of agreement errors mentioned in the previous section, is a feature common to some nonstandard dialects. Often, in fact, it appears in conjunction with the *He don't* agreement error, as in (9.i).

(9) (i) He don't have *no* excuse for being late.
 (ii) We do not have *no* time today.

The double negative can, of course, appear independently of such agreement errors, as it does in (9.ii). This error, like the phrase *blue in color* discussed earlier, can be considered an example of redundancy since those who use the double negative apparently fail to see that they need only *not* or *no,* rather than both. But because the double negative is considered incorrect, not merely unnecessarily repetitious, it can be classified as a usage error.

SECTION 3. SPEECH VERSUS WRITING

One could argue that all the problems writers face are the result of differences between speech and writing. Conventions governing punctuation are of no concern to speakers since they can rely on inflection, tone, and pauses to indicate, for example, where sentences end or whether they are asking a question or making a statement. Writers, on the other hand, must learn to use puncutation not only to approximate the rhythm and tone of speech, but also to conform with non-speech-related conventions. For example, writers must learn to use the semicolon instead of the comma to join two independent clauses not joined by a coordinate conjunction or to use colons to introduce formal lists or certain explanatory clauses. Similarly, spelling is important only to written language; it simply does not apply to speech. The organization of discourse into paragraphs is another feature of written language with which speakers need not be concerned. And in conversation, we are less concerned with the use of transitions to indicate shifts of ideas or of cohesive ties to suggest the relationship of one idea to the next. Such devices matter little in speech since normally our conversations are based on an interplay among the participants: Speakers and listeners trade roles, and listeners can ask for clarification of ideas that they do not understand. Even when one person does most of the talking, listeners provide cues as to whether they understand, cues which can be physical, such as a puzzled or inquiring look, a nod or shake of the head, and cues which can be verbal, such as saying *I see,* or *yes,* or *uh huh*. In writing, where such interplay and feedback are not possible, writers have the task of providing cues in the form of words and phrases which help readers understand how ideas are related to one another.

In the following pages, the kinds of differences between speech and writing just mentioned will be distinguished as **print-code** and **non-print-code** features. The former include features such as capitalization and puncutation, which are conventions of written langauge and are governed by rules, while the latter refer to matters of coherence, context, voice, and so on, which the lack of interplay between writer and reader makes necessary. The third part of this section will analyze the relationship between dialect and standard written English.

3.1. Print-Code Features

In order to record language so that it is intelligible to others, writers learn and conform to certain conventions necessary only because they are writing rather than speaking. These print-code conventions are visual clues to readers which enable them to understand the marks on the page. One of the more obvious print-code conventions is the formation of letters. The instruction in handwriting which is a part of the curriculum of elementary school students enables them to participate in written communication by mastering the shapes of letters and the means of connecting individual letters to form words that others will be able to read. As we all know from a variety of personal experiences, the more idiosyncratic a person's handwriting, the more difficult it is to understand what that person wants to communicate. A similarly fundamental print-code convention is that of leaving space between words to indicate their boundaries. Asentenceinwhichwordsarenot-separatedbyspacesmaybeintelligible, but only if the reader is willing to make an extraordinary effort. And most readers, understandably, are not willing to do so. The print-code convention of spacing between words is so fundamental that even the most unskilled writers conform to it most of the time, and most writers either learn to form letters clearly enough that they can be read or avoid the problem by typing or by dictating for someone else's transcription. Thus neither of these print-code conventions causes writers or readers major difficulty. Such is not the case with the print-code conventions of capitalization, punctuation, and spelling.

In speech, proper nouns are not identified any differently from other words, but in writing, conventions of the print-code in English require writers to capitalize the first letter of these words, as well as the first letter in the first word of a sentence. Capitalization of names usually offers little difficulty, even for unskilled writers. Errors are more likely to occur when a proper name is used in conjunction with a title, such as *Uncle Jack*. Two common errors, both the results of the writer's overgeneralization of an imperfectly learned convention, may occur with such titles. First, the writer may fail to capitalize the first letter of the title because he does not recognize that it is considered part of the person's name and because he knows that while proper names do have the first letter capitalized, words modifying them do not. The possibility of error is compounded by the fact that many words that show kinship are not usually used as titles or do not have the first letter capitalized: (10.i) is incorrect, but (10.ii) is correct.

(10) (i) My *S*ister Jane is coming to visit.
(ii) My *U*ncle Jack is coming to visit.
(iii) My *U*ncle, Jack, is coming to visit.

At the same time, (10.iii) is incorrect because the word *uncle* is not being used as a title or part of a proper name. When the word *uncle* and similar titles are used independent of proper names, the first letter is not capitalized. This distinction leads to the second common error caused by overgeneralization of a rule: the capitalization of the initial letter in such words wherever they appear. For instance, a writer who has learned to capitalize in such titles when they appear with a proper name might also produce sentences such as (11.i–ii) if he has not learned the limits of the capitalization rule.

(11) (i) My *A*unt gave me her old car.
(ii) His *U*ncle and *A*unt moved to Arizona recently.

Some kinship titles produce additional difficulty because they are often used in place of proper nouns or names. Capitalization conventions dictate (12.i–ii).

(12) (i) I'm always glad when *M*om and *D*ad phone me.
(ii) I'm always glad when my *m*om and *d*ad phone me.

In the first sentence, *Mom* and *Dad* are used as proper names; they are how the writer addresses his parents—instead, we presume, of calling them John and Mary. In the second sentence, the writer's use of the possessive pronoun *my* changes *mom* and *dad* from proper names to simple titles.

The writer who masters the rules for capitalizing the first letter of kinship titles can safely apply them to other titles, such as "*P*rofessor Smith," but "my economics *p*rofessor." Of course, these rules have exceptions, for instance, the convention of capitalizing the initial letter in exclusive titles, those that apply to only one person at a time, as in (13).

(13) The *P*ope will be traveling to South America soon.

It is beyond the scope of this study to survey all the conventions of capitalization by which writers must abide. Many seem inconsistent, such as those that dictate that the first letter is capitalized in the names of days of the week or months while this is not the case for seasons, or that the names of directions (*north, south, east,* and *west*) have an initial capital only when they refer to specific regions, not when they refer to compass headings. Other conventions may confuse writers who fail to see the difference between the name *Main Street* and the use of the word *street* as a common noun in *The name of that street is Oak.*

One additional element of capitalization which must be mentioned is the apparently random capitalization of letters, especially initial letters of words, which characterizes some writers. Shaughnessy (1977) offers several explanations for random capitalization. First, she suggests, writers may capitalize to emphasize a particular word or group of words. Second, she proposes, apparently random capitalization may be connected with the writer's sense of where new ideas or sentences begin. Thus, writers who do not use terminal punctuation consistently or correctly may nevertheless use capital letters where they wish to indicate a new sentence. Shaughnessy's third explanation of incorrect capitalization, like her first two, emphasizes the distinction between speaking and the print-code demands of writing: She points out that for some writers, making the uppercase letter may be easier than making the lowercase one. And though she does not say so, one can infer that the failure to capitalize may in some cases be the result of the opposite phenomenon.

Punctuation, like capitalization, is clearly a print-code convention, and like capitalization follows rules that have no bearing in speech. As mentioned earlier, sometimes punctuation parallels speech patterns. This is particularly true of exclamation points and question marks, which are intended to duplicate intonation. It is also true of periods and commas used to indicate pauses between sentences or parts of sentences. But many handbooks of grammar and usage caution writers against using 'natural pauses' as a guide for punctuation, and certainly such pauses cannot account for the large number of rules governing correct punctuation or the variety of punctuation available to writers, or the options available within the bounds of the rules. It may, for example, seem logical to have two forms of punctuation, periods and commas, to indicate the difference between sentence boundaries and smaller units of meaning within sentences. Such distinctions may seem to be based on differences one can also detect in speech as major and minor pauses. But colons, semicolons, hyphens, dashes, quotation marks, and apostrophes serve print-code functions that are not bound to any specific parallel in speech. Often they help readers interpret what is meant in the same way context or intonation may do in speech, as in the case of the quotation marks (or absence of them) in (14.i–iii).

(14) (i) He said John said it was too late to go.
(ii) He said, "John said it was too late to go."
(iii) He said, "John said, 'It was too late to go.'"

In (14.i), the absence of quotation marks indicates indirect reporting of speech. There is no indication that the writer is conveying the exact words of either character, *he* or *John*. In (14.ii), the quotation marks tell readers that the speaker identified as *He* spoke the words about John and what John said, but there is still no indication that John spoke the exact words attributed to him. (14.iii), with two sets of quotation marks, provides readers with different information. They are told both what *He* said and the exact words John spoke, the latter indicated by the internal quotation marks. In speech, stress and intonation would probably provide the listener with the cues that the quotation marks provide in writing. These examples, by the way, also demonstrate the purely conventional, rule-governed nature of punctuation in the way periods are placed inside the closing quotation marks.

Indeed, as often as punctuation suggests a tie to speech or offers a way of interpreting meaning clearly, it more often is governed by rules that are purely conventions of the print-code. As was suggested earlier, the rule dictating that a semicolon be used to join two independent clauses not connected by a coordinating conjunction has no bearing to spoken language. In writing, the semicolon is intended to suggest a syntactically more complex unit than does the comma, but it does so only because that is a convention users of written English have accepted. The comma splice, which most usage handbooks and English teachers interpret as a major error, may occur not because the writer fails to recognize two syntactic units—the very fact that the writer has used punctuation between the two clauses indicates that he realizes the need for separation. Instead, it may be that the writer does not know the print-code rule that makes the comma an incorrect choice of punctuation. Even if the comma splice does occur because the writer fails to see that he is joining two independent clauses, such recognition matters only in writing since speakers do not have to indicate clause endings in any particular way. (In fact, as will be discussed later, speakers often do not use complete clauses or sentences. Conversation is filled with fragments.)

Apostrophe-related errors are another example of punctuation problems caused by print-code conventions. The use of the apostrophe to mark omitted letters in contractions has no parallel in speech, and in writing it is usually superfluous, since it does not indicate a pause or otherwise contribute to our understanding of the word when we read silently or our pronunciation when we read aloud. *Doesnt* looks odd to us only because we are used to the convention of using the apostrophe, not because it is hard to understand or read. Similarly, the use of the apostrophe to indicate possessive case is a print-code convention which is only partially related to pronunciation. In speech, we recognize the difference between possessive and plural by context. In writing, we have a variety of rules that govern whether we use *'s* or *'* to indicate possessive case. And although in isolated sentences the apostrophe may make meaning more clear, in actual discourse context provides sufficient information to allow readers to understand what the writer intends. For example, in (15), the omission of the apostrophe makes it impossible to determine if one boy or more than one boy are being identified.

(15) The *boys* hats are on the shelf.

One might assume that since *boys* is plural, the hats of more than one boy are on the shelf, but that assumption could not be made with much confidence. However, sentences such as this do not appear without a context, and earlier in the discourse (or perhaps later, if this were the first sentence of a text) readers would find out how many boys were being written about. Indeed, one might argue that the apostrophe is more trouble than it's worth, especially considering the inconsistencies of its correct use. In the previous sentence, for example, the contraction *it's* is consistent with the rule for using apostrophes to form contractions, but the possessive *its,* like other possessive pronouns, is formed without an apostrophe. Frequently writers, especially inexperienced writers, are confused by this inconsistency and use the contraction to indicate the possessive or, if they are aware that *it's* is the equivalent of *it is,* use *its'* as a possessive pronoun. Similarly, the convention of using *'s* to indicate the plural of letters, numerals, and words used as words (as in "Do not make your *a's* look like *o's*") not only adds a third use of the apostrophe to the print-code, but also leads, through overgeneralization, to the incorrect formation of other plurals by adding *'s.* Signs such as *Clean Used Car's Sold Here* are common evidence of this confusion.

What has been said about quotation marks, semicolons, and apostrophes is also true of most other marks of punctuation. Our use of colons, hyphens, and dashes is dictated by print-code conventions, not by an effort to duplicate speech. Such is also true of dividing discourse into paragraphs and indenting the first line of each new paragraph. Paragraphing, like the capitalization of the initial letter in the first word of a sentence and like punctuation, provides readers with cues about how ideas are organized in a text. Initial-letter capitalization and punctuation indicate the beginning and ending of individual sentences and the links between ideas within those sentences. The convention of spacing between or indenting paragraphs indicates larger units of meaning, the boundaries of which are determined conceptually and which have no equivalent in speech.

A final print-code feature that distinguishes writing from speech is spelling. Like the other features mentioned here, spelling is relevant to writers and readers, but not to speakers. Conventionalized spelling enables writers to communicate not only with a contemporary audience but also with an audience in the future. Were spelling to be idiosyncratic or were it to change dramatically over a relatively short period of time, written communication would not be possible. Difficulties with English spelling are often the result of its frequent independence from pronunciation and the variety of ways the language allows us to make the same sound. Examples of words spelled quite differently from how they are pronounced include *often,* the preferred pronunciation of which, according to Webster's *New World Dictionary,* is *ôf'n,* and other words with unpronounced letters, like *knock* or *knight*. The word *night* is commonly misspelled *nite,* and although this misspelling can probably be attributed to a deliberate intention on the part of advertisers to draw attention to the word, the frequent use of this spelling has led to its becoming accepted as correct by a large number of people who seem to use it unself-consciously. The current interest in diet and fitness has resulted in a similar deliberate misspelling of the word *light* as *lite* (perhaps with the intention of making the word itself lighter by a letter). This misspelling, too, possibly because it is so widespread, is used frequently by writers who otherwise conform to standard spelling. In fact, *lite* replaces *light* not only in situations referring to weight, but also when the writer is concerned with visible light, as in *Please turn on the lite*. What makes these misspellings seem logical is that they more closely reflect the pronunciation of the word than do the correct spellings with the silent *gh*. Adding to the complexity of English spelling is the fact that the same sound can be designated by a variety of spellings. Shaughnessy (1977) points out that the spellings of phonemes such as *sh, er, f,* and *j,* the long vowels, and the schwa sound—which has twenty-two spellings—are especially hard to predict. Some errors, though not involving the actual incorrect spelling of words, seem to occur both because the same sound can be represented by more than one spelling and because pronunciation differs from spelling. *Could've,* the contraction for *could have,* is frequently written as *could of,* reflecting both the pronunciation of the contraction and the fact that *'ve* and *of* sound similar. Similarly, many writers omit the *d* to indicate the past participle in phrases like *used to* and *supposed to* because in speech the final *d* blends with the initial *t.* Thus reliance on sound and pronunciation leads to error. Homophones such as *their, there,* and *they're; by* and *buy;* and *two, too,* and *to* can also cause problems for writers and readers, whereas in speech, context enables listeners to understand which word is meant and the identical pronunciation of the words is of no concern to the speaker.

Spelling, like punctuation and capitalization, is also governed by rules writers must follow which, however, have no bearing on speech. For example, one rule dictates that to form the plural of a noun ending in *y,* one must drop the *y* and add *ies,* (e.g., *baby/babies*). Another rule explains when to double the final consonant of a word before adding a suffix beginning with a vowel. Others govern whether the final silent e is retained or dropped before a suffix is added to a word. Like the other print-code conventions mentioned in this section, such spelling rules are scribal features of written language which exist to make written communication possible but which are irrelevant in spoken language.

3.2. Non-Print-Code Features

As we have seen, print-code features are physical qualities of written language, the actual marks on the page which enable writers to record and readers to process language. But while the conventions of the print-code account for some of the differences between speech and writing, they certainly do not account for all of them. Spoken and written language also differ in ways which cannot be attributed merely to the physical requirements of encoding, but which instead reflect the different dynamics of oral and written communication. Such non-print-code differences include the presence of extraverbal clues in speech, and differences in context and coherence between speech and writing.

When we speak, we rely not only on words to convey meaning, but also on what E. D. Hirsch has called "extra-verbal clues" (1977:7). These include physical clues—gestures and facial expressions—which enable us to emphasize, to express emotion, and to suggest how we wish our listeners to perceive us. Coupled with clues provided by intonation, these physical clues enrich our speech. For instance, the word *no* can be said loudly and quickly, accompanied by a frown or by pounding on the table, to indicate firmness, anger, or displeasure. But it could also be said quietly, slowly, and with a smile, as when a teacher responds to a student's incorrect response in class, in order to indicate that while the response is wrong, the nay-sayer is not angry, and in fact may be sympathetic. *No* can even be said gleefully, as when one responds to an incorrect answer in charades or a competitive quiz game. As actors and comedians must learn, timing is also an important extraverbal clue. The amount of time between the narrative of a joke and its punch line or between a comment and another's response to it can be as meaningful as the words themselves. When we speak, we use timing to make ourselves clear, and when we listen to others speak, our interpretation of what they say is influenced by their timing as well as by their words, gestures, intonation, and facial expression. When these nonverbal clues are missing, as they are in literary dialogue, the dialogue differs from actual speech because it must be more complete and coherent (Hirsch, 1977:21–23).

Actual speech always occurs within a context. We speak to someone else and in so doing establish an immediate context or situation for what we will say. We are aware of our surroundings, our relationship to the other person or people with whom we speak, and thus are also aware of much of what we can assume or not assume about how our listeners will interpret us. And the fact that our listeners are present allows them to respond to what we say, to give us feedback both through language and through nonverbal clues. As speakers, we learn to interpret a puzzled facial expression and to try to explain ourselves more fully or to ask a question like *Do you understand?* or *Am I being clear?* Because the participants can speak to one another, conversations tend to be made up of fragments, phrases, and isolated words. Speakers often fail to complete sentences before someone else, anticipating what the first speaker will say, interrupts. Hirsch (1977:21–22), citing the example of the transcripts of taped conversations used by the House Judiciary Committee during the Watergate investigation, emphasizes the difficulty of interpreting spoken discourse when one is unfamiliar with the context in which it has taken place. He points out that the committee members eventually had to listen to the tapes because the transcripts were frequently unintelligible. The words themselves could not convey information about how things were said—that is, the nonverbal clues were missing—and the fragmented nature of real speech made reading the transcripts an ineffective way to discover what the tapes revealed.

Because it does not occur within an existing context, writing must supply a context of its own (Britton 1970; Emig 1977; Hirsch 1977; Kantor and Rubin 1981). Kroll explains that "writing *typically* involves the production of texts which are explicit and autonomous, and hence distinct from conversational utterance" (1981:53). Writers and their readers do not share the same immediate temporal situation that people engaged in conversation do, nor can writers be as sure as speakers about what their audience will know. Thus written texts must be more complete and coherent than speech. Formal speeches, sermons, lectures, and so on are exceptions to this point: Although speakers and listeners generally share the same temporal and physical situation, the independent nature of these discourses, coupled with the lack of immediate feedback from listeners, makes formal oral discourse more like written language than like ordinary conversation. Indeed, because writing lacks the extraverbal clues of gesture, intonation, and expression, and because writers must compensate for the lack of feedback from and interplay with their audience, the advice often given to beginning writers to write as they speak is misleading. Spoken and written texts are not the same: The latter must be more explicit if they are to be effective, and the naturalness sought by those who give that advice cannot be attained simply by trying to imitate speech patterns in writing.

3.3. Dialect

Another reason that the advice to write as one speaks does not, as its adherents claim, lead to effective writing is that written language is far more standardized and fixed than spoken language. Each speaker's language patterns are slightly different from those of anyone else; more important, groups of native speakers of the same language speak different dialects from those of other groups (Lindemann 1982). These dialects may be socially, economically, ethnically, regionally, and/or racially influenced, and they may share features with one another. Further, although each dialect may have a distinct and distinguishable vocabulary, pronunciation, syntax, and grammar, dialects of the same language are, for the most part, mutually intelligible by native speakers of that language. Although the native of The Bronx and the native of Baton Rouge may have some initial difficulty adjusting to one another's dialect, they will be able to understand each other—or be able to make themselves understood by relying on shared vocabulary. Thus the easterner who uses the word *soda* and the midwesterner who uses the word *pop* to refer generically to any carbonated nonalcoholic beverage will be able to understand each other, if in no other way, by using the more widespread term *soft drink* or by using a specific brand name, like *Coke* or *Pepsi*. Dialects that differ in syntax or grammar may be more difficult to understand for those who do not speak the dialect, but native speakers of English, despite their differences in dialect, generally can communicate effectively with one another. (Of course, the fact that various dialects have different vocabularies or define words differently from one another can also mean that speakers of a dialect *can,* if they wish, use dialectal differences to avoid being intelligible. Smitherman (1975) gives examples of Black English that require translation in order to be understood by those unfamiliar with that dialect.) Furthermore, dialects are dynamic, changing more rapidly than written language, especially lexically. And the boundaries of dialects are fluid: As speakers are exposed to other dialects, they adopt features from them and incorporate those features into their own dialect.

Written English, on the other hand, is much more standardized, not just for American users, but for all who write in English. The print-code features discussed earlier account for part of this standardization, as do historical features like increased literacy, the growth of public education, increased and cheaper publication of books and magazines, and the greater speed with which written communications can travel over wide geographical areas (Hirsch 1977). Such standardization of the written language is necessary if the language is to reach a wide contemporary audience and if it is to endure over time. Hirsch (1977), following Haugen (1966), and Epes (1985) uses the term **grapholect** to refer to the national written standard language. Hirsch explains that "a grapholect is a normative language in ways that cannot be attributed to any dialect" (1977:44). Thus all dialects differ from the grapholect although some dialects may resemble it more closely than others.

For teachers of writing, the actual differences between dialects and the grapholect may not be as important as the recognition that such differences exist and the attitude one takes on the basis of that recognition (for a more complete discussion and bibliography, see Giannasi 1976). One of the more important points to recognize is that dialects are not merely error-filled versions of the grapholect. Linguists have pointed out that native speakers, by virtue of knowing their language, have internalized the rules governing its use (Chomsky 1957). Along these lines, Hirsch explains that "the study of oral languages in the twentieth century has demonstrated that oral speech (when uncontaminated by the influences of literacy) follows linguistic rules which are no less rigorous than those of any literate language" (1977:40). What is important to realize is that such linguistic knowledge applies to the *dialect* the speaker uses, not to the grapholect, which must be learned by *all* speakers. Of course, some dialects are more similar to the grapholect than others. Those sharing most features with the grapholect are often referred to as **standard** while those that differ greatly are called **nonstandard** (Epes 1985; Lindemann 1982), though the pejorative connotation of **nonstandard** leads many to avoid both terms, preferring instead to use phrases like 'Edited American English' or 'Standard Written English' rather than 'standard English' and to identify dialects by their users, for instance, Black American English, or simply Black English. Regardless of the names, speakers whose dialect is close to the grapholect have less difficulty mastering it, and those whose dialect is quite different have more difficulty because they must learn linguistic conventions which differ from those they use most often and know intuitively. But teachers who understand that dialects differ from the grapholect will be more likely to understand why some of their students make consistent errors when they write: They are carrying over dialect features into their writing or are attempting to adhere to an imperfectly known convention of the grapholect. (The concept of dialect interference is not accepted by all scholars. For a recent discussion of the debate, see Hartwell 1980, 1985; and Morrow 1985.)

In the 1970s, debate over the social status of dialects, especially of minority dialects, coupled with the knowledge that dialects follow internal linguistic rules of their own and that therefore all dialects are equally correct, led many teachers and scholars to question the propriety of teaching a standard dialect or of expecting students to write a version of English that differed dramatically from their dialect. At issue was the idea of whether forcing students to use a dialect other than their own establishes a prestige dialect or denigrates other dialects. Although Hirsch's differentiation between dialect and grapholect and his subsequent discussion of this issue go far toward resolving it, the issue is nonetheless one to which writing teachers must be sensitive.

Hirsch's explanation is lucid and reasonable, and should be read in its entirety. He points out that the notion of equal correctness applies to individual dialects, that since they adhere to conventions which can be codified as rules, dialects are internally correct. Further, internal correctness is the only legitimate test of correctness: Dialects are correct in their own terms, not in terms of an external standard. But, Hirsch explains, a national language, particularly a national written language, is *not* a dialect: It is, as noted before, a **grapholect,** and is "transdialectal in character, an artificial construct that belongs to no group or place in particular" (1977:44). Though this may seem like terminological sleight-of-hand, it is not. Distinguishing between a national written norm and a variety of dialects which are primarily oral allows us to recognize that teaching the conventions of the grapholect need not be seen as critical of any dialect. The written language serves the function of allowing writers to communicate with others despite differences in dialect and, as suggested earlier, despite differences in time and situation. The stability of written language and its widespread comprehensibility are what make it valuable as a communicative construct, but linguistically it is not superior to dialects of the language. The effective composition teacher will recognize that it is important to teach students to conform to the conventions of the standard written language because the ability to use it is liberating, opening doors to opportunities available to those who are able to write well. But as we teach this accepted version of the language, we must be cautious not to denigrate students' dialects, not to consider them inferior or incorrect. Certainly, some dialects have more prestige than others, and some students may find it personally useful or desirable to modify their speech by adopting features of another dialect, but it is not the task of the composition teacher to encourage dialectal changes or to imply that one dialect is superior to another. Besides being insensitive, such behavior may be counterproductive to the goal of teaching students to become skilled users of written language, since students who are made to feel inferior or inadequate often lack the motivation to learn. Instead, they may become discouraged or hostile.

This discussion of differences between speech and writing has, by necessity, gone beyond the limits implied by the title of this chapter. Many of the differences between spoken and written language are apparent in syntax and in whole discourses, not in individual words. To the extent this is so, a number of the issues raised here will be discussed from different perspectives in later chapters.

CHAPTER 2

The Sentence

SECTION 1. GRAMMAR AND SYNTAX

Syntax refers to the relationship among words in a sentence. Although writing teachers often define the word *syntax* loosely, to mean sentence structure or the order of words in a sentence (see, for example, Lanham 1979), when they discuss syntax with their students or when they identify a problem in a sentence as syntactic, they generally are concerned with meaning as much as with sentence structure or word order. Thus while this discussion of syntax will begin with a consideration of syntactic problems writers encounter, it will also include a discussion of syntactic options that are primarily stylistic.

1.1. Sentence Boundary Problems

Fragments, comma splices, and fused sentences are considered by most writing teachers to be among the most serious syntactic errors writers can commit. Perhaps because it has become traditional to think of the sentence as the basic unit of meaning (regardless of whether it is correct to think so), errors that suggest that the writer is not aware of the grammatical boundaries of sentences are often interpreted as indications that the writer's thinking is flawed. A more accurate view of sentence boundary errors takes into account several of the ideas mentioned in the previous chapter. First, we should recognize that sentence boundaries, indicated by punctuation, are in part features of the print code, not of speech. As was suggested earlier, periods and commas substitute for pauses in speech, but their specific use, along with the use of other punctuation marks which separate clauses, is based on conventions that exist only when we write. In addition, research into the syntactic patterns of conversation suggests that much of actual speech consists of phrases and clauses that are not complete or discrete sentences (Hirsch 1977; Shaughnessy 1977). Thus written sentences do not consistently imitate the syntactic patterns people use when they speak. Finally, as Lindemann (1982), Schafer (1981), Shaughnessy (1977), and others have pointed out, Chomsky's distinction between **linguistic competence** and **linguistic performance** suggests that while people may have the inherent grammatical knowledge of their native language, their ability to use the language may not match what they know about it. Thus students might be able to distinguish between grammatical and nongrammatical sentences, but they still may produce fragments, comma splices, or fused sentences. Their skill with the print code is not consistent with their native knowledge of grammar.

Most people have learned at one time or another a grammatical definition of sentence which asserts that a sentence "is a string of words that contains a subject and a verb and is not grammatically dependent on anything outside itself" (Flynn and Glaser 1984:147). Of course, being able to use this definition to identify and correct fragments depends on whether or not a person also understands what 'subject,' 'verb,' and 'grammatically dependent' mean. Fragments rarely occur because a writer has simply omitted the subject from what would otherwise be a grammatically correct sentence. Flynn and Glaser cite examples of such fragments, for instance, *This is the most reliable lawnmower I have ever seen. Starts every time.* (1984:149). In the fragment *Starts every time,* we recognize the informality of speech in which we add afterthoughts and explanations without concern for grammatical connections because the context provides a semantic connection. *Starts every time* is a comment on the word *reliable* used in the preceding sentence, and though it is not a sentence, its meaning is clear. In writing, such unacceptable fragments can be corrected either by providing the missing subject, ***It*** *starts every time,* or in some cases by connecting the fragment to the previous sentence, a technique often used to correct other kinds of fragments.

More frequently, among both unskilled and moderately skilled writers, fragments occur when a phrase or dependent clause is punctuated as a sentence. Verbal phrases are especially troublesome since they contain words that look like main verbs but are not (1.i–iii).

(1) (i) The sprinter collapsed onto the track. Exhausted by his efforts. (past participle phrase)
  (ii) She served deep and rushed to the net. Anticipating her opponent's weak return. (present participle phrase)
  (iii) Most people yearn for the same thing. To be respected by others. (infinitive phrase)

Prepositional phrases and appositives, though they may not contain verbs or verbals, can also be separated from the sentences they modify, resulting in fragments (2.i–ii).

(2) (i) He mustered his courage and took the first step. Into the dark passage. (prepositional phrase)

(ii) After only a few steps, he heard a sound. A low, steady, mechanical hum. (appositive)

Each of these phrases can be joined to the preceding sentence and the fragment will be eliminated. Of course, fragments may occur when phrases precede the sentence they modify, in which case the fragment can be joined as an introductory phrase. This could occur if the participle phrases in the examples above preceded the main clause (3.i–ii).

(3) (i) Exhausted by his effort. The sprinter collapsed onto the track.
(ii) Anticipating her opponent's weak return. She served deep and rushed to the net.

Because dependent clauses contain both a subject and a verb, they are frequently punctuated as sentences. Writers who use only the partial "a sentence must have a subject and a verb" criterion to define a sentence do not realize that relative pronouns or subordinating conjunctions transform independent clauses to dependent clauses. It may be difficult for these writers to see that while (4.i) is correct, (4.ii) is wrong.

(4) (i) Everything depended on him. He was the only one left.
(ii) Everything depended on him. Because he was the only one left.

Logic would suggest that the subordinating conjunction used to make explicit a relationship which is implicit and clear without it should not have so dramatic an effect as to turn what was a correct sentence into a fragment. Yet that is exactly what happens. Similarly confusing for some writers is the difference between (5.i) and (5.ii).

(5) (i) I decided to buy the blue car. It is the one I looked at yesterday.
(ii) I decided to buy the blue car. Which is the one I looked at yesterday.
(iii) Which car did you buy?
(iv) When did you make up your mind?

In (5.i), the pronoun *it* serves as the subject of the second clause, which is independent. In (5.ii), the pronoun *which,* referring, like *it,* to *car,* functions differently. *Which* fills the subject slot of the clause, but also identifies the clause as dependent. And because relative pronouns and some subordinating conjunctions also serve as interrogatives, introducing questions such as (5.iii) and (5.iv), writers cannot assume that any clause beginning with one of these words is dependent. (Of course, dependent clauses beginning with these words can also precede the independent clause to which they are properly attached, so a string of words beginning with an initial-capitalized subordinate conjunction or relative pronoun may be a perfectly correct complex sentence.) Flynn and Glaser (1984) point out the particularly troublesome nature of *that,* which can be used as an adjective (6.i), as a pronoun serving as a subject (6.ii), and as a relative pronoun which introduces a dependent clause (6.iii).

(6) (i) That boy is my nephew.
(ii) That is my house.
(iii) There is the house that I bought.

A further complication for the novice writer trying to avoid fragments is the fact that most writing texts and usage handbooks are honest enough to confirm what the writer has observed from his own reading: Sometimes fragments are acceptable, especially when a writer is trying to capture the tone of normal conversation, imitate thought, punctuate an exclamation, or create special emphasis.

Comma splices and fused sentences are sentence boundary errors of the opposite nature of fragments. While a fragment is something less than a complete sentence which has been capitalized and punctuated as if it were a sentence, comma splices and fused sentences occur when writers punctuate more than one independent clause as a single sentence. Both errors, like fragments, are violations of print-code conventions. The comma splice, as mentioned in the previous chapter, occurs when two sentences are joined by a comma instead of being joined by a semicolon or by a comma and a coordinating conjunction or being punctuated as separate sentences. The fact that the writer uses punctuation indicates that he is aware of joining two syntactical or semantic units, even though he may not realize that he is joining two independent clauses. And it is reasonable to speculate that most comma splices occur because writers wish to indicate a close relationship between two ideas. Perhaps the same justification could be used to explain fused sentences, which occur when a writer joins independent clauses without using any punctuation. But while the writer who creates fused sentences may be trying to suggest that his ideas are related, the absence of any linking or separating punctuation indicates that the writer is not conscious of or certain about where one idea or sentence ends and the next begins. Fused sentences and comma splices, as Shaughnessy (1977) points out, may be a way for an insecure writer to postpone closure or to illustrate a relationship between ideas when he is not sure that the relationship is clear.

1.2. Problems Within Sentences

Sentence boundary errors, though considered serious and not always easy for writers to learn to avoid or correct, are at least easy for teachers to identify and categorize. But a grammatically complete, discrete sentence can go wrong in ways that are much harder to classify or explain. Our intuitive syntactic knowledge enables us to recognize that something is wrong with a sentence like *The art of good writing is a very difficult level to reach,* even if we cannot immediately identify the problem. Often, we rely on the marginal comment 'Awk' to tell students that something is wrong with a particular sentence, even though we know that such a comment does not help the student decide how to revise the sentence or avoid the awkwardness in the future. In this section, relying in part on Shaughnessy's taxonomy of the syntactic problems of basic writers, we will classify some of the syntactic derailments that can occur in grammatically complete yet nevertheless flawed sentences.

1.2.1. Blurred Patterns. Shaughnessy uses the phrase **blurred patterns** to refer to what others often call mixed constructions (Axelrod and Cooper 1985; Woodman and Adler 1985). Shaughnessy explains that blurred patterns are those "that erroneously combine features of several patterns" (1977:49). For example, the student who wrote "*At least I can say* is that I will have a college degree" has confused *The least I can say is* and *At least I can say that* (Shaughnessy 1977:49–50). In this case, the writer has blended two similar phrases into one which is not meaningful. Often such patterns occur when a writer begins a sentence with one syntactic pattern and ends the sentence with another, as in *By being in too big a hurry can lead to mistakes.* This sentence begins with a modifying phrase which cannot serve as a subject for the predicate *can lead to mistakes.* The error can be corrected either by turning the opening phrase into a noun phrase—*Being in too big a hurry can lead to mistakes*—or by adding an appropriate subject to the predicate—*By being in too big a hurry, you can make mistakes.*

1.2.2. Consolidation Errors. Shaughnessy (1977) uses the term **consolidation error** to refer to syntactic derailments that occur when writers unsuccessfully attempt to pack information into a single sentence through coordination, subordination, or juxtaposition. She suggests that such errors are signs that a writer is making the effort to write sophisticated sentences and show relationships between ideas, but that he has not mastered the syntactic patterns he wishes to use.

In her discussion of **coordinate consolidations,** Shaughnessy distinguishes between the use of coordinating conjunctions to join complete sentences and the use of the same conjunctions "to coordinate smaller units than sentences" (1977:54). This latter use of coordination is a form of consolidation. Shaughnessy provides (7) as an example of how coordinate consolidation can function.

(7) (i) They believe they can become leaders in their field.
(ii) They believe they can get good secure jobs.
(iii) They believe they can become leaders in their field and get good secure jobs.
(iv) They believe they can become leaders in their field and a good secure job.

(7.i) and (7.ii) can be consolidated into (7.iii) by creating a compound verb phrase. Consolidation errors occur when writers ignore the constraints of parallel structure, as in (7.iv). Here, Shaughnessy points out, the author has ignored the constraints placed upon him by beginning the coordinate construction with *leaders,* the complement of *become.* Doing so limits the writer's choice of the second element in the construction to "another sentence, another verb, or another animate noun that will fit into the concept of people in general becoming certain kinds of people (*leaders, well-paid professionals,* etc.)" (1977:54–55).

Such errors in coordinate consolidations occur whenever a writer fails to use the same grammatical form for each item in a pair or series. Special problems arise with paired coordinating structures such as *both/and, either/or,* and *not only/but also* because writers often forget the constraints the first member of the pair places upon them. The following is an example of such a consolidation error in a sentence written by a very inexperienced writer.

(8) Students attending college are *not only* benefiting [*sic*] themselves but it will eventually benefit the community in which they live. (Shaugnessy 1977:56)

In this example, the writer has apparently forgotten that he has used *not only* and has thus committed himself to a syntactic pattern that demands a verb phrase, not a complete clause, in order to be parallel. Misplacing one part of the coordinating pair can also lead to a consolidation error, as in (9.i). Here, the first pair precedes a prepositional phrase while the second precedes a verb. (9.ii) and (9.iii) are two possible correct versions.

(9) (i) Errors occur *not only* at sentence boundaries, *but also* appear within sentences.
(ii) Errors *not only* occur at sentence boundaries, *but also* appear within sentences.
(iii) Errors appear *not only* at sentence boundaries, *but also* within sentences.

Subordinate consolidations, like coordinate consolidations, allow writers to combine ideas into one sentence which would otherwise be expressed in two. Although subordination does not require the writer to wrestle with the subtleties of balance, like coordination, it does demand that the writer forestall closure on an idea and keep in mind the main thrust of a sentence while he adds qualifiers or modifiers. Shaughnessy points out that problems with subordinate consolidations usually "occur at or near the junctions where subordinate and independent structures intersect" (1977:59). For example, a writer who begins a sentence with an adverbial clause may omit the subject of the independent clause in the belief that the introductory clause has provided the grammatical subject (10.i). This blurred pattern can be corrected by providing a grammatical subject (10.ii).

(10) (i) Even though he may lose the game should still play his best.
(ii) Even though he may lose the game, he should still play his best.

The word *which* is particularly troublesome. Shaughnessy explains that it is often used as a catchall subordinator, as it is in (11), where it substitutes for *because*.

(11) All he talked about was actors and actresses *which* he wished he was a professional actor. (1977:63)

Shaughnessy also provides examples of the problems that occur because of the idiomatic use of *which* with some prepositions, as in *the paper in which I read the announcement,* or *to which I subscribe,* and so on. She identifies three errors involving *which* plus a preposition (12.i–iii).

(12) (i) The use of *which* in situations where it is inappropriate: *I intend to go to college to try to find another field in which to take.*
(ii) The use of *which* plus a preposition where *which* alone will serve: *You know what you want and you can just about demand the price in which you will receive.*
(iii) The redundant use of the preposition in cases where the preposition might appear in either of two places: *The college-bound student would like to find out in which field he or she would be most interested in.* (Shaughnessy 1977:64–65)

By **juxtaposition consolidation,** Shaughnessy refers to the expedient use by some inexperienced writers of ignoring coordination or subordination as ways to link ideas in favor of simply placing ideas next to one another. One form of juxtaposition takes the form of identifying a topic, then following it with a sentence of comment or explanation not grammatically connected to it, as in (13.i–ii).

(13) (i) Retail buying and merchandizing, there is a tremendous demand.
(ii) The job that my mother has, I know I could never be satisfied with it.

Shaughnessy explains that this structure enables the writer "to center the attention of his reader on the real subject of his discourse and then go on to make statements about it" (1977:66–67). Redundant subjects, common to speech but inappropriate in formal writing, are another example of a juxtaposition consolidation (14).

(14) The boy *he* ran away after he broke the window.

1.2.3. Inversions. Inversion errors occur when writers deviate from the **Subject–Verb–Complement** syntactic pattern most common in English. Of course, such deviation is often stylistically or semantically desirable, and these errors often reflect efforts by writers to expand their repertoire of syntactic options. Shaughnessy includes within this category of errors sentences such as (15.i–iii).

(15) (i) *The things they want you to know* you do not know *this* in high school.
(ii) I am getting able to discuss many differents [*sic*] points of view in this course *which* I could not do *it* before.
(iii) The more education that one gets its [*sic*] better for them the more experience they get.

In (15.i–ii), redundancy occurs because the writer, after inverting the direct objects, uses pronouns to repeat them in the more typical postverb position. In (15.iii), the author does not have control of the balance required by the *the more X, the more Y* pattern.

The use of the direct-question pattern instead of the indirect-question pattern is another common inversion error, occurring in sentences like (16.i) which are used in place of (16.ii).

(16) (i) We wanted to know when would the test be.
(ii) We wanted to know when the test would be.

SECTION 2. MEANING AND SYNTAX

Though of course the syntactic problems discussed in the previous section affect interpretation of a sentence, they are essentially grammatical problems. Often, however, a sentence is difficult to understand even though it is grammatically correct. Sometimes, as we will discuss in the next section, the difficulty stems from an opaque or wordy style. Sometimes unclear modification and ambiguous reference make it hard to understand what a sentence means. Writers use modifying phrases and clauses not only to consolidate ideas, but also to expand them by adding details and explanation. And writers can use pronouns and other words which refer to a previously mentioned concept in order to provide coherence and avoid repetition. But when modifiers and reference words have ambiguous referents or fail to modify clearly, they create confusion for readers.

2.1. Dangling and Misplaced Modifiers

Dangling modifiers obscure meaning because they violate our expectation that modifying phrases will give us information about a specific word in a sentence. But dangling modifiers are phrases or elliptical clauses that have nothing to modify in the sentence to which they are attached; thus they 'dangle.' And since dangling modifiers often appear at the beginning of a sentence, in the form of introductory verbal phrases, they mislead readers by beginning a message that the sentence does not complete. For example, in (17.i), the participial phrase prepares readers for a subject describing a person or people, for example (17.ii–iii).

(17) (i) Hiking all afternoon, my legs felt tired.
(ii) Hiking all afternoon, the girls reached the cabin.
(iii) Hiking all afternoon, I felt my legs tiring.
(iv) After hiking all day, the mountain seemed no nearer. (Flynn and Glaser 1984:80)

The word *hiking* refers to a human activity, not to an activity in which part of a human (legs) can partake. In this case, readers would probably understand what the writer intended, despite the dangling modifier, but in (17.iv) the writer's point is more obscure. In this example, the main clause does not contain any word with the human qualities necessary for *hiking* to serve as a modifier. The subject of the sentence, *mountain,* cannot hike; thus the modifier dangles because it does not modify the subject it seems to refer to. And the sentence is confusing (and funny) because its opening phrase prepares the reader for a clause about a human activity, not a statement about an inanimate object.

When the subject or subject and verb of a modifying clause are omitted, the reader expects the subject of the main clause to identify the subject of the modifying clause, as in (18.i).

(18) (i) When only seven, she started to write novels.
(ii) When only seven, her father changed jobs.
(iii) When she was only seven, her father changed jobs.

But when the subject of the main clause does not identify the subject of the modifying clause, the modifier dangles, as in (18.ii). Since it is unlikely that her father changed jobs when he was seven, readers will recognize that the subject of the main clause differs from the subject of the introductory clause. Thus, for the sentence to be clear, it should probably be revised to (18.iii).

Misplaced modifiers are the source of similarly unclear and sometimes humorous sentences. It is possible to identify a word in the sentence that the misplaced modifier is supposed to comment upon, but the modifier is placed so that it appears to modify another element in the sentence or so that it seems to modify more than one element. For example, in (19.i) the modifier is placed too far from the word it is supposed to modify. Though it is possible that the writer intends to distinguish his house with the loud radio from other houses he owns, it is more likely that the phrase *with the loud radio* should refer to the car, as in (19.ii). Adverbs are also frequently misplaced, as in (19.iii). This sentence is confusing because *almost ate* does not specify whether the writer actually ate any sandwiches at all. It may mean that he contemplated eating three sandwiches but decided to eat none, or one, or two, or two and a half. It is likely that the writer meant (19.iv), which more clearly indicates that the author ate two complete sandwiches and nearly all of a third.

(19) (i) The car passed my house *with the loud radio.*
(ii) The car *with the loud radio* passed my house.
(iii) I *almost* ate three sandwiches.
(iv) I ate *almost* three sandwiches.

Misplaced modifiers that might modify either of two elements in a sentence are often called **squinting modifiers.** In (20.i), *when she was twenty* could refer to the time the subject made a decision or it could be part of the decision she made at an earlier time. The modifier could be placed elsewhere to clarify the intended meaning. For example, (20.ii) suggests that the decision to move to an apartment when she was twenty was made at some earlier time, but (20.iii) implies that the decision was made when the daughter was twenty. Though one might argue that all of the versions are ambiguous, placing the modifier between the two elements it might modify gives the reader the least chance to interpret the sentence accurately. In general, writers must learn to place modifiers as close as possible to the word or phrase they modify to avoid confusing their readers.

(20) (i) My daughter decided *when she was twenty* to move to her own apartment.
(ii) My daughter decided to move to her own apartment *when she was twenty.*
(iii) *When she was twenty,* my daughter decided to move to her own apartment.

2.2. Ambiguous Reference

Syntactic reference usually concerns the necessity of pronouns standing for a clearly identifiable antecedent, and while we discuss pronoun reference here, we also include what we call **semantic reference.** As we will explain, this second type of ambiguous reference helps identify the awkwardness of sentences such as *The art of good writing is a difficult level to achieve.*

Pronouns allow writers to be more concise and less repetitious since by using them writers can avoid repeating a word that is usually longer than the pronoun itself. But if the pronoun does not refer to a clearly identifiable word, its use may lead to ambiguity. Sometimes a writer may use a pronoun that has no antecedent, as in (21).

(21) We visited the site where *they* found the relics.

The pronoun *they* has no specific antecedent in this sentence. It is impossible for a reader to know, unless the antecedent has appeared in a previous sentence, who *they* refers to—archaeologists, builders who happened to stumble on relics while excavating, children who were exploring a cave, or others. The pronoun *you* often appears without an antecedent, especially when the appropriate antecedent is a general group of people or people in general, as (22.i) illustrates.

(22) (i) *You* had to study hard to get high grades at my high school.
(ii) To become an astronaut, *you* must train and study for years.

In (22.i), *you* does not refer to the reader; it refers instead to students at the writer's high school at some time in the past. A sentence such as (22.ii) is likely to be imprecise too, since the author probably is not addressing a group of potential astronauts with the pronoun *you,* but instead is using the pronoun to refer generally to those people who wish to become or have become astronauts. A similar ambiguity occurs when the antecedent is implied, but not stated, as in (23).

(23) When the mayor held his press conference, *they* asked him about his reelection bid.

Because readers understand the context of the sentence, that is, they understand that at a press conference reporters ask questions, they will understand who is implied by the ambiguous *they*. But the antecedent does not appear in the sentence, and thus the sentence is, potentially at least, ambiguous. Ambiguity can occur also if a pronoun refers to a whole clause rather than one particular word. For example, in (24) the pronoun *which* has no clear antecedent, but instead refers to the entire clause *we missed the beginning of the film*.

(24) We missed the beginning of the film, *which* made us angry.

Ambiguity occurring when antecedents are missing, are only implied, or are whole clauses is a common feature of speech and even in writing does not often render discourse unintelligible. More troublesome is the case in which a pronoun has more than one potential antecedent in a sentence, as in (25).

(25) Jim told John that *he* was mistaken.

He can refer to either Jim or John; the context of the sentence provides no clues about which name the writer intends to serve as the antecedent.

Another type of reference problem does not involve pronouns, but instead occurs when a writer fails to recognize the semantic effects of a particular syntactic pattern. In (26.i), the author associates the word *level* with the quality *good writing*.

(26) (i) The art of good writing is a difficult level to reach.
(ii) Good writing is difficult.

For the author of this sentence, writing is an art or skill that can be thought of as having a series of levels: poor, adequate, good, and so on. But the syntax of this sentence follows the pattern of **Subject–Linking Verb–Complement,** and in this pattern, the complement renames or is the equivalent of the subject. Thus the complement (*level*) refers to the subject (*art*), and not, as the author seems to think, to the object of the preposition (*writing*). Semantically, *art* does not contain the concept of *level,* or at least *art* unmodified is not a *level,* as the sentence implies. This sentence may have gone awry because the author was trying to sound formal or to avoid short, direct sentences. But his point could have been made clearly and concisely had he simply written (26.ii). Instead, his sentence is confusing because the semantic reference he wishes to make cannot be made with the syntactic pattern he has chosen.

SECTION 3. STYLE AND SYNTAX

Style, like **syntax,** is a word used casually to mean just about anything the user wishes. Corbett (1976) and Winterowd (1975), in essays surveying the relationship of stylistic studies to rhetoric and composition, indicate that two broad views of style have dominated stylistic scholarship. One view is that style concerns the features of prose specific to an individual. Scholars such as Milic and Ohmann, though with different theoretical perspectives, support this notion that style involves those individual choices a writer makes when selecting from the lexical and syntactic options available to him. The second major view of style, held by Enkvist (1964) and Riffaterre (1959, 1960), suggests that style involves departures from a linguistic norm. When we speak of Hemingway's style or Joyce's style we acknowledge our sense that style can be a matter of individual choices. When we consider style generically, speaking for instance of plain or ornate styles, of bureaucratese, of dramatic or ironic styles, we are accepting the idea that there are norms governing the appropriate style for a particular discourse, and that thus one's style can depart from a particular norm. Enkvist draws another useful distinction between textual contexts and extratextual contexts, the former concerned with matters such as phonetic, morphemic, lexical, and syntactic elements, and the latter concerned with genre, situation, reader/writer relationship, and so on (Enkvist 1964, discussed in Corbett 1976). This distinction enables us to see that style can be discussed rhetorically as well as linguistically and that stylistic appropriateness can be viewed as determined by considerations which extend beyond an individual's particular linguistic preferences. As it applies to whole discourses, style will be discussed in later chapters; here we will limit ourselves to several specific syntactic elements of style.

Perhaps what can most confidently be said about style is that it exists. Individual writers do seem to have specific lexical and syntactic preferences which make up their individual styles, and specific genres demand that writers follow particular conventions which comprise the style for the genre. Beyond this, we recognize that some texts are more pleasurable and clearer to read than others, even though both texts may be grammatically correct and neither may contain the problems of modification, reference, and so on discussed in the previous section of this chapter. At the level of the sentence, we can identify variety, clarity, and conciseness as positive stylistic features. We can also identify syntactic patterns that allow writers to emphasize ideas they wish to stress. Although writing teachers may not be able to help all of their students become great stylists, we can emphasize these general principles that make writing more effective and clear.

3.1. Variety. It is commonplace to say that texts composed of sentences that are for the most part nearly the same length are boring or hard to read. Texts composed of one short sentence after another not only seem childish and choppy, but also strike readers as being conceptually simple and unsophisticated. On the other hand, texts composed exclusively of long, heavily embedded sentences may confuse readers, especially if the individual sentences are not carefully constructed. However, as desirable as it may be for a writer to vary the length of his sentences, a more important feature of syntactic variety concerns the syntactic patterns the writer uses.

English provides its users with a fairly small number of basic sentence types or patterns, often presented in writing texts or handbooks diagrammatically as **S(ubject)–V(erb), S(ubject)–V(erb)–O(bject), S(ubject)–V(erb)–C(omplement), S(ubject)–V(erb)–I(ndirect) O(bject)–D(irect) O(bject),** and so forth. Depending on the source, one can find five, seven, eight, or more patterns listed as 'basic.' These basic, simple sentence types can be expanded in many ways, by coordinating elements within them, by coordinating whole sentences, by subordinating one sentence to another, by adding modifiers in the form of single words or phrases, and so on. Hunt (1965), Mellon (1969), and others have studied the natural development in the variety of sentence types used by writers as they grow older. They, as well as Christensen (1963), have analyzed the syntactic patterns of skilled adult writers, identifying features they believe are indicative of a mature syntactic style. Mellon and Christensen and O'Hare (1973) have proposed pedagogical approaches for teaching students to increase what Mellon (1969) has called 'syntactic fluency,' that is, the range of sentence types a writer uses. Some of these pedagogical techniques will be discussed in chapter 12.

3.2. Conciseness and Clarity

As writers develop syntactic fluency, either through normal growth or through instruction and practice, they begin to write longer sentences. But with increased length comes the potential for sprawling, confusing sentences, particularly if the writer takes as a model the heavily nominalized, passive style of so much of the prose written by people in business, government, and the professions. Lanham (1979) and Williams (1985) have written textbooks providing suggestions for writing and editing clear and concise sentences. Williams is particularly helpful in identifying sources of wordiness and confusion, and much of the following discussion will be derived from his categories and examples.

As experienced readers, most writing teachers can identify excessive wordiness, but as with the syntactic problems we often mark 'Awk,' the sentences we mark as being wordy are often easier to see than to analyze. In chapter 1 we discussed one source of wordiness, redundancy, but wordiness has other sources. Some modifiers lead to wordiness because they usually fill space without adding meaning. Single-word modifiers such as *very, many, basically, generally,* and *certain* fall into this category, as do phrases such as *kind of* and *each and every*. For example, (27.i) can be rewritten more concisely as (27.ii).

(27) (i) This *kind of* terrorism affects *each and every* one of us.
(ii) Terrorism affects us all.

Modifiers such as these do sometimes have a legitimate function, but often we use them unconsciously when they are unnecessary. The same is true of some phrases that can often be replaced by single words. Williams offers over two pages of such common phrases and the words that can replace them, including *due to the fact that* and a number of other . . . *the fact that* . . . phrases, which can be replaced by *because* or *since; as regards, in reference to,* and *concerning the matter of,* which can be replaced by *about;* and so on (Williams 1985:77–79).

Writers can sensitize themselves to these modifiers and phrases and learn to avoid them when they write or replace them when they edit. It is more difficult to avoid wordiness that results from stating the obvious or including unnecessary details since what is obvious or unnecessary depends on one's audience. Williams (1985:74), however, points out that examination of prose may reveal wordiness based on semantic similarity, as (28.i) suggests. Williams revises the sentence to (28.ii) and offers (28.iii) as his explanation.

(28) (i) Imagine a mental picture of someone engaged in the intellectual activity of trying to learn what the rules are for how to play the game of chess.
(ii) Imagine someone trying to learn the rules of chess.
(iii) *Imagine* implies a mental picture; *trying to learn* implies being engaged in

the activity of; we know chess is intellectual; chess is a game, and games are played. (Williams 1985:74)

This explanation relies on two kinds of knowledge: knowledge of words—that *imagine* implies a mental picture—and knowledge of the world—that chess is a game. For readers who possess these kinds of knowledge, as most native users of English would, the first version of the sentence contains phrases that state the obvious.

(29.i) demonstrates how excessive, unnecessary detail can lead to wordiness. Williams suggests pruning this sentence to (29.ii).

(29) (i) Baseball, one of our oldest and most popular outdoor summer sports in terms of total attendance at ball parks and viewing on television, has the kind of rhythm of play on the field that alternates between the players' passively waiting with no action taking place between the pitches to the batter and exploding into action when the batter hits a pitched ball to one of the players and he fields it.
(ii) Baseball has a rhythm that alternates between waiting and explosive action. (Williams 1985:75–76)

One need not agree that Williams's revision makes the same point as the original to recognize that eliminating obvious statements like *to the batter* and *a pitched ball* improves the sentence. And clearly the long appositive following the subject is filled with details that have no bearing on the point of the sentence. The decision of whether details are necessary or not depends, of course, on the writer's purpose and his knowledge of his readers, but the background information about baseball contained in the appositive is too far removed from the main idea of the sentence to be an appropriate addition to it. Were the author to feel that his readers needed this information, he would be better served by placing it in a separate sentence.

Not only are **passive constructions** usually longer than active constructions, they also are often less vigorous and clear, as (30.i–ii) illustrate.

(30) (i) John threw the ball.
(ii) The ball was thrown by John.

Because (30.ii) is passive, it is longer than (30.i) by two words. In an isolated sentence, two words may not matter, but over the course of a longer text, one passive construction after another can rob the prose of its forward motion. This occurs in part because the person performing the action is not named until the end of the sentence, and readers must hold in mind what occurs (the verb) and to what it occurs (the object) until they finally learn who or what is responsible for the action. Another potential problem with the passive voice is that it allows writers to avoid stating who or what is responsible for an action. (31.i) exemplifies this feature of the passive voice.

Of course, sometimes writers do not know who performs an action and sometimes that information is irrelevant. And sometimes writers do want to avoid identifying the source of an action in order to hide responsibility. We can see the value of hiding responsibility if we embed a clause (31.ii) into (30.i).

(31) (i) The ball was thrown.
(ii) John threw the ball which broke the window.
(iii) The ball which broke the window was thrown by John.
(iv) The ball which broke the window was thrown.

John would probably prefer (31.iv) since his responsibility for breaking the window is no longer obvious; however, writers who do not intend to hide meaning need to be sensitive to the potential of confusing their readers if they use this construction.

Nominalizations, nouns derived from verbs or adjectives, can also reduce the clarity and crispness of a writer's style. The following examples (32.i–iii) from Williams's text illustrate how nominalizations can rob a sentence of vigor by removing action from the verb.

(32) (i) There is a *need* for *reanalysis* of our data.
(ii) There is a data *reanalysis need.*
(iii) We *must reanalyze* our data.

In the first two versions, the nominalizations *need* and *reanalysis* describe the action which must occur, and the expletive *there* plus the verb *is* add only length, not meaning, to the sentences. The third version, in which the action is stated in the verb and the actor in the subject, is both more concise and clearer. (32.ii) also illustrates how nominalizations and other nouns can be piled up one after another, creating a turgid style which seems to be especially common in scientific and technical writing. In addition, nominalizations, like passives, allow agents to be dropped out. Compare (33.i) through (33.v).

(33) (i) A doctor should reevaluate his condition. (active)
(ii) There is a need for his condition to be reevaluated by a doctor. (passive with agent)
(iii) There is a need for his condition to be reevaluated. (passive without agent)
(iv) A need for a reevaluation of his condition by a doctor exists. (active voice wth nominalizations, agent present)
(v) A need for a reevaluation of his condition exists. (active voice with nominalizations, agent dropped)
(Sentences adapted from Williams 1985:12–13)

The passive and nominalized versions are 50–100% longer than the active version, depending on whether or not the agent, *doctor,* is present. But conciseness alone does not account for the preferability of the first version; it clearly states the important information by following Williams's sensible advice about syntax: "State who's doing what in the subject of your sentence, and state what that 'who' is doing in your verb" (1985:8).

3.3. Emphasis

As Williams recognizes, even such sensible principles as the one just stated do not always apply. In English, we tend to place information that we want to emphasize at the end of a sentence. For example, (34.i) lacks the emphasis of (34.ii).

(34) (i) She was only thirteen when she published her first novel.
(ii) She published her first novel when she was only thirteen.

Although English allows us to subordinate either clause and to place either clause first, the word *only,* coupled with our knowledge that most writers are much older than thirteen when they publish their first novels, suggests to us that the important information concerns her age. Placed at the beginning of the sentence, that information seems introductory and less important.

Efforts to structure sentences so that what we wish to emphasize comes toward the end may require us to violate the "state who's doing what in the subject" principle. Williams (1985:57–59) gives examples of four syntactic devices which allow writers to increase the emphasis at the end of a sentence, each of which removes the actor from the subject position:

(35) (i) The use of *there: There are a few grammatical patterns in English whose specific intention seems to be to throw special weight on the end of a sentence* versus *A few grammatical patterns in English seem to have a specific intention to throw special weight on the end of a sentence.*
(ii) The use of *what: What this country needs is a monetary policy that will end the violent fluctuations in money supply, unemployment, and inflation* versus *This country needs a monetary policy that will end the violent fluctuations in money supply, unemployment, and inflation.*
(iii) The use of *it* as an anticipatory subject: *It once seemed inevitable that domestic oil prices must eventually rise to the level set by OPEC in order to force oil conservation* versus *That domestic oil prices must eventually rise to the level set by OPEC in order to force oil conservation once seemed inevitable.*
(iv) The use of *it* as an expletive: *It was in 1933 that this country experienced a depression that almost wrecked our democratic system of government* versus *In 1933 this country experienced a depression that almost wrecked our democratic system of government.*

Of course, it is not always necessary to employ one of these techniques to place emphasis at the end of a sentence. In the preceding sentence, for example, the introductory phrase *of course* could have appeared after the word *sentence*), but the result would not have been as emphatic. Emphasis alone, however, does not determine where such movable phrases or clauses should appear. As we shift our attention away from isolated sentences and to whole discourses, we will examine the relationship between the structure of individual sentences and the coherence of the texts they form.

CHAPTER 3

Discourse

SECTION 1. THE ARRANGEMENT OF DISCOURSE

For writing teachers, the topics discussed in the previous two chapters are important primarily as they relate to how we can help students write whole discourses. Occasionally a word or sentence in isolation can make up an entire discourse—the single word *Yes* written as a response to a request; *Excellent* written across the topic of an exam; *Please call John when you get home* written as a telephone message. But these short discourses are usually written within a particular context as a response to another written or oral communication. In writing classes, our focus is on longer discourses, and although the papers our students write are usually responses to assignments we make, our intention is to teach them skills to enable them to write effectively in a variety of situations, not all of which will necessarily be prompted by another discourse.

In this chapter, our general concern will be with how written discourses convey meaning. Though our focus will be on language, such a discussion must touch upon all of the elements of any communication, the encoder (writer or speaker), the decoder (audience, reader, or listener), the subject, and the language (or code or signal) through which the encoder communicates a message to the decoder about the subject. This relationship is traditionally depicted as a triangle and referred to as the **communications triangle.**

(1)

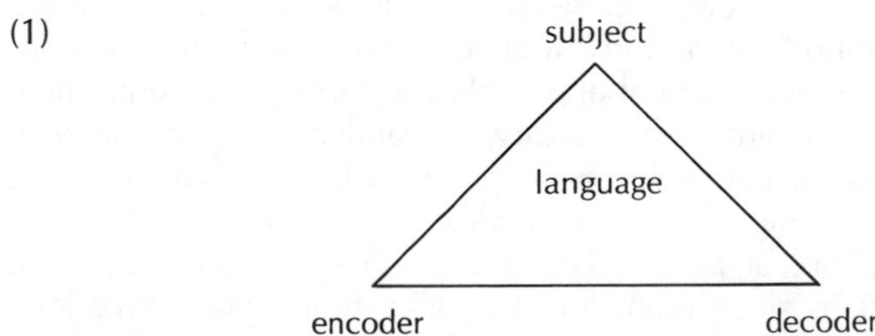

Though its concepts are as old as Aristotle's *ethos* (concerning the speaker), *pathos* (concerning the audience), and *logos* (concerning the subject), the communications triangle has proven to be a rich heuristic for modern rhetorical theory and pedagogy (see Weiser in press-a, in press-b). The communications triangle is valuable in part because it reminds us to consider each element of any communication and in part because it reminds us that writer, reader, subject, and language are interwoven and ultimately cannot be thought of in isolation from one another.

As we suggested above, the role of language in a discourse is to convey the writer's message to the reader. (Since our focus here is on written discourse, we will use the terms 'writer' and 'reader,' but what we say will in general hold true for oral discourses as well.) In more specific terms, the lexical and syntactic choices a writer makes establish his voice or persona in the discourse and enable him to identify his relationship with his audience. Skilled writers make these choices readily, varying their diction and syntax as the situation demands. It is not difficult to recognize that the same person writing about the same subject for different readers will be likely to write differently for each audience. Informal letters to friends or family will differ from reports or letters written to business associates, and reports to business associates may differ from one another if the writer is the supervisor of one audience and the subordinate of another. Thus linguistic choices are influenced by a writer's understanding of his relationship with his readers.

The meaning of a discourse also depends on its arrangement or organization. Corbett (1971) traces the classical plan of arrangement to Cicero and Quintilian. Their plan, designed for formal oration and primarily persuasive, includes five parts: **introduction, statement of background facts, support for the writer's view, refutation of opposing views,** and **conclusion.** We see the influence of this five-part plan in the traditional 'five-paragraph theme' approach to teaching writing (which is now recognized as limited because it leads to mechanically structured discourses). Most advocates of this approach neglect the specific function of the background, support, and refutation sections, substituting instead the general label 'body' for the section of the essay between the introduction and conclusion. The term 'support' is frequently used to refer to the content of the body of an essay and to the sentences that elaborate on the topic sentence of a paragraph.

The concepts of introduction, body, and conclusion, or beginning, middle, and end, are the more general approaches to discussing the arrangement of discourse. In the nineteenth century, Alexander Bain established an approach to categorizing specific **forms** or **modes** of discourse. According to Bain, all discourse fell into one of five modes: description, narration, exposition, argumentation, or poetry. The poetic mode has generally been ignored by rhetoricians since Bain, and the other four modes have long served as the standard classification of discourse types. In a brief, extremely lucid summary of Bain's modes, D'Angelo points out that "each form is assumed to have its own function, its own subject matter, its own organizational patterns, and its own language" (1976:115). Bain includes as language categories denotative, connotative, figurative, literal, objective, impressionistic, factual, and emotive. As patterns of organization he mentions space and time (for narrative and descriptive writing), analysis and classification (for exposition), and induction and deduction (for argumentation).

Both the concepts of the four modes of discourse and the patterns of organization have remained dominant in current approaches to teaching writing. Many composition texts and readers are organized by modes or patterns or by both. Conventional composition course sequences take students through a semester of writing which is primarily narrative and descriptive followed by a semester that focuses on exposition and argumentation, or assign papers based on specific organizational patterns such as cause and effect, comparison/contrast, process, and so forth. Such pedagogical approaches have come under criticism within the last fifteen years as emphasizing the written product rather than the writing process. One recent rhetorician who has treated the patterns of organization more holistically is D'Angelo (1975, 1985). He suggests that the organizational patterns are reflections of conceptual patterns. Thus comparison/contrast is not simply an artificial way of organizing a discourse; instead it is a reflection of the fact that we compare and contrast items, concepts, and experiences as a way of understanding them. The same is true for other patterns of organization such as analysis, classification, and so on. Further, D'Angelo suggests that the patterns can be connected with invention since each pattern implies certain questions that can be asked about any subject. Comparison/contrast invites a writer to ask how a subject is like or unlike similar subjects; classification allows the writer to ask if the subject is part of a larger category of subjects or if it can be subdivided into smaller groups of subjects; description encourages questions about the physical characteristics of the subject; and so on. Thus D'Angelo argues that the arrangement of a discourse is not divorced from its meaning or its origins in the writer's mind.

In addition to the traditional modes of discourse and the patterns of organization, the concept of *genre* can be used as a basis for discussing arrangement. Thus the typical arrangement of any particular type of discourse—a book review, a personal essay, a proposal, a sonnet, a business letter, or a research report—could be analyzed and a model of its structure used to guide writers as they compose similar texts. Though this approach could lead to the mechanical adherence to a pattern, it need not, especially if the specific requirements of voice, style, and audience of each genre are considered along with the typical arrangement of texts in that genre. For instance, in addition to noting that book reviews typically begin with a summary of the book and include the reviewer's evaluation, a generic analysis might also mention that reviewers must consider that their audience is composed of people with varying degrees of familiarity with the book, ranging from those who have read the book to those who have never heard of it or its author before. An analysis of a research report would mention the typical structure of introduction, including a statement of the problem and review of the literature; method, including the identification of subjects, materials, and procedures; results; and discussion. But it would also discuss the conventional style of such reports, particularly as regards lexical and syntactic choices. Such an approach to genre—like D'Angelo's approach to the organizational patterns—rather than isolating arrangement incorporates it into the larger consideration of discourse.

SECTION 2. THE AIMS OF DISCOURSE

Any theory of discourse limited to the forms of discourse or patterns of arrangement can give only an incomplete idea of what a successful discourse is. The relationship among writer, reader, subject, and language suggested by the communications triangle implies not only that a writer uses language to communicate to a reader about a subject. Implicit in the idea of communication is also the concept of **purpose, intention,** or **aim.** The author's purpose is at the heart of any discourse: We write about a subject because we have something we wish to say to our readers. Their emphasis of form over purpose is another reason that mode-centered and pattern-centered theories and pedagogies have been the target of recent criticism. Such criticism usually includes the charge that people describe, narrate, compare, analyze, evaluate not for the sake of describing, narrating, and so on, but in order to accomplish a particular purpose. Further, most discourses are not exclusively description, narration, comparison, or classification. Instead, writers are likely to use several modes or patterns in a single discourse, choosing those that help them attain their larger purpose.

D'Angelo (1976) points out that Bain, an associationist psychologist as well as a rhetorician, included the concept of aim in his theory. According to Bain, the three aims—to inform, to persuade, and to please—corresponded to the three faculties of the mind—the understanding, the will, and the feelings. D'Angelo also reminds us that Bain's modes originally included poetry as a fifth category and that "thus description, narration, and exposition relate to the faculty of the understanding, persuasion relates to the will, and poetry to the feelings" (1976:116). But Bain's primary interest was in the forms of discourse, not the purposes.

Kinneavy (1971) emphasizes the importance of the aims. Using the communications triangle and the relationships it suggests as a basis for his theory, Kinneavy identifies four aims of discourse: **expressive, persuasive, referential,** and **literary.** Expressive discourse emphasizes the writer, whose purpose is primarily self-expression. Expressive discourses include diaries, journals, and prayers on the individual level, and manifestos, protest statements, and constitutions on the level of larger communities or groups. Persuasive discourse is audience-oriented. Its primary purpose is to convince or persuade an audience to act or change. Examples include advertising, editorials, sermons, and political speeches. Referential discourse is subject-centered and can be divided into three subcategories: exploratory, informative, and scientific. Exploratory discourse includes proposed solutions to problems, tentative definitions, and dialogues. Informative discourse includes news articles, reports, textbooks, and instructions. Scientific discourse is comprised of discourse that proves a point by arguing from accepted premises or by generalizing from particulars, or discourse that combines both of these methods. Literary discourse emphasizes language and includes—in addition to fiction, poetry, and drama—jokes, ballads, movies, and TV shows (Kinneavy 1971:61). As these examples suggest, each aim encompasses a variety of forms of discourse, each with a pattern of arrangement and style most appropriate to it.

Kinneavy's is the best-known work on purpose or aims, but it is not the only work emphasizing the aims of discourse rather than the modes. Earlier, Jakobson proposed what he called "the six basic functions of verbal communication" (1960:357), which he diagrammed as follows:

(2)

	REFERENTIAL	
EMOTIVE	POETIC	CONATIVE
	PHATIC	
	METALINGUAL	

These functions, which we shall explain shortly, are related to Jakobson's version of the fundamental elements of any verbal communication, just as Kinneavy's aims are related to the four elements of the communications triangle. Jakobson presents his six elements as follows:

(3)

	CONTEXT	
ADDRESSER	MESSAGE	ADDRESSEE
	CONTACT	
	CODE	

Jakobson's addresser, addressee, context, and code correspond to the encoder, decoder, subject, and language of the communications triangle. **Message** refers to the point the author wants to make about the context, and **contact** refers to the "physical channel and psychological connection between the addresser and the addressee, enabling both of them to enter and stay in communication" (1960:353). Each function emphasizes one of these elements. Thus, emotive (or expressive, as Jakobson also calls it) communication is focused on the addresser, conative on the addressee, referential on the context, and poetic on the message. Phatic communication, which emphasizes contact, includes language designed "to establish, to prolong, or to discontinue communication" (Jakobson 1960:355), such as *I see, Uh-uh, Are you listening?* and so on. The metalingual function focuses on the code itself; it is communication about the language being used, such as *What does that word mean?* and *I don't follow you.*

Though Kinneavy recognizes the similarity between his work, Jakobson's, and that of Hymes, who has applied Jakobson's schema, he points out that his system of aims was derived independently of (and in part before) that of Jakobson and Hymes (Kinneavy 1971:59). Britton and his associates (1975) have derived their **function categories** more directly from Jakobson and Hymes, and from Sapir. Britton derives from Sapir the notion that all speech is essentially expressive, but becomes more explicit as the need to communicate increases (Britton et al. 1975:10). Thus Britton places the **expressive** function at the center of his model (4), flanked by the **transactional** and **poetic** functions.

(4)

TRANSACTIONAL——————EXPRESSIVE——————POETIC

Britton's idea of expressive writing is similar to Kinneavy's, focusing on the writer and his immediate concerns and feelings. Transactional writing includes Kinneavy's referential and persuasive aims; it emphasizes the writer in relationship to the larger world and includes a variety of subcategories, which we will examine later. The poetic function corresponds to Kinneavy's literary aim. These function categories, Britton explains, "are an attempt to provide a framework for the question 'Why are you writing?'" (1975:76).

Britton's work is also influenced by that of Moffett (1968), whose scheme for classifying discourse is based primarily on the distance in time and space between the writer and his audience and between the writer and his subject. Moffett's categories are essentially a cognitive-based reordering of the modes, but Britton adopts Moffett's categories of writer-subject distance, **recording, reporting, generalizing,** and **theorizing,** in his subdivision of the transactional function. Britton divides the transactional category into two main subcategories, the **conative** and the **informative,** and explains that "informative language is used to make information available; conative language is an instrument of the writer's intention to influence the reader" (1975:94). The conative is further divided into **regulative,** including orders, advice, and instructions one is obligated to obey, and **persuasive** subcategories. The informative is subdivided into seven smaller categories, ranging from the most concrete to the most abstract. Although we will not discuss these categories in detail, we have presented them in (5).

(5)

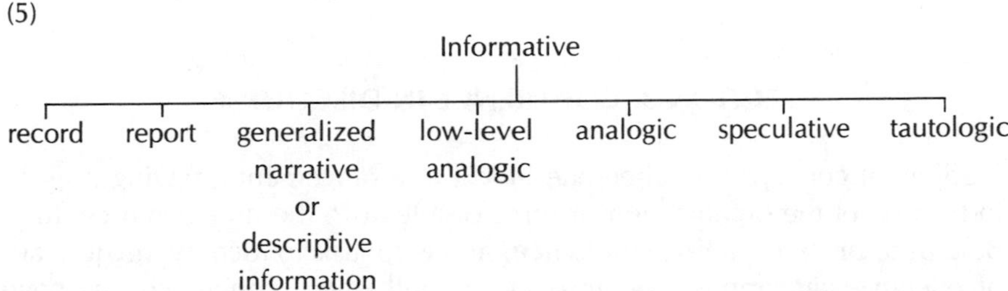

The first three categories are grounded in fairly concrete observations: The writer records what he observes at the moment, reports on past observations (either his own or of others), or offers general information in the form of facts or instructions. Low-level analogic discourse involves the presentation of generalizations without the attempt to explain the relationship among the generalizations. Analogic discourse relates generalizations hierarchically or logically; speculative discourse focuses on the generalizations themselves; and tautologic discourse involves the writer in theorizing. Thus the movement in these categories is from the simplest and most concrete recording of observations to the most complex and abstract ways of thinking, from what is immediate in time and space to what may not exist temporally or physically.

Kinneavy's emphasis on the purpose or aim of discourse and Britton's functional categories are an important corrective to the almost exclusive emphasis on arrangement in recent pedagogy. But such categories are subject to the same kinds of criticism as have been leveled at arrangement- and mode-centered approaches: Discourse is no more likely to be exclusively expressive as it is to be exclusively narrative or descriptive. A writer may have persuasion as his major aim when he writes a particular discourse, but that does not mean that he will not at the same time inform his readers. Novels fall under the literary aim, but of course some novels are clearly and intentionally didactic or persuasive. Whether that means they should no longer be considered literary is not as important as whether the author attains his purpose. (Of course, we are able to say legitimately that a novel that is blatantly propagandistic is not good literature, particularly if it has none of the qualities we attribute to successful novels. But it is also possible that a propagandistic novel is at the same time good literature, and it is equally possible that a novel with no informative or persuasive purposes may be bad art. Authors may succeed at achieving more than one goal and may fail at achieving a single goal.) It is important to recognize, as Kinneavy and Britton have done, that any attempt to classify discourse according to aim, mode, or organizational pattern can be successful only in describing what dominates the discourse. In reality, discourse ignores the lines between categories. Writers often have multiple purposes and incorporate multiple strategies of arrangement to achieve them.

SECTION 3. COHERENCE IN DISCOURSE

Traditional concepts of coherence link it to arrangement, viewing it as an indication of the organization or form of a text. In the nineteenth century, Bain used the terms **unity, coherence,** and **emphasis** to identify the qualities of effective paragraphs, and through his influence, coherence has been referred to in most composition texts vaguely as a quality of paragraphs which helps establish unity (**emphasis** receives little emphasis in most texts). Researchers and theorists interested in coherence have attempted to identify the features of paragraphs that make them coherent, focusing primarily on structural patterns such as coordination and subordination (Christensen 1965); intersentential links (Winterowd (1970:226) is typical and also noteworthy because he uses the terms **coherence** and **form** synonymously); functional patterns (Becker 1965; Larson 1967; Young and Becker 1965). (For other recent concepts of the paragraph, see the "Symposium on the Paragraph" in *College Composition and Communication* 17:2 (1966). All of this work on coherence shares two features. First, it treats coherence as something found in texts, identifiable as grammatical, lexical, or semantic features. Second, although all of these researchers limit their work to the paragraph, all suggest that what they propose about coherence in paragraphs holds true for longer texts and for whole discourses.

Within the last decade, both of the shared features of the previously cited work have gained the attention of other composition theorists and researchers. Basing their work on concepts borrowed from text linguistics and pragmatics, Bamberg (1983), Phelps (1985), and Witte and Faigley (1981) have begun to explore coherence in whole discourses. In doing so, they have recognized the limitation of viewing coherence as exclusively textual and have distinguished between the concepts of coherence and cohesion, which have been and still are often used synonymously.

The view that coherence is a textual quality ignores the fact that a coherent discourse is one that is consistent in content, purpose, voice, and style. More important, coherence is determined as much by a reader's perception of a text as it is by a writer's intention or by the text itself. Fahnestock calls coherence "the quality enabling a reader to sense a 'flow' of meaning" (1983:400). Bamberg (1983), Phelps (1985), and Witte and Faigley (1981) point out that coherence is both textual and extratextual in that it depends both on textual clues and on the ability of readers "to draw on their own knowledge and expectations to bridge gaps and to fill in assumed information" (Bamberg 1983:420). Thus coherence is a feature of the whole communication process and involves the writer, the subject, the text, and the reader.

We will return to more theoretical definitions of coherence when we distinguish it from cohesion. First, however, we should note that despite the recognition that coherence is different from cohesion, few scholars have been able to point to specific features that may lead to coherence. In a report of research designed to identify such features, Bamberg (1983:428) presents the following criteria for a coherent essay (6):

(6) (i) Writer identifies the topic;
(ii) Writer does not shift topics or digress;
(iii) Writer orients the reader by describing the context or situation;
(iv) Writer organizes details according to a discernible plan that is sustained throughout the essay;
(v) Writer skillfully uses cohesive ties such as lexical cohesion, conjunction, reference, and so forth to link sentences and/or paragraphs together;
(vi) Writer often concludes with a statement that gives the reader a definite sense of closure;
(vii) Writer makes few or no grammatical and/or mechanical errors that interrupt the discourse flow or the reading process.

These criteria include some of the more conventional concepts about coherence such as identifying and not disgressing from the topic, organizing details according to a clear plan, and avoiding errors. More important, they refer to the role of the reader in determining coherence: the writer orients the **reader,** gives the **reader** a definite sense of closure, does not make errors that interrupt **reading.** By including these references to the reader in her criteria, Bamberg emphasizes the contextuality of coherence: Although it is a textual feature, it is not exclusively textual.

The recognition that coherence has extratextual features has made it possible to distinguish between coherence and cohesion. Until fairly recently, the terms were used interchangeably. For instance, Winterowd recently acknowledged that "the most serious weakness in 'The Grammar of Coherence' is its failure to distinguish between *cohesion* and *coherence*" and stated that the piece "was talking about the grammar of cohesion, not coherence" (1985:100–101). Winterowd's admitted confusion of the two terms does not undercut the importance of his earlier essay, but it does underscore that coherence and cohesion have only recently been differentiated from one another. The discussion of coherence thus far has hinted at the difference: **Coherence refers to the consistency of purpose, voice, content, style, form, and so on of a discourse as intended by the writer, achieved in the text, and perceived by the reader.** Cohesion, on the other hand, is a textual quality which contributes to coherence through verbal cues. Witte and Faigley explain the distinction as follows: "Cohesion defines those mechanisms that hold a text together, while coherence defines those underlying semantic relations that allow a text to be understood and used" (1981:202). Among the "mechanisms that hold a text together" are conjunctions of all kinds, including conjunctive adverbs, pronouns, and the words and phrases typically called transitions (such as *first, second,* etc.), as well as parallelism, the repetition of words, and the use of words that are typically associated with each other, including synonyms, near synonyms, antonyms, and words with semantic connections (such as *word, sentence, paragraph,* or *fire, hot, burn*). Such cohesive ties, as these mechanisms are called, can occur within sentences, but most research has concentrated on cohesion between sentences and in larger texts.

To illustrate the difference between coherence and cohesion, we can examine (7), from Witte and Faigley (1981:201).

(7) The quarterback threw the ball toward the tight end. Balls are used in many sports. Most balls are spheres, but a football is an ellipsoid. The tight end leaped to catch the ball.

These sentences are cohesive; that is, they are related to one another through a number of semantically similar words. The word *ball* appears in each sentence. The words *quarterback* and *tight end* in the first sentence are echoed by the word *sports* in the second sentence and the word *football* in the third. The words *threw* in the first sentence and *caught* in the fourth create a cohesive link between those two sentences. But despite the cohesiveness of these sentences, they do not comprise a coherent text. Most readers would agree that this series of sentences does not appear to have a purpose, that it is not consistent in terms of the content it provides. The first and fourth sentences seem to belong together because they describe a complete action, one that readers can interpret on the basis of their knowledge of the real world, but the second and third sentences do not seem part of that same world, nor do they seem to belong to the same world as one another. (It might be possible to imagine a coherent text that would include the second and third sentences—a text about different kinds of balls used in sports, perhaps—but even the act of imagining such a text demands that the reader participate in creating its coherence.)

The example of a series of cohesive sentences which are nevertheless not coherent points out that cohesion contributes to coherence, but does not assure it. Cohesion is an internal quality of texts; Halliday and Hasan suggest that "cohesion occurs where the INTERPRETATION of some element in the discourse is dependent upon that of another" (1976:4). For example, in the sentence just quoted, the interpretation of the word *that* depends on the presence of the word *interpretation* earlier in the sentence, and the interpretation of *another* depends on the presence of *element*. Coherence is a larger, more global quality of discourse, one that depends on features outside the text as well as within it. Coherent discourses announce or imply their topics, are governed by an overall plan, provide readers with enough information to allow them to understand the writer's meaning and purpose, and incorporate cohesive devices which create links between words and ideas. Thus coherence depends not only on internal interpretability of a text, but on its interpretability in terms of the world of the reader as well. This does not mean that any discourse that contradicts the reader's knowledge of reality is incoherent. If it did, science fiction and fantasy would be impossible, but they are interpretable because they include details and information that create a self-contained context. A text can, however, be incoherent if it assumes that the reader has more knowledge than he does or if, as in the football example cited earlier, it does not allow the reader to interpret the writer's intention.

The concept of coherence brings us full circle in our discussion of discourse. In a coherent discourse, the writer successfully communicates his message to his reader, using language not only for what it denotes, but for how it creates wholeness. His decisions about diction, syntax, and arrangement combine with his sense of purpose and his knowledge of his reader in the discourse he produces. The following chapters will present in detail the linguistic concepts that can enhance our understanding of the complex process of creating effective, coherent discourses.

CHAPTER 4

Language as a Human Phenomenon

SECTION 1. LANGUAGE AND LINGUISTICS

Linguistics is the scientific study of language. It is not concerned with any particular language, a language, but rather with language as a human faculty. In other words, this approach assumes that all the extant (i.e., live or dead but recorded) languages, whose number can be estimated at 5,600, share some basic traits. These traits are known as **language universals,** or—less accurately—**linguistic universals,** and linguistics has been interested in them for the last three or four decades. Before that, the obvious differences among languages, resulting in the lack of mutual intellegibility between virtually any two languages, obscured the common nature and basic properties of all human, or natural, languages. A few obvious examples of linguistic universals are listed below.

(1) (i) Every language has vowels and consonants.
(ii) Every language has verbs and nouns.
(iii) Every language has the triple organization, namely, from bottom up: sound → word → sentence.

The element of language organization mentioned in (1.iii) is one aspect of the main function of language, namely to pair certain sound sequences with certain meanings and therefore to enable speakers to convey or express the latter while uttering the former. If a one-to-one correspondence between all the possible sound sequences and all the possible meanings were available or feasible, the pairing process would be a matter of mechanical enumeration. In that case, communication could proceed by indicating a place on the list, for example by number, for each intended meaning. It so happens, however, that this organization is formidably complex, primarily because language has to, and does, have a potential for conveying infinitely many meanings with rather limited means.

A typical language has only a few dozen sounds, and various combinations of those sounds make up the words of the language. The number of words in a language is much greater—in a good dictionary, the number of entires may reach 500,000 or even more. However, more practical dictionaries may contain only 120,000 or even fewer words and still suffice. Even in such a dictionary, many if not most words are too special (2.i), exotic (2.ii), rare (2.iii), or outdated (2.iv) for most speakers. On the other pole of the scale, in a number of developed countries, a vocabulary of under 5,000 words is required from a high school graduate, while a 50,000-word potential enables one to pass easily for an intellectual.

(2) (i) allophone, combinatorial, deoxyribonucleic, feedbag, raceme
(ii) burnoose, busby, koto, phylactery, tournedos
(iii) jejune, monition, polonaise, serendipity, vociferous
(iv) beseem, felly, highboy, thou, velocipede

The number of sentences any language is capable of is infinite even if the individual vocabularies are limited, simply because—theoretically—there is no cap on the number of words in a sentence. No matter how many words a sentence has, a new adjective can be added to a noun, a new relative clause can be added to a noun phrase, or another sentence can be conjoined to the given one with the help of *and*. Even if the number of words in a sentence is limited to, say, 20 and the basic vocabulary is assumed to be 5,000, the number of possible sentences runs into millions.

In other words, the organization of language is such that a few dozen sounds can be combined in millions of ways to correspond to millions of complex meanings, each conveyed by a sentence. On top of that, sentences are combined into paragraphs and texts in millions of ways, resulting in even more complex meanings. This impressive organization job is made possible by a multileveled structure of language. In (3), the linguistic entities of each level are shown on the left and the basic linguistic disciplines that study them are on the right. From sound to text/discourse on the left, each higher entity consists of one or (usually) more lower entities, that is, each morph consists of one or more sounds, each word of one or more morphs, and so on. Meaning, however, is a different category—it does not consist of sentences. Meaning is a property possessed by all the entities on the list from discourse down to morph.

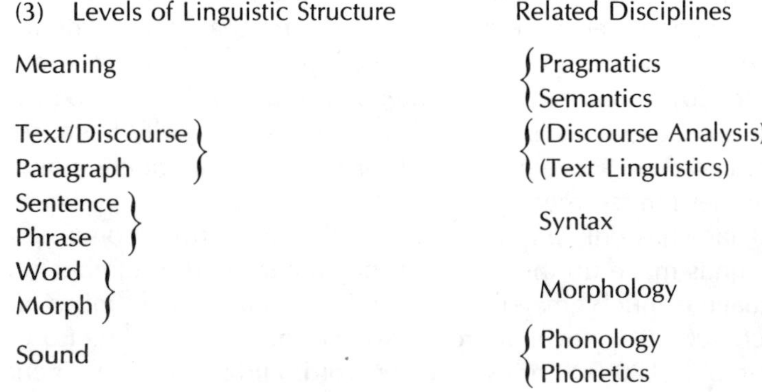

(3) Levels of Linguistic Structure
Related Disciplines
Meaning
Pragmatics
Semantics
Text/Discourse
Paragraph
(Discourse Analysis)
(Text Linguistics)
Sentence
Phrase
Syntax
Word
Morph
Morphology
Sound
Phonology
Phonetics

The disciplines on the right are central within linguistics, but the list is far from exhaustive. The disciplines in parentheses are perfectly legitimate but less well established than the others on the list. There are, however, other linguistic disciplines as well. Thus, for instance, borderline phenomena between sound and morph are studied by morphonology. All of the disciplines listed can study a certain language historically, thus constituting historical linguistics, with comparative linguistics within it trying to reconstruct the ancestors of extant languages, such as the Indo-European language for most European and many Asian languages. Each of the disciplines on the right in (3) can be applied to one particular language or group of languages, yielding such particular disciplines as English linguistics (phonetics, phonology, etc.), Germanic linguistics (phonetics, etc.), Semitic linguistics, and so on. Typology studies similarities and dissimilarities among languages which do not have the same origin.

There are specialized areas, such as dialectology and sociolinguistics and psycholinguistics. Immediately adjacent to linguistics proper, there are linguistic applications to the teaching of languages, lexicography (the making of dictionaries), natural-language artificial intelligence, humor research, sign language, animal communication, and, of course, rhetoric and composition. It can in fact be argued that sociolinguistics and psycholinguistics are applications of linguistics to sociology and psychology, respectively. Chapters 4–9 will deal briefly with each of the above-mentioned linguistic disciplines, but the bulk of the exposition will be devoted to the central (nonparenthesized) disciplines in (3), which form the foundation of the science of language.

SECTION 2. FACETS OF LANGUAGE

Language is a multifaceted phenomenon. It has biological and psychological, social and cultural, physical and historical, structural and formal facets, and each of these will be commented upon briefly in this section.

Language has a **biological** facet in three senses. First, speech is produced orally with the help of the so-called organs of speech. Natural-language sounds result from the passage of air, pumped out by the lungs, through the vocal chords in the larynx in the throat, and then through either the oral cavity (the mouth) or the nasal cavity (the nose). The uvula in the very back of the mouth is the valve that directs air to either cavity while blocking its way to the other. In the mouth the tongue, teeth, lips, and palate contribute in various combinations to the articulation of particular sounds.

Second and more important, human biological equipment includes the so-called speech center in the brain, usually in the left temple region. Apparently this is where utterances are formed and transmitted to the organs of speech for actual production and where perceived utterances are relayed for interpretation. What is known is that in the case of brain injuries, if a lesion occurs in that region, the speech ability is affected. Moreover, injuries to certain areas within the region may affect the victim in a specific way, causing a different sort of speech disorder or aphasia. Thus, depending on the exact location and seriousness of the lesion, the victim can lose a part of his or her vocabulary (a minor and usually temporary aphasia of this sort may occur to uninjured persons, leading to their groping for a name or a word they are sure they know) and use incorrect words (e.g., *mother* for *sister* or *apple* for *orange*). A different aphasia leaves the vocabulary intact but makes it impossible for the victim to combine words into sentences. A third kind affects the production commands, and the person utters nonsensical sounds while being under the impression that he or she is talking properly. Numerous other forms of aphasia have been observed, studied, and treated—not necessarily in this order—in the last half-century.

While the location of the speech center is known and there are some good hypotheses about its internal structure, it has not been possible to observe the mental mechanisms underlying language at work, primarily because the electrochemical processes that can be observed and measured do not relate to language or thought in any regular or clear way. This is why the observation of the product of the center's activity, namely of speech, remains the only way to get to know something about those mental mechanisms.

In the 1960s Chomsky suggested that people are born with a natural predisposition to language, in other words, that the human brain contains at birth the knowledge of all linguistic universals, of everything that all languages have in common, and that this innate knowledge is then activated by exposure to a particular language, resulting in the acquisition of that language. There has been a great deal of philosophical debate about this hypothesis. The alternative theory, favored by the behaviorists in psychology, is that babies are born with a clean slate and acquire a language by listening to samples of speech uttered by the parents and other speakers in their environment. Obviously, if the innate-language hypothesis prevails, language will be recognized as a much more biological phenomenon than the behaviorists would like to think.

Whether language is in fact innate bears heavily on the third issue with regard to its biological facet, namely, whether **language is species-specific,** whether it is exclusively human. Two major features are often put forward as possessed exclusively by human language and not by any system of animal communication—they are **creativity** and **freedom from external stimuli.** What is meant by creativity is much simpler and more accessible than writing poetry or novels—it involves the fact that just about any sentence one utters or perceives, including this very sentence, is uttered or perceived for the first time ever. Practically every sentence, therefore—ritual formulae such as *How do you do?* and various clichés and direct quotes excepted—is novel in this sense. Natural language is set up in such a way, as we saw in the previous section, that infinitely many novel sentences can be produced out of a very limited inventory of sounds and a less limited but clearly finite inventory of words.

Freedom from external stimuli is understood in this context as the situation in which, given an external stimulus such as hunger, the speaker can say *I am hungry* or *Let's go back* or *I can wait* or any number of other things, including nothing.

Animal systems of communication are often described as having a finite and limited number of signals, each of which must be uttered in the situation it describes, so that if the animal is hungry or in danger, the unique hunger or unique danger signal must be uttered. The reality defies these conclusions, at least in part. Reconnaissance bees are capable of producing an infinite number of signals in the direction and duration of their "dance" when they report to worker bees back in the hive on the exact location of a source of nourishment. Dogs and other animals are capable of play, which may be a kind of "unnecessary" behavior related to freedom from external stimuli.

The main thrust of research in animal communication, with most groups focusing on the primates, is to produce evidence that the animal can consciously produce a novel signal out of the known elements, for example, something along the lines of "I am hungry *and* in danger." They are constantly challenged on such findings by the opponents, who often claim that some surreptitious cuing takes place in the purported cases of animal language creativity, reducing the alleged new signal to a Pavlovian conditioned reflex.

The **psychological** facet of language should include all the complex links between human psychology and language. We know, for instance, that speech delivery, intonation, rate, pitch, and articulation depend strongly on the state of mind or on the mood the speaker happens to be in. A borderline discipline between psychology and linguistics, psycholinguistics, is supposed to study all these phenomena. However, so far it has been exclusively an experimental field, whose agenda depends heavily on the efficiency of the available and often fashionable techniques. Recently, a popular subject has been the so-called semantic memory, and the experiments have been designed to find out what kinds of semantic information can be recalled faster and what more slowly. The resulting concept of short-term and long-term human memory must have been influenced by the computer design with the similar distinction built into it.

There are two basic facts associated with the **social** facet of language. First, every language must have a **speech community** associated with it. The speech community must use the language monolingually and exclusively for all the domains and registers of its life. The size of speech communities ranges from hundreds of millions—for Mandarin Chinese, Spanish, English, Hindi/Urdu, Swahili, and Russian—to a few hundred native speakers—for such languages as Hinalug, a member of the Lezghin group in Azerbaijan in the Soviet Union. If a language loses its speech community, it becomes a dead language, though even in the case of such well-known dead languages as Greek, Latin, and Sanskrit, technically a few hundred monolingual native speakers can usually be found (usually these are orphans raised in enclosed religious communities in monasteries, for instance). However, there is a certain threshold and if the size of the speech community falls below it, the language loses its viability and becomes an "endangered species."

The threshold is not so much purely numerical—though it can be safely predicted that when the speech community is down to single thousands, the language is in trouble—but rather the indirectly but strongly related ability of a small society to maintain all the necessary institutions in its language. Thus, in Hinalug, an isolated mountain village with 1,700 inhabitants, it is impossible to get a higher education or learn any contemporary skill in the native tongue. The result is that the new generations grow up bilingual or trilingual (Hinalug, Azeri, Russian), and the native tongue reduces its sphere of application to family life, household chores, and village gossip, though a switch to a different language—**code switching**—occurs almost invariably in the latter when the story involves an episode outside the village.

The moment certain kinds of situations, or registers, fall beyond the scope of a language, it stops being a full-fledged, viable language and is likely to die out within a few generations. The process is usually irreversible, unless circumstances are favorable for deliberate efforts, based on a political consensus, to revive such a semidead language—the twentieth century witnessed some spectacular successes in this kind of endeavor, probably for the first time in history. Hebrew has been revived from the status of almost exclusively the language of prayer to become a live, vibrant, fully developed language of Israel. The Celtic languages—Welsh, Irish Gaelic, Scottish Gaelic, and Brittan—are staging a comeback probably in this order of progress made so far. These are all exceptions, however; usually a disappearing language cannot be helped. Since Franz Boas, an American anthropological linguist of German extraction and a pioneer of such efforts with regard to native American languages, linguists have felt obliged to record and describe each such language before it becomes extinct.

Second, the social facet of language is manifested in the **social differentiation** of national languages, reflecting the socioeconomic differentiation of the corresponding societies. This phenomenon is the subject of sociolinguistics, which studies the **social dialects** and the various phonetic, morphological, syntactical, and lexical phenomena characterizing them.

Thus, the pronunciation of *would you* as *wouju* or of *nothing* as *nothin'* and the use of *ain't* or of a double negative such as *I don't know nothin'* would attribute the speaker of American English to a nonprestigious group. Phrases such as *It's cool* or the ones interspersed with *man* were associated with the counterculture in the recent past. The use of rare words, such as the ones in (2.iii), is often associated with a more prestigious group of speakers. The use of such linguistic social identifiers is common in fiction, drama, and film.

The **cultural** facet of language is immediately related to the social one. Language is the vehicle of all institutional and creative culture the society has. Language and culture are inseparable, and since the former reflects the latter, the study of the language will provide invaluable clues into the culture underlying it. On the other hand, no real understanding or use of a language is possible without a considerable familiarity with its culture. How can a foreigner understand the meaning of such an English cliché as *to touch base* or even of an individual word such as *lobbyist* without some knowledge of baseball and the American political system, respectively? Language and culture as a combined phenomenon has been the subject of **anthropological linguistics.** Earlier in this century, following the example of the British anthropologist Malinowski (1923), the linguistic anthropologists tried to discover a "primitive" culture with an equally "primitive" language serving it, so that all the links between the two would be much more feasible to describe in full. However, while they did discover tribes that had never heard of automobiles, the complexity those cultures exhibited was of the same order of magnitude as in the "civilized" world. Later, the anthropological linguists started comparing small and closed groups of related words, such as the systems of kinship in various languages, with the cultures those languages served; the focus on some such semantic fields (see chapter 8, section 2.1)—color terms, words for love, terms of endearment, curses, and so forth—characterizes much current work in linguistic anthropology.

The **physical** aspect of language involves the acoustical nature of sound, and acoustics is, of course, a branch of physics. Acoustics will be dealt with briefly in the next section, so it will suffice to mention here that linguistic sound is a kind of vibration (i.e., a frequent alternation of impulse with no impulse, of "up" and "down") and as all other vibrations, such as radio or TV waves, it is characterized by volume, or amplitude, or range, and by frequency (i.e., the number of cycles between two adjacent "ups" per unit of time). The volume is usually measured in decibels, and the frequency in cycles per second (cps). The human ear perceives the frequency range between approximately 16 and 10,000 cps and is uncomfortable with a sound louder than 80 decibels. Naturally, human organs of speech are designed to produce sounds within this comfortable perception range.

The **historical** facet of language is also simple enough. Languages change in time, they undergo historical changes. These changes are an interesting combination of change and continuity. Languages tend to change somewhat with each new generation. Children tend to talk differently from their parents and, even more obviously, from their grandparents. The English of Shakespeare is very hard for modern speakers of English, who live some 350 years later; to understand Chaucer's English of over 600 years ago is accordingly even harder for a modern reader, let alone speaker, to understand. On the other hand, parents and children must be able to communicate, and they most certainly do, so the generational changes have to be small enough. The mechanism of change in languages depends on gradual accumulation, accelerated by historical and social cataclysms, such as wars, revolutions, and mass migrations. The first two cause class transpositions and regrouping of social dialects, leading to substantial changes in the prestigious standard dialect. Migrations bring language interference and borrowings. Language change will be discussed in somewhat more detail in chapter 9.

The **structural** facet of language is central to what language is all about. Language structure is what makes the elaborate organization, necessary for the efficient pairings of sound sequences and meanings, possible and efficient. The linguistic disciplines of phonetics/phonology, morphology, syntax, and semantics/pragmatics, discussed in chapters 5–8, study the various levels of linguistic structure and make up the bulk of any linguistic introduction. Linguistic structure is characterized by intricate networks of relations within each level and among the various levels. Every single entity in language is what it is because of its relations with other entities. In a certain sense, each such entity is a bundle of relationships. The triple organization of every natural language—sound→word→sentence; see (1.iii)—is the foundation of linguistic structure.

While it seems obvious now, the realization that language is an elaborate structure did not occur until early in the twentieth century, and when it did, thanks to the independent efforts of Ferdinand de Saussure in Switzerland, Jan Baudouin de Courtenay in Poland and Russia, and Franz Boas in Germany and the United States, it led to the emergence of an entirely new approach to linguistics. Known as structural linguistics, it dominated the field until at least the 1950s and was characterized by a clear preference for precise, mathematicalized methods, a tradition inherited by contemporary linguistics. Mathematical reasoning is formal, and therefore, with structural linguistics, language acquired a **formal** facet. Formality does not necessarily mean the use of prohibitive formalism—what it does mean is explicitly and clearly stated definitions and rules, which can be used and applied without resorting to any intuitive knowledge on the part of the user; this is not the case in traditional grammars and descriptions, which appeal to the reader's intuition all the time.

In traditional description, a reference can be made to 'verbs of motion' as a group and an observation made about them. Whether or not a given verb belongs to such a group or not is up to the reader to decide, and his or her ability to make a correct attribution (e.g., is *to stop* a verb of motion or not?) without any guidance or control on the part of the linguist will thus determine whether the description will be understood or misunderstood. A structural description, on the other hand, would typically list all the verbs of motion and state a rule with a reference to this list. The use of the rule would thus be rendered mechanical: To determine whether the rule applies to a given verb the user simply looks it up in the list. In French, whether a verb is one of motion determines whether it is used with the auxiliary *être* 'be' instead of the standard *avoir* 'have.' This conception of formality suggests the setting up of rules for mechanical use, without thinking and without knowing anything about the language in question. The only knowledge required is the ability to interpret the straightforward notational conventions in the rules and to manipulate language entities in strict accordance with the rules. Needless to say, an enormous amount of thinking has to go into the way the rules are set up in order to render their mechanical application meaningful.

Structural linguistics attempted to exclude the native speaker and his or her intuition from this scheme of things. Its motto was "Whatever the speaker says *in* his language is sacred; whatever he says *about* it is nonsense." Practically, structural linguists always tried to elicit as much language matieral from the native informant as possible, often using themselves as their own informants and applying introspection to provide the necessary **corpus** of language samples, and then to apply their formal methods of segmentation and distribution (see chapter 5) to the material, trying to obtain the complete information about the language in this way. The structural techniques did not prove very effective outside phonetics, phonology, and some morphology, partly because the structuralists' study of syntax and especially semantics was crippled by their exclusion of the native speaker's intuition from consideration.

A much more natural balance between formality and intuition was discovered by Chomsky in the mid-1950s. While having inherited the formal, mechanical-rule orientation from structural linguistics (which he is popularly believed to have dethroned, practically single-handedly, at that time), he suggested that the purpose of any such system of formal rules postulated by linguists was to model the native speaker's intuition in some important respect, and where the output of a formal theory or description deviated from the native speaker's judgment, the former had to be made to fit. Chomsky's transformational grammar, a syntactic theory, is the best example of this approach, and it will be discussed in chapter 7. The "post-transformational" linguistics of the 1970 and 1980s has been experiencing an acute "identity crisis" concerning the nature, role, and degree of formality in its perception of linguistic theory.

SECTION 3. MAJOR LINGUISTIC DICHOTOMIES

Since de Saussure, linguistics has distinguished between language and speech, synchrony and diachrony, and syntagmaticity and paradigmaticity.

Language and **speech** are inseparable but distinct. Language is the abstract system internalized in the minds of native speakers. Language makes speech possible and it is manifested in and as speech. However, language as such cannot be heard or uttered. Speech, on the other hand, is observable as uttered and perceived utterances. Language can be studied only through the observation of speech, but speech is not an ideal input for such a study because utterances can contain elements characterizing them but not the linguistic mechanisms underlying them. Thus, real speech may contain slips of the tongue, such as the famous spoonerisms in (4); however, their perpetrator does have the same words free of error in his internal lexicon, and making the slip does not at all mean that his knowledge of the language is somehow deficient. Speech may, and does, contain sentences that are ungrammatical because of a change of plan in the middle of a sentence (5.i) or because the speaker forgets the beginning of the sentence halfway through it (5.ii). Finally, in speech, extremely long sentences or sentences with a structure burdensome for our memory ((6) is an example made up by Victor Yngve in the 1950s to illustrate his then famous hypothesis that the speakers have a short-term memory which can handle only 5 to 9, i.e., 7±2, 'regressive syntactic structures, of which (6) has exactly 7—the sentence has proven to be virtually universally impossible to comprehend when presented orally, and, of course, from the point of view of language, it is a perfectly well-formed sentence), are not used because they are not effective, while in the abstract system of language, they exist in the same realm of grammatical possibilities as the more acceptable shorter and simple sentences (this sentence is a good example of an overlong and overloaded sentence, which is less acceptable in speech than the shorter and simpler sentences are).

(4) (i) You hissed my mystery lecture.
(ii) You have tasted the whole worm.

(5) (i) Let me tell about my own experience in the Sahara desert when I was young, and I mean like—they drive me crazy, those old-sounding wise guys the teenagers tend to be these days, because I did not wear my first pair of trousers until my prom—you just look at all those made-up fourteen-year-old girls these days.

(ii) The result I am talking about is not so much in terms of money because money is much less important than the ideas because ideas can generate money but not vice versa, so that's why they are more important.

(6) If what going to a clearly understaffed school really means is not appreciated we should be concerned.

The more contemporary terms for language and speech are **linguistic competence** and **linguistic performance,** respectively, and the structuralist notion of linguistics as being the study of the former to the total exclusion of the latter is still accepted widely. Both Bloomfield and Chomsky used this view to exclude certain parts of linguistics from its permitted agenda—for Bloomfield, it was semantics; for Chomsky, much semantics and all pragmatics.

Synchrony and **diachrony** involve a conceptually simpler distinction between a descriptive and historical approach in linguistics. Synchronic linguistics studies any single stage in the development of a particular language or group of languages, without comparing that stage to any other preceding or following it. Thus, a study of contemporary American English is synchronic, and so is a description of the language of Chaucer if no comparison is made. If such a comparison is the goal of the research, it is of a diachronic nature. Chapters 5–8 deal exclusively with synchronic linguistics.

Syntagmaticity and **paradigmaticity** refer to the study of linguistic entities within the same actual utterance and as lists of phenomena not occurring in the same utterance, respectively. Thus, saying that *you* and *have tasted* are the subject and predicate, respectively, of (4.ii) is to make a syntagmatic statement, while saying that *you* is a personal pronoun in English, along with *I, he, she, it, we,* and *they,* is paradigmatic because this statement is not made relative to any particular segment of speech. This last dichotomy is less important but the terms tend to be misused and their meaning somewhat mystified in the literature.

SECTION 4. LANGUAGE AS COMMUNICATION

Finally, language is the primary means of human communication. In general, communication involves the message, the sender, and the recipient. Linguistic communication has the utterance, the speaker, and the hearer, as shown in (7).

(7)

Naturally, the speaker and hearer constantly change places in the process of communication, and it has been realized recently that turn-taking is an important communicative skill and the one acquired the earliest by babies. While interruptions are possible in both friendly and hostile environments, they are perceived as aberrations and violations of the rule.

When the speaker and hearer coincide in one person, as in the case of inner speech or keeping a diary, communication gives way to thought expression; language is, of course, used for that purpose as well, competently but somewhat marginally as far as its relation with thought is concerned. While very little reliable evidence on the complex relation between thought and language is available, even simple introspection seems to suggest that people hardly ever think in complete sentences. It is believed that linguistic "shorthand," such as one-word labels or short and incomplete phrases, is used in thinking quite effectively, along with pictorial images not related to language.

To summarize this chapter, linguistics emerges from this brief and general discussion as the study of linguistic competence, of mental mechanisms underlying language, and of the primary means of human communication. Other perspectives on language and linguistics will emerge from the next four chapters.

CHAPTER 5

Phonetics and Phonology

SECTION 1. SOUND

The sounds of natural language are the smallest observable entities in speech. What the native speaker hears when listening to speech is a continuous flow of sound. There are no pauses between sounds, and even pauses between words are not necessarily there, despite the fact that blanks between written words are a common convention. In real speech, pauses can be more reliably predicted between phrases and, even more so, between sentences. However, the native speaker distinguishes separate, discrete sounds in this continuous flow of speech and identifies sequences of them as words.

The sound of natural language is studied by two disciplines, phonetics and phonology. The former does it empirically, the latter theoretically.

SECTION 2. PHONETICS

Phonetics provides the tools of empirical analysis of language sound. The phonetics of a particular language pursues the following goals:

(1) **Goals of Phonetics:**

- (i) to segment the continuous flow of sound into discrete, identifiable, and recurring units, thus matching the native speaker's intuitive phonetic abilities;
- (ii) to make a complete inventory of the sounds of a language;
- (iii) to describe each sound in terms of its articulation and acoustics;
- (iv) to describe the elements of pronunciation besides the sounds (the suprasegmental elements).

2.1. Transcription

After the continuous flow of sound is successfully segmented into discrete sounds, the result should be presented in a system of notation in which every sound is represented by one symbol and every symbol always stands for the same sound. In principle, so-called **phonetic systems of writing,** or phonetic orthographies, are supposed to be based on the same principle. In practice, however, the ideal one-to-one correlation between letters and sounds is very hard to discover. Orthographies range from a few good approximations of the ideal, such as the use of the standard Latin alphabet for Italian or Swahili, to the disastrous irregularity of English spelling. The reason for this in English is primarily that the spelling was "frozen" with the advent of the printing press, at which time the orthography was not too bad, but numerous ensuing changes in pronunciation have not been accompanied by corresponding changes in spelling. In many languages, the problem is that there are more different sounds than there are Latin characters. Those languages resort to various additional, 'diacritical' signs over certain letters, such as the umlaut ¨, hachek ˇ; accents ´, `, or ˆ, the tilde ˜; and so on, or to much rarer signs under the line, such as the cedilla ¸ , or the syllable-forming dot ̣. The ultimate criterion of the accessibility of a phonetic orthography is, of course, one's ability to pronounce a written word while knowing only the conventions of the orthography but not the word itself. The English orthography would score very low on this test because the same sound in it can be represented by numerous letters or combinations of letters (2.i) and the same letter can stand for a number of sounds (2.ii). George Bernard Shaw, however, went too far when he claimed that *ghoti* should read as *fish* in English because of the availability of such spellings of the three sounds in the latter word as in (2.iii)—those spellings are somewhat marginal and positional: Thus *gh* as *f* is impossible at the beginning of a word, and *ti* can stand for *sh* only in suffixes such as *-tion*.

(2) (i) m**ee**t, m**ea**t, m**e**ter, bel**ie**ve, rec**ei**ve, **I**ssey, C**ae**sar
(ii) **a**lone, **a**nd, ab**a**te, f**a**ther, **a**ll
(iii) lau**gh,** w**o**men, na**ti**on

(Shaw bequested a considerable sum of money to a future reformer of English spelling, and while many proposals have been made, the money remains unclaimed because of the stipulation that everybody adopt the new alphabet.)

Unable to use the spelling, linguists developed their own system of expressing sounds with symbols on a strict one-to-one basis. In the 1920s, they adopted the **International Phonetic Alphabet (IPA)**, which was supposed to contain enough different symbols for all the sounds of all extant languages; various modifications and additions have been made since.

Every particular language uses a small portion of all the known sounds and, therefore, of the IPA symbols. The process and result of rendering the sounds into IPA is called transcription. The list in (3) contains the symbols necessary for American English, with a few relevant examples.

(3) IPA Symbols	Examples of Spelling
p	**p**in, s**p**in, sim**p**le, zi**pp**er, hicou**gh**
b	**b**in, am**b**le, ni**b**, ni**bb**le
t	**t**in, s**t**ick, ca**t**er, la**tt**er, walke**d**
d	**d**in, la**d**en, **d**i**d**, shove**d**, la**dd**er
k	**k**in, **q**ui**ck**, **c**ro**ck**, s**ch**eme, fi**x**[1]
g	**g**oat, fi**g**, **g**i**gg**le, **gu**est, e**x**act
f	**f**in, tri**f**le, i**f**, tou**gh**, **ph**iloso**ph**er
v	**v**eal, e**v**il, e**v**e, o**f**, sa**vv**y
θ	**th**in, pi**th**y, ba**th**, tee**th**
ð	**th**en, fa**th**er, ba**th**e, tee**th**e
s	**s**in, **ps**ychology, **sc**ion, re**c**eive
z	**z**ip, **x**erox, ro**s**e**s**, pea**s**, e**x**act
š	**sh**in, **s**ure, o**ce**an, lu**x**ury, con**sci**ous
ž	trea**s**ure, a**z**ure, bei**g**e, gara**g**e, preci**si**on
h	**h**en, **wh**o, re**h**ash
č	**ch**in, pi**tch**er, righ**te**ous, na**tu**re
ǰ	**j**u**dg**e, **g**in, a**dj**acent, su**gg**est
m	**m**u**m**, i**m**possible, co**m**e, co**mb**
n	**n**ip, **gn**at, **kn**ee, si**gn**, **pn**eumatic
ŋ	fi**n**ger, si**n**k, si**ng**er, a**n**xious, thi**ng**
l	**l**itt**l**e, si**ll**y, sa**l**t, ca**ll**
r	**r**ip, fai**r**y, gi**r**l, **rh**ythm, **r**ight
w	**w**in, q**u**een, lang**u**age, ch**o**ir, **w**itch
ʍ[2]	**wh**y, **wh**ale, **wh**ich
y	**y**ou, f**e**w, d**u**e[3], b**e**auty, m**u**se
i	m**ee**t, m**ea**t, m**e**t**e**, rec**ei**ve
ɪ	b**i**t, **i**mpossible, pr**e**tty, w**o**men
e	ab**a**te, b**ay**, st**ea**k, v**ei**n, g**au**ge
ɛ	m**e**t, obsc**e**nity, s**ay**s, l**ea**d, fr**ie**nd
æ	m**a**t, th**a**t, d**a**d, r**a**t
u	d**o**, r**u**de, thr**ough**, t**o**, t**oo**, tw**o**
ʊ	b**u**ll, p**u**t, f**oo**t, w**o**lf
o	m**oa**t, m**ow**, b**eau**, d**ough**, s**ou**l
ɔ[4]	b**ough**t, c**augh**t, **awe**, b**o**re, **o**r
a	b**o**ttle, kn**o**wledge, n**o**t
ə	b**u**s, d**oe**s, l**u**ck, **u**s; **a**lone, harm**o**ny, wom**a**n
ay	b**i**te, f**igh**t, **ai**sle, ch**oi**r, d**ie**
aw	b**ow**, d**ow**n, d**ou**bt, c**ow**
ɔy	b**oy**, f**oi**l, t**oi**l

[1]Here and below, the letter *x* stands for the sound in question and an additional sound.

[2]The sound [ʍ] is not present in all American dialects. The diagnostic test is provided by the words *witch:which*. Those people who pronounce these two words identically do not have [ʍ] in their phonetic repertoire.

[3]In some American dialects, the sound [y] is missing from this and many similar words. Everybody, however, keeps it where confusion is possible, for example, *beauty:booty*.

[4]In some American dialects, this sound is not distinct from the next one. The diagnostic test is *caught:cot*. Those who pronounce the two words identically have one sound instead of two. Everybody, however, keeps the distinction before [r]: *car* and *core* are never pronounced identically, for example.

The boldface letters in the examples indicate, often very roughly, what letters represent the sound in question. Thus, for instance, the sound [y] gets no representation in the spelling of some words. The three separated groups of sounds in (3) constitute the consonants, single vowels, and diphthongs of English, respectively. These terms will be formally introduced in the next subsection.

In (4.ii), a whole sentence (4.i) is transcribed (it is conventional to have a pair of square brackets at the beginning and end of the transcription).

(4) (i) It is extremely important to remember that each word consists of sounds represented by its transcription and not at all by its spelling.
(ii) [ɪt ɪz ɪkstrimli ɪmpɔrtənt tu rɪmɛmbər ðæt ič wərd kənsɪsts əv sawndz rɛprɪzɛntɪd bay ɪts trænskrɪpšən ænd nat æt ɔl bay ɪts spɛlɪŋ]

(4.i) is, in fact, a very important statement. Unfortunately, most people can be completely "hypnotized" by the customary spelling and talk and think of the letters instead of the sounds. Such people are likely to insist that they pronounce a sound like [ǰ] differently in all the examples in its line because all the spellings are different. The electronic analysis of their pronunciation (see section 2.3), however, will always prove them wrong. Spelling is not a linguistic phenomenon but rather an external convention (cf. chapter 1, section 3.1), and it is ignored by linguistics entirely beyond this point.

2.2. Articulatory Phonetics

After the sounds are segmented, identified, and transcribed, they are studied by articulatory phonetics from the point of view of how exactly they are pronounced. Articulatory phonetics sets up a number of distinctive features, in terms of which the sounds are characterized. We will set up just six main features, two for both vowels and consonants together, and two each for consonants and vowels separately.

The first articulatory feature for all sounds is Vowel versus Consonant, or ± Vowel. All the sounds in the first portion of (3) are consonants, and all the others are vowels. The difference in the pronunciation is in the presence of an obstruction to the passage of exhaled air. If the obstruction is there, the result is a consonant: if it is not, a vowel is articulated.

The second articulatory feature is Voiced versus Voiceless, or ±Voice. All the vowels and some of the consonants are voiced but some other consonants are not. The vocal chords are tense and they vibrate in the case of the voiced sounds; they are loose and quiet in the case of the voiced ones. The vibrations can be felt if one puts a couple of fingers to one's throat at the collar level, and they cease immediately when one switches to an unvoiced sound, for example, from [z] to [s]. These two sounds are a typical voiced/unvoiced pair, and many others are available in English. The articulation of the two members of a pair is identical, except for the use of the vocal chords. The consonants in (3) are, in fact, listed in pairs, with the unvoiced ones coming first. The exceptions are [h], which does not have the voiced counterpart, and the last eight consonants on the list, which are all voiced and have no voiceless counterparts in English.

The next two articulatory features concern obstruction, and they are therefore applicable only to consonants. The third main articulatory feature for consonants is the place of the obstruction. Unlike the previous two articulatory features, it is not binary, that is, it does not have just two values, plus and minus. Instead, there are seven places where the consonantal obstruction may be created in English. For the bilabial consonants (from the Latin *labia* 'lips'), it is created by the two lips coming together (see (5) for the listing of this and other types of consonants). For the labiodental consonants, the obstruction is created by the combination of the lower lip and upper teeth. For the interdentals, the tip of the tongue goes between the teeth, protruding for some speakers. The alveolar consonants are articulated by creating an obstruction resulting from a contact or near contact of the tip of the tongue and the high ridges above the upper teeth, called the alveolae. The palatal consonants are formed by raising the front part of the tongue to the part of the palate immediately behind the alveolae. The obstruction for the velar consonants is created by the back part of the tongue against the back part of the palate called the velum. And, finally, even farther back into the throat, in the glottis, the glottal consonants are articulated.

The fourth and final main articulatory feature for consonants concerns the manner of obstruction. If the passage of air is blocked altogether as part of the articulation and the consonant results from the 'explosion' of the obstruction, it is called the stop, or the explosive. If, on the other hand, the passage of air is never blocked entirely and the air is allowed to escape all the time in the process of articulation, the consonant is created by friction of the air against the organs of speech brought closely together and is called the fricative. The third type, the affricate, is a combination of a stop and a fricative—the two English affricates, [č] and [ǰ], combine the articulations of [t] and [š] and of [d] and [ž], respectively. One diagnostic test for a stop is that it cannot be made to last long, while any fricative can. The affricate cannot be made to last long without its slipping into its second, fricative component; thus, any attempt to pronounce a "long" [č] results in a [t] and a long [š]. Generally, there are no long consonants in English, and the double spelling always signifies a single consonant.

In (5), the English consonants are listed with regard to their third and fourth main articulatory features.

The consonants that share the same slot in the chart are further distinguished by auxiliary articulatory features. Thus, [m, n, ŋ] are the three nasal consonants in English—they are stops in the oral cavity but the air is allowed to escape through the nasal cavity, so they can be made to last as

(5) Manner	Stop	Fricative	Affricate
Place			
Bilabial	p, b, m	w, ʍ	
Labiodental		f, v	
Interdental		θ, ð	
Alveolar	t, d, n, r, l	s, z	
Palatal		š, ž, y	č, ǰ
Velar	k, g, ŋ		
Glottal		h	

fricatives. To accommodate the situation, if these further distinctions are important, sometimes the fourth main feature for consonants is set up as two features, ±Stop and ±Fricative (with a special provision for the affricates), and then the nasals are characterized as either +Stop, +Fricative, or −Stop, −Fricative, while the regular stops and fricatives are +Stop, −Fricative, and −Stop, +Fricative, respectively. [r, l] are also characterized as stops with reservations; Known as the laterals, they are pronounced with a complete obstruction formed, but the air is allowed to escape around the lowered sides of the raised tongue.

The nasals and the laterals each form a natural class of consonants. Other natural classes share special articulations as well—there are the sibilants (from the Latino *sibilare* 'to hiss') [s, z, š, ž, č, ǰ]; the sonorants [m, n, r, l, ŋ]; the glides, or semivowels [r, w, y]. In the articulation of the latter class, it is not entirely clear whether the organs of speech are brought together to create friction as for fricative consonants or a very narrow passage without friction as for some vowels. The solution is run along the lines of stops and fricatives; the first main feature for all sounds can be divided into two, ±Vowel and ±Consonant, and then the semivowels can be described as either +Vowel, +Consonant or −Vowel, −Consonant.

Thanks to the auxiliary articulatory features and natural classes, each consonant on chart (5) obtains a unique combination of articulatory features, and in general it is typical of languages not to have two different sounds with very close articulations unless they are variants of the same phoneme (see section 3).

Two main articulatory features are set up for vowels as well. The third feature for vowels is loosely denoted as "Front-Back," and it is concerned with the part of the tongue that gets tense and is raised considerably or slightly to shape the column of air for a particular vowel. The feature has three values, front, central, and back. The fourth feature, "height," is concerned with the degree of raising the tongue. For English, it is useful to set up three levels, high, mid, and low, with two intermediate ones in between, high-mid, and mid-low. The chart in (6) assigns the corresponding values of these two features to each American English vowel.

(6) Front-Back Height	Front	Central	Back
High			
High-Mid	i		u
Mid	ɪ		ʊ
Mid-Low	e		o
Low	ɛ	ə	ɔ
	æ		a

As the chart shows, the central area, at least in its lower region, is taken over by the indefinite vowel called the schwa, or shwa (from its name in Hebrew). As its line in (3) shows, in some examples it is stressed, in others it is not. Until rather recently, most American dialects differentiated between these two cases and maintained a separate low central vowel, denoted as [ʌ], in the stressed position, while limiting the indefinite, reduced schwa to the unstressed position.

Diphthongs are vowels consisting of one half of a single vowel and one half of a semivowel. Some phoneticians treat every possible combination of an English vowel with an English semivowel as a diphthong, and it is true that many native speakers of American English hear, and somewhat fewer pronounce, somewhat different vowels before [r]; it is hard for those people to accept that the vowel in *bed* and *bear* is the same, namely [ɛ].

Each vowel in a word forms a syllable, and the word has as many syllables as there are vowels. (In some languages, and marginally in English, the sonorants are also capable of forming syllables. In English, the alternative theory postulates a schwa before every sonorant "suspected" of forming a syllable, e.g., in *possible* [pasəbəl], thus simplifying the English syllabics.) (7.i) contains one-syllable, or monosyllabic, words; (7.ii) two-syllable, or bisyllabic, words; (7.iii) three-syllable, or trisyllabic, words; and (7.iv) words with over three syllables, or polysyllabic words, which are much rarer in English than in some other languages. Each syllable consists of one vowel either alone or preceded and/or followed by one to three consonants. The English language does not tolerate heavy combinations of consonants, or consonantal clusters, and four consonants together is probably the maximum, as in *extra [*ɛkstrə], in which case the cluster is usually divided between two syllables. Where the syllabic boundary is drawn is not very important in those languages which like English do not favor dividing a word in spelling between the end of one line and the beginning of the next one. Other languages, like Russian, insist on doing it often and strictly along the syllabic boundaries. The number of syllables in a word is important for stress in linguistics and for meter in poetry.

(7) (i) dóg, bóok, áwe, mét, whíte

(ii) desíre, wríting, sólid, stréetwise, dictáte

(iii) ùncóver, líbidò, búrgundy, élephant, òverdó
(iv) ùndeírable, òverprodúction, electrónically, elèctrocárdiogrȁm

In each English word, one syllable is pronounced stronger than all the others and is defined as stressed. The accents over some vowels in (7) indicate where the stress falls; it is simpler to treat the only syllable of a monosyllabic word as stressed as well. Besides that, in American English more than in British English and as is not the case in most other languages, a polysyllabic word is likely to contain a second-strongest syllable, which carries the secondary stress marked as ` in (7). The tertiary (̏) and quartiary stress are not unheard-of either.

Besides not favoring the nonprimary stresses, languages other than English may have much stronger preferences as to the place of the stress in a word. Such fixed-stress languages as French or Polish always stress the same syllable of the word, the last and the last but one, respectively. A somewhat weaker regularity is exhibited by Italian or Latin, both of which stress the next to last syllable unless it is formed by a short vowel, in which case the preceding syllable, if there is one, gets the stress. Some languages keep the stress on the same syllable of the word, independent of its form; others like English may deviate from that, for example, *lúxury:luxúrious*. Still other languages, such as Swedish, Chinese, Thai, and many others, add a musical tone to the sheer strength of simple dynamic stress such as English stress. In Thai, for instance, the same sound sequence [paa] means 'rice paddy,' 'maternal uncle,' and 'face,' when pronounced with the rising, falling, or flat tone, respectively.

So far we have discussed word stress. In a sentence, there is sentence stress: Certain types of words are allowed to keep their word stresses when they enter the sentence and other types have to lose theirs. Thus, in (8.i) only the third and fifth words keep their stresses. They are a verb and a noun, respectively, and two other 'independent' parts of speech, adjectives and adverbs (see chapter 6), typically keep their word stresses as well.

(8) (i) I am réading a bóok
(ii) *Í* am réading a bóok
(iii) I *ám* réading a bóok
(iv) I am réading *á* bóok
(v) I am *réading* a bóok
(vi) I am réading a *bóok*

(9) (i) I am reading a book, not anybody else
(ii) I am reading a book right now
(iii) I am reading one book
(iv) I am reading a book, not learning it by heart
(v) I am reading a book, not a magazine

Stressing a word in a sentence that should not be stressed renders the sentence emphatic (8.ii–iv), with additional meaning implied. A similar effect is achieved by double-stressing a word that is already stressed (8.v–vi). The additional meanings implied by (8.ii–vi) are exemplified by (9.i–v), respectively.

In many languages including English, the words in a sentence are characterized by pitch, the sentence counterpart of musical tone in a stressed syllable. Typically, a "regular" nonemphatic sentence (e.g., (10.i)) has a falling pitch pattern (10.ii). A general question (10.iii) has a rising pitch pattern (10.iv), while a special question (with an interrogative word) follows (10.ii). Sentence (11.i) has the usual meaning if pronounced roughly as (11.ii) and an absurd and funny meaning if the pitch goes sharply up on the last word (11.iii).

(10) (i) I am reading a book

(ii)  — — — —

(iii) Are you reading a book?

(iv) — — — — —

(11) (i) What did you put in my drink, Jane?

(ii) 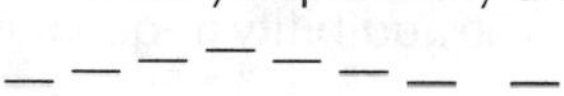 — — — — — — — —

(iii) 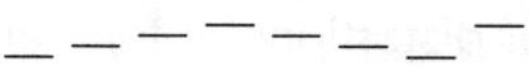 — — — — — — — —

The word and sentence stresses, emphasis, pitch, rate of speech delivery, and a few more or less simple factors make up language intonation, which characterizes every language and sets it apart from any other language as much as, if not more than, its actual sounds do. Comedians who poke fun at various accents pay a great deal of attention to the intonation, real or alleged, of a dialect or a language, and, for the listeners' recognition, often depend on it more than on distorted pronunciations.

2.3. Acoustic Phonetics

Acoustic phonetics studies the sound of language as a physical, acoustic phenomenon, namely as vibrations. It establishes correlations between articulations and acoustic properties of various sounds.

Thus, vowels are characterized by tone while consonants are noises. The latter are harder to describe acoustically because they are not regular vibrations, or waves.

Every native speaker's voice is characterized by a unique basic tone of a certain frequency. People are aware of this when they knock on the door and answer *It's me* to the question *Who's there?* Since the answer itself is devoid of any content, its function is simply to produce a sample of the familiar voice and thus to gain admission. Nobody would say *It's me* if the person inside is a stranger.

Male voices are lower than female voices; their basic tones are close to 100 cps. For female speakers, tones are closer to 200 cps. Each vowel uttered by a given speaker is a combination of the basic tone and a few dozen overtones, all sounding at the same time, at least in principle. Each overtone is a multiple of the basic tone. Thus, if a man's basic tone is 110 cps, his overtones are 220, 330, 440, 550, . . . cps, all the way to the upper limit of the human frequency range, around 16,000 cps. A female with the basic tone of 220 cps will have twice fewer overtones within the range, 440, 660, . . . cps.

Most of the overtones have an amplitude close to zero. For all practical purposes, only a handful of overtones are actually audible. What makes every vowel unique is the combination of audible overtones. Each vowel is characterized and actually constituted by two or more groups of overtones, each such group around a certain frequency. These frequencies are constant for all speakers but every individual speaker accommodates them with his own overtones. This elegant arrangement allows for both the uniqueness of pronunciation for each individual speaker and the certainty of recognition for each vowel, no matter who pronounces it. The audibility frequencies for each vowel are called the formants.

Consonants are unique combinations of distortions of tone and pauses. Electronic equipment has been available to present speech visually for a few decades now. It has recently given way to much more advanced computerized equipment. The pictures that both old oscillographs and spectrographs and new digital computers present on their screens demonstrate two basic facts. First, consonants are much more complex acoustically than vowels. Second, the human ear seems to remain a better analyzer of human speech than any machine.

SECTION 3. PHONOLOGY

Like phonetics, phonology is concerned with language sound. However, quite unlike phonetics, it is a highly theoretical discipline, which postulates abstract concepts and operates with them formally to match that aspect of the native speaker's linguistic competence that is the phonological competence. The goal of phonology is to provide a formal theory on which the phonological description of every particular language would draw. The goals of the phonological description of a language are stated in (12).

(12) **Goals of Phonology:**

(i) to provide the complete phonemic inventory of a langauge, that is, the list of all word-distinguishing invariants;

(ii) to discover and formulate all the phonological processes and rules of the language;

(iii) to ensure that the results of (i) and (ii) are compatible with the results of (1) for the same language as well as explaining, determining, and having limited predictive powers about the phonetic description of the language obtained in line with (1).

3.1. Phonological Competence

Unlike the goals of phonetics in (1), (12) requires a serious explanation and building-up to. We will start with the central notion of phonology, the **phoneme.** The formal apparatus, set up to define the phoneme, is the first example in this book of a formal linguistic theory trying to match a native linguistic ability. What is the phonological competence of the native speaker? We will first describe what the theory is trying to match and then we will demonstrate how it attempts to achieve that.

The basis of the native speaker's phonological competence is the ability to identify purely intuitively two or more different, often quite different, sounds as the realizations, tokens, or variants of the same invariant sound. Thus, if a speaker of English were to utter a regular English sound, such as [k], 100 times in a row, 100 slightly or not so slightly different sounds would result. Some of the differences would be audible to the speaker himself, others only to a trained phonetician, a few would be detected only by advanced electronic equipment. However, without any doubt, the speaker and any other speaker of English would uniformly identify all the 100 sounds as [k]. Apparently, each occurrence of the sound is intuitively compared with the "gold standard" and/or the permissible range for it still to be an occurrence of the sound in question. Since exactly the same is true of the other sounds as well, the native speaker can be postulated to have internalized a list of such gold standards for the language, and phonology is after that list.

It is that list as well that makes it possible for a native speaker to accept as passable a phonetically deviant foreign accent or a very different native dialect as long as all the different sounds are kept apart. In other words, foreigners or dialect speakers can do whatever they like with their [k] sounds as long as these cannot be confused with any other sound of English. When a native speaker of French pronounces the English word *table* as [tebl], with the [t] dental as in French instead of alveolar as in English and unaspirated as in French instead of aspirated as in this English word (see below), the native

English hearer will still perceive it as a pronunciation, possibly very strange, of the word *table* and not of any other word. However, when an Oriental speaker pronounces a sound somewhere between [r] and [l], because the two sounds are the same in Chinese, Japanese, and Korean, the native English hearer cannot distinguish between words like *read* and *lead*. The French speaker will get away with an accent in this particular case but not so the Oriental, because the former's aberrance, unlike that of the latter, does not result in any word confusion. (The French will, however, be in the same kind of trouble if [t] and [θ] are confused because then *tick:thick* or *pat:path* will not be distinguished.)

The native speaker realizes intuitively that some differences between sounds are word-distinguishing while others are not. The latter example is provided by the aspirated variants of [p, t, k] in English. The three voiceless stops in English are the only sounds in the language that are aspirated, or pronounced with an additional friction somewhat similar to the articulation of [h], at the beginning of words and before vowels—as in *pin* [p^{h}n]—for all speakers, and anywhere between two vowels—as in *caper* [kep^{h}er]— for some. [p^h, t^h, k^h] are the standard notations for the aspirated pronunciations. What will happen if the incorrect, unaspirated pronunciation is substituted for the correct one in *pin,* and conversely, the inappropriate, aspirated pronunciation is substituted for the correct one in, say, *spin* [spɪn], resulting in [pɪn] instead of [p^{h}ɪn] and [sp^{h}ɪn] instead of [spɪn], respectively? Any native speaker will respond to this question immediately by noting the odd pronunciation of the two words, but it will never cross his or her mind that a different word was pronounced each time. The reason is that there is no word in English that differs from [p^{h}ɪn] in having [p] instead of [p^h] at the beginning and that is otherwise identical, and the same is true of any word containing [p^h] or, conversely, [p]. In other words, the native speaker intuitively possesses all the evidence necessary to establish that the difference between the aspirated and unaspirated pronunciations of the English voiceless stops is not word-distinguishing. On the other hand, the difference between [p] and [b] distinguishes many words, such as *bin:pin* or *tab:tap,* and any native speaker will confirm that these are different words.

What follows from this is that the native speaker is intuitively aware of all the word-distinguishing sound invariants, such that every actual sound is a manifestation of one of them and only those two sounds, the manifestations of different invariants, can distinguish words. This is the concept that phonology is trying to capture by postulating the formal notion of the phoneme—the sounds that distinguish words are different phonemes, the sounds that do not may be variants of the same phoneme. A few preliminary definitions are needed to build up to the definition of the phoneme, namely, definitions of the concepts of position and of distribution.

3.2. The Phoneme: Formal Theory

Every sound of natural language occurs within certain words, that is, in certain positions. What kind of position the sound does or does not occur in is important for its phonological status. Each sound is affected the strongest by its position relative to the word boundaries and by the immediately preceding and following sounds. How many adjacent sounds should be taken into account is an open question, and it varies from language to language and, within the same language, from occasion to occasion. It also matters at what level of detailization the discussion is held: The deeper the level the larger the environment for each sound. The level of detailization also determines whether the adjacent sounds are identified merely as vowels and consonants, or as members of certain natural classes, or even as particular sounds. For the purposes of this introduction, it will suffice to stay at the least deep level of detailization (see, however, the discussion in section 3.3). We will, therefore, define **position** as follows:

(13) **Definition 1. Position:** The position of a sound in a word is the combination of the following three factors:
 (i) whether the sound occurs at the beginning, in the middle, or at the end of the word (the terms are the initial, intermediate, and final position, respectively);
 (ii) whether the sound is preceded by any sound and, if so, whether the preceding sound is a vowel or a consonant;
 (iii) whether the sound is followed by any sound and, if so, whether the following sound is a vowel or a consonant.

Using the symbols Vw and C for vowels and consonants, respectively, and # for the word boundary, that is, the customary blank in the spelling before or after each word, and reserving the blank slot marked as__for the sound whose position is described, the possible types of position can be summarized as follows (14):

(14) **Types of Position:**
 (i) **Initial-Final:** #__#
 (ii) **Initial:** #__C, #__Vw
 (iii) **Intermediate:** C__C, C__Vw, Vw__C, Vw__Vw
 (iv) **Final:** C__#, Vw__#

(14.i) includes, of course, only the very few one-sound words in English, which can consist only of a vowel (but not every vowel makes up a word). *I* or *eye* [ay] and *awe* [ɔ] are the best examples. The sound [s], being a consonant, cannot occur in the initial-final position but it does occur in all the others, as shown in (15), with (15.i–iii) corresponding to (14.ii–iv), respectively:

(15) (i) stay, song
(ii) ecstasy, mixer [mɪksər], excite, assign
(iii) purse, lease

The examples in (15) prove that [s] occurs in all types of positions, with the exception of the initial-final one, and this information constitutes the distribution of [s] in English. **Distribution** is defined as follows (16):

(16) **Definition 2. Distribution:** The distribution of a sound in a language is the complete list of all the positions in which it occurs in the language (at the predetermined level of detailization).

At the least detailed level, distributions can be presented as (17):

(17) The distribution of [s] in English = #__C, #__Vw; C__C, C__Vw, Vw__C, Vw__Vw; C__#, Vw__#

In other words, at this level of detailization, one example of a type of position leads to the inclusion of the entire type in the distribution. If no example of a type can be found for the sound, the type is omitted from, or not listed in, the distribution.

Two sounds can be compared as to their distributions. Since each distribution is a list, the most meaningful question is whether the two lists overlap. The following two definitions depend on the response to this question.

(18) **Definition 3. Complementary Distribution:** Two sounds are said to be in complementary distribution if and only if their respective distributions do not overlap, that is, if there is not a single (type of) position (at the selected level of detailization) in which both sounds may occur.

(19) **Definition 4. Contrastive Distribution:** Two sounds are said to be in contrastive distribution if and only if they are not in complementary distribution or—more substantively—if their respective distributions overlap, that is, if there is at least one (type of) position in which they both may occur.

The aspirated and unaspirated pronunciations of [p, t, k] are obviously in complementary distribution because their distributions can be shown to be as in (20), with the second type of position in (20.i) optional for some speakers. However, for each speaker, no matter whether the distribution of [pʰ] includes one or two types of position, the distribution of [p] consists of all the others and nothing but them, which is indicated by using the word *otherwise* instead of actually listing in (20.ii) the remaining types of position.

(20) (i) Distribution of [pʰ] = #__Vw(, Vw__Vw)
(ii) Distribution of [p] = otherwise.

On the other hand, the strongest case of contrastive distribution is provided by the so-called **minimal pairs**:

(21) **Definition 5. Minimal Pair:** A minimal pair for $Sound_1$ and $Sound_2$ is a set of two words that differ only in that, in exactly the same position, the first word has $Sound_1$ and the second $Sound_2$ (and that are otherwise identical).

Thus, *pin:bin, repent:rebent,* and *tap:tab* are all minimal pairs for [p:b]. Obviously, the sounds for which a minimal pair is a minimal pair may occur initially, intermediately, or finally. The existence of just one minimal pair for a couple of sounds puts the two sounds in contrastive distribution because, in accordance with (19), the minimal pair provides proof that there exists at least one identical position in which both sounds do occur.

The last item to discuss before the final set of definitions is the physical similarity of sounds. While there is no formal criterion of similarity, it is usually thought of in terms of sharing the articulatory features, especially the main ones. A possible approach is to postulate that any two sounds that differ in no more than one articulatory feature are similar.

The concepts of physical similarity and complementary distribution play a crucial rule in defining first the concept of **allophone** (22) and then of **phoneme** (23).

(22) **Definition 6. Allophones:** Two sounds are allophones, or variants of the same phoneme if and only if the following two conditions obtain:
(i) the two sounds are physically similar;
(ii) the two sounds are in complementary distribution.

(23) **Definition 7. Phoneme:** A phoneme is the set of its allophones.

Thus, obviously, since [p^h] and [p] share all the articulatory features with the exception of the auxiliary feature of aspiration, and since they are in complementary distribution (20), the two sounds are allophones of the phoneme usually designated as /p/, whose relation to its allophones is shown in (24).

(24)

```
      /p/
     /   \
  [pʰ]   [p]
```

3.3. Phonemic Description

Equipped with a battery of concepts and definitions from section 3.2, a linguist whose task it is to describe practically the phonology of a language after the phonetic description is completed has a sharp eye for all the pairs of sounds that can be suspected of being allophones of the same phoneme. He does that in order to be able to reduce the list of all sounds to that of important invariants (with a list of variants associated with each, though many have just one) that can distinguish words. Allophones cannot distinguish words because, being in complementary distribution, they exclude the possibility of a minimal pair for them.

The phonologist goes for the physically similar sounds as most suspect, always willing to bend the adopted criterion of similarity to include more candidates rather than fewer. For each pair of suspects, the question is: Are $Sound_1$ and $Sound_2$ allophones or different phonemes? This is, without any doubt, the main question of phonemic description, and it has to be answered for each possible pair before the complete phonological inventory is arrived at. It is convenient to answer this question by following the flow chart in (25).

(25) **Flow Chart for Deciding if $Sound_1$ and $Sound_2$ Are Allophones or Different Phonemes:**

(i) Is there a minimal pair for $Sound_1$ and $Sound_2$?
If yes, stop. $Sound_1$ and $Sound_2$ are different phonemes.
If no, proceed to (ii).

(ii) Are $Sound_1$ and $Sound_2$ physically similar?
If yes, proceed to (iii).
If no, stop. $Sound_1$ and $Sound_2$ are different phonemes.

(iii) Are $Sound_1$ and $Sound_2$ in complementary distribution?
If yes, stop. $Sound_1$ and $Sound_2$ are allophones.
If no, stop. $Sound_1$ and $Sound_2$ are different phonemes.

The specific answers are not necessarily easy to obtain. Thus, one's failure to think of a minimal pair does not necessarily rule out its existence in the language. However, it is customary to treat this failure as "no" and to proceed to the next question, partly because the issue will be brought back in (25.iii). Certain fuzziness is associated with (25.ii). The inability to think of a certain example may, in principle, handicap one's response to (25.iii). The flow chart does work very smoothly, nevertheless, for most clear cases. Many pairs are declared as different phonemes on the grounds that they have a minimal pair—for instance, *pin:bin* for [p:b]; *bad:bed* for [æ:ɛ]; *by:boy* for [ay:ɔy]. Other cases may be more problematic.

The question of whether [ŋ] and [h] are allophones or different phonemes is a real issue in English phonology, and it illustrates the complete dependency of the answer on the adopted definitions and criteria. No minimal pair will be discovered for the two. The question of their physical similarity can be answered either way, depending on the adopted set of articulatory features and criterion of similarity. Thus, if one follows the list of main articulatory features in section 2 and their values for the two consonants set up in (5), as well as the criterion of zero-one different features for similarity, the two sounds differ in voice, place, and manner (voiced vs. voiceless, velar vs. glottal, and stop vs. fricative, respectively). However, some phoneticians lump velar and glottal consonants together for English, on the one hand, and, on the other hand, being nasal, [ŋ] is actually a fricative in the nasal cavity. The remaining voice distinction may then turn out to be the only one, in which case it will not be redundant to answer (25.iii).

In terms of distribution, while [h] tends to occur initially and not finally, and [ŋ] the other way around, both may occur intermediately. At the superficial level of detailization adopted in (14), both sounds occur in the Vw__Vw type of position as in *singer:rehash*. Now, at a deeper level, the actual vowels turn out to be not identical. Much more important, it turns out that, true to their final or initial preferences, [h] occurs intermediately primarily at the beginning of a morph (see chapter 6), while [ŋ] at the end of a morph. At the superficial level, then, the two sounds are different phonemes; at a more sophisticated one, they do not occur in the same position. Only the existence of a minimal pair can settle the question of distribution finally, and no minimal pair is available for them.

In the case of [ŋ] and [h] and in general, it is much more important to realize what is at stake for each alternative answer to the main question of phonemic description rather than to know the "correct" answer. Convenience may dictate the choice, and in this particular case, [ŋ] and [h] are usually treated as different phonemes. It must be clear now that the transcription in (3) was phonemic rather than phonetic because no aspirated/unaspirated allophones were provided for [p, t, k], nor were any other known variants provided for other English phonemes that have more than one allophone (see section 3.4).

3.4. Phonological Rules

The formal apparatus introduced in section 3.2 makes it possible to give a precise expression to various phonological phenomena. This expression usually takes the form of a rule. Most phonological rules state the terms and conditions for the realization of a phoneme as one or another of its allophones. All the rules are simply translations of "plain English" into the formal conventions.

Thus, if we assume that the phonemes /p, t, k/ are aspirated only in the initial position when followed by a vowel, this fact can be presented as a formal rule (26):

(26)
$$\# \begin{bmatrix} /p/ \\ /t/ \\ /k/ \end{bmatrix} + \mathrm{Vw} \rightarrow \# \begin{bmatrix} [p^h] \\ [t^h] \\ [k^h] \end{bmatrix} \begin{matrix} + \\ \mathrm{Vw} \end{matrix}$$

Another known phonological rule states the fact that in many American dialects, especially in fast and informal speech, the phonemes /t/ and /d/ may come to sound the same, and neither as [t, t^h] or [d]. It happens between two vowels or between a vowel and a sonorant, and the resulting pronunciation is often called the flapper because it sounds like a click. Its transcription symbol is [ʔ], the question mark without the dot underneath. When the flapper is pronounced, words like *writer:rider* are no longer distinguished. This phenomenon, when two different phonemes share a common allophone and word confusion is possible because of that, is called **syncretism,** and it is clearly counterproductive as far as the word-distinguishing function of the phonemes is concerned. Such phenomena tend to be or become marginal and to disappear in languages—in other words, languages are better off without them. However, as long as the flapper exists, a straightforward phonological rule about it can be stated:

(27)
$$\text{Vw} + \begin{bmatrix} /\text{t}/ \\ /\text{d}/ \end{bmatrix} \begin{Bmatrix} \text{Vw} \\ +\text{Sonorant} \end{Bmatrix} \rightarrow \text{Vw} + [\text{ʔ}] \begin{Bmatrix} \text{Vw} \\ [+\text{Sonorant}] \end{Bmatrix}$$

The last example involves the two allophones of the diphthong [ay], possible in a large number of English dialects. The diphthong tends to sound shorter and more frontal, something like [ʌy] rather than [ay] before final voiceless consonants and as [ay] otherwise. The phonological rule in (28) states this formally.

(28) /ay/ + [−Voice]# → [ʌy] + [−Voice]#

Similar formalisms can capture historical phonological processes (see chapter 9).

Rules (26) through (28) are typical results that linguistics is trying to achieve, namely, to discover and explicate the rules characterizing the native speaker's competence. The speaker follows such rules unconsciously because they are internalized, encoded in his mind—they are part of his knowledge of the language. Linguistics wants a complete and accurate list of these rules. Another good example of a simple rule that determines the native speaker's output and that linguistics discovers and formalizes is (6) in chapter 6. Language is perceived and treated by linguistics as a rule-governed behavior, and linguistics is the systematic and complete study of those rules.

CHAPTER 6

Morphology

SECTION 1. MORPH

There are many words in natural language that can be divided into two or more meaningful parts called **morphs.** Thus, the English words in (1.ii) consist of two morphs each, the ones in (1.iii) of three morphs each, and a few of the much rarer words in English—with 4 or more morphs—are listed in (1.iv). Very many words in English consist of just one morph, as in (1.i).

(1) (i) desire, table, dog, walk, red, elephant
(ii) desirable [dɪzayr + əbl]; tables [tebl + z]; doggish [dɔg + iš]; walking [wɔk + ɪŋ]; redder [rɛd + ər]; elephantine [ɛləfənt + ayn]
(iii) undesirable [ən + dɪzayr + əbl]; reframed [ri + frem + d]; inconsistent [ɪn + kənsɪst + ənt]
(iv) inconsistently [ɪn + kənsɪst + ənt + li]; nationalization [næsən + əl + ayz + e + šn]; antidisestablishmentarianism [ænti + dɪs + ɪstæblɪš + mənt + ərɪ + ən + ɪzm]

The division of words into morphs is completely unrelated to and much more important than the syllabic division. While all that a syllable needs is a vowel, the morph should satisfy a number of conditions before it can be distinguished as such in a word.

(2) **Conditions for Distinguishing Morphs Within a Word:** A word can be divided into two or more morphs if and only if all of the following conditions obtain:
(i) each candidate for a morph has a meaning;
(ii) each candidate for a morph occurs with the same meaning in other words as well;
(iii) the meaning of the word is the "sum" of the morph meanings.

If a word cannot be divided into morphs according to (2), it is a one-morph word. In (1.ii), what makes it possible to divide *undesirable* into three morphs is that all three have a meaning (3.i) and occur with the same meaning in other words (3.ii) and the meaning of the whole word consists of the three meanings (3.iii).

(3) (i) *un-* reverses the meaning of the word it is attached to; *desire* means a certain feeling; and *-able* means roughly 'capable of [causing]'

(ii) unhappy, undo, unpleasantly; to desire, desirability, desired; likable, capable, movable
(iii) undesirable 'the opposite of + the meaning of *desire* + capable of causing'

Words like (1.i) do not even have a candidate for a second morph but other words may have. If these candidates fail the test in (2), then the word has to be described as a one-morph word. Thus, *cran-* in *cranberry* fails (2.i), *goose-* in *gooseberry* fails (2.ii), and *understand* fails (2.iii) for *under-* and *stand* as the two candidates for a morph.

The morphs can be divided into two important classes, lexical and grammatical. The lexical morphs in (1) include the entire (1.i) line and then *frame, consist, nation,* and *establish*. All the other morphs in (1.ii–iv) are grammatical (*un-, -able, re-, -d, in-, -ent, -ly, -al, -ize, -a-, -tion, anti-, dis-, -ment, -ari-, -an, -ism*). The difference between the two classes is both in meaning and usage.

The lexical morphs denote directly objects, actions, qualities, and other "pieces" of the real world. The grammatical morphs can modify only the meanings of the lexical morphs by adding a certain element to them—this is why their meanings are more general and vague and become clearer and more specific within a particular word. Grammatical morphs pluralize nouns, put verbs in the past tense, switch adjectives to adverbs or nouns to verbs, and so on. Accordingly, the lexical morphs can, as a rule, occur without grammatical morphs, as in (1.i) (see, however, section 3 on the zero morpheme), but the opposite is impossible—each grammatical morph must accompany a lexical morph, which can, in fact, be accompanied by several grammatical morphs, as in (1.iii–iv). Because of this difference in usage, the lexical and grammatical morphs are sometimes referred to as free, or independent, and bound, or auxiliary, respectively.

It has also been noticed that while new lexical morphs are created almost daily, within new words known as neologisms, which enter the vocabulary of a language with the new objects and concepts (see chapter 9), hardly any new grammatical morph ever emerges. When the word *sputnik* was borrowed from Russian into English in 1957, the Russian suffix *-nik,* which has roughly the meaning of the English *-er* in *writer* or *speaker,* seemed for a while to be a candidate for a new grammatical morph in English. The word *beatnik,* with the same suffix, was still used at the time. A similar suffix *-chik,* with a diminutive meaning, was also used very marginally in some dialects of American English under the influence of Yiddish, as in *boychik* 'little boy' (in fact, *-nik* in *beatnik* came from Yiddish rather than directly from Russian, from which Yiddish had borrowed it long ago). Neither of the suffixes "made it," which is typical, and one reason was that they were not at all necessary for English, which had its own means of expressing the same meanings. The more important reason, related to the first one, is that the grammatical morphs constitute a very conservative component in any language and resist any "intrusion." The logic seems to be that all the grammatical meanings that a language needs are taken care of well by the native means, and the language does not want anything it does not have already. When an exception to this orthodox conservatism is possible, grammatical innovation does occur, but it is indeed very rare. For this reason, the grammatical morphs are sometimes referred to as the closed-list morphs while the lexical ones make up the open list.

There are traditional names for some morphs, depending on their role and position in the word. The lexical morph of the word is often called the root, or the radical. The prefix occurs before the root and the suffix after the root. It is customary to designate the former with a hyphen after it and the latter with a hyphen before it, as has been done in the examples above.

SECTION 2. ALLOMORPH AND MORPHEME

Typically, some grammatical morphs in languages fulfill the same function and carry the same meaning. A situation similar to the allophone/phoneme situation can be observed in morphology as well. Thus, three English suffixes, /-s, -z, -ɪz/, are used regularly to pluralize English nouns; (4.i–iii) contain relevant examples.

(4) (i) books, cats, caps, baths
(ii) dogs, lads, tabs, clothes, tins, drums, things, ties
(iii) classes, quizzes, lashes, garages, churches, judges

It is easy to observe that the choice of one of the three suffixes seems to be closely related to the final sound of the singular form of the noun. In (4.i) these sounds are all voiceless; in (4.ii) they are all voiced; in (4.iii) however, some are voiceless and the others are voiced but they all belong to the natural class of sibilants (see chapter 5, section 2). Other examples would also corroborate the observation, but there are exceptions, exemplified in (5).

(5) (i) children, oxen
(ii) men, women, geese, mice, lice
(iii) sheep, fish
(iv) syllabi, formulae, apparati, data, criteria

The exceptions constitute a very limited and closed list. No new words are added to it, and in fact, some words on it seem to be defecting—plurals like *formulas* are becoming increasingly acceptable (see chapter 9). New words always follow the appropriate line in (4). The complete rule of English noun pluralization can then be formulated in the following flow chart.

(6) **Flow Chart for English Noun Pluralization.** In order to determine how a given English noun N forms its plural, answer the following questions:
(i) Is N on the list of exceptions?
If yes, form the plural as indicated on the list.
If no, proceed to (ii).
(ii) Is the final sound of N a sibilant?
If yes, form the plural by adding /-ɪz/.
If no, proceed to (iii).
(iii) Is the final sound of N voiceless?
If yes, form the plural by adding /-s/.
If no, form the plural by adding /-z/.

Obviously, (6) deals with the phonemic composition (and transcription) of the plural noun forms rather than with their spelling. However, the spelling conventions are quite straightforward as far as the regular plurals are concerned: *-s* is added to all nonexceptional words except for those with sibilants at the end, which do not have a mute final *-e* in the spelling; those words, for example *church,* have *-es* added.

In (6.iii), it does not matter whether one asks the question about the voiced or voiceless sounds because the "no" answer will take care of the other possibility. It was phrased as it was because there are many fewer voiceless sounds in English and the purely mechanical check is accordingly easier.

Now, (4) and (5) clearly indicate a situation with regard to the nonexceptional plurals, which is similar to complementary distribution in phonology, and it is indeed the case that /-s, -z, -ɪz/ are in complementary distribution in exactly the same way. The concept of allomorph can be defined, then, similarly to (22) in chapter 5, with the concept of physical similarity, useless in morphology, replaced by the same meaning or function, as in (7). The concept of morpheme is defined accordingly in (8).

(7) **Definition 1. Allomorph:** Two morphs are allomorphs, or variants of the same morpheme, if and only if the following two conditions obtain:
(i) the two morphs have exactly the same meaning or function;
(ii) the two morphs are in complementary distribution.

(8) **Definition 2. Morpheme:** A morpheme is the set of its allomorphs.

Any two of the three noun plural morphs are allomorphs, so all three of them are allomorphs. The morpheme of which they are all variants is referred to as the Noun Plural morpheme and is denoted as Pl. Its relation to the allophones (9) is only slightly more complicated than in (24), primarily because it has to include as allomorphs all the various exceptions.

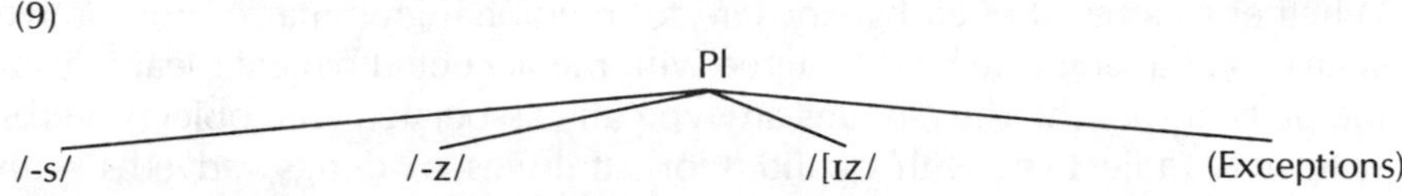

Interestingly, there are two other, totally different morphemes in English, which have the same allomorphs as Pl. The first is Poss, for the Possessive Noun case, as in (10), and the second is PresThirSg for the third-person singular form of the Present Tense of the verb, as in (11). Examples for each of the corresponding allomorphs are provided in (10.ii) and (11.iii). Unlike Pl and PresThirSg, Poss does not have exceptional allomorphs.

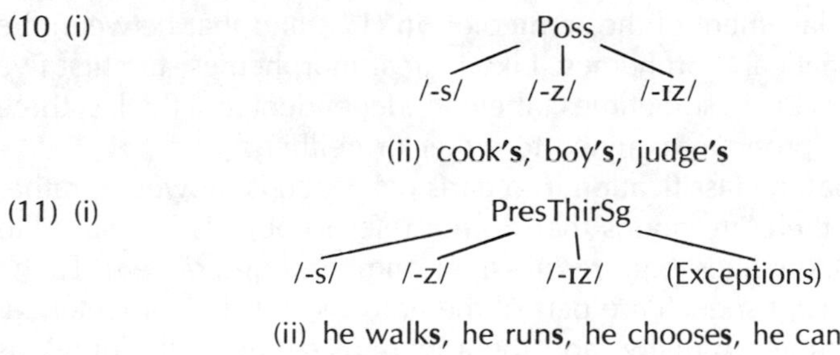

SECTION 3. PARTS OF SPEECH

Since Aristotle, grammarians have been classifying words into parts of speech. A standard list of parts of speech, with the customary symbols denoting them in parentheses, is given in (12).

(12) **Parts of Speech:** Noun (N), Verb (V), Adjective (Adj), Adverb (Adv), Numeral (Nu), Pronoun (Pron); Determiner (Det), Preposition (Prep), Conjunction (Conj)

There are numerous classifications of and arguments for or against each of them in the traditional grammar of any particular language and in traditional linguistics in general. Thus, numerals can be eliminated as a part of speech and divided between the nouns and adverbs. Particles may be added to the list, especially for languages other than English. Interjections, it might be argued, constitute a part of speech as well, rather than a unique, non-propositional speech act (see chapter 8, section 5).

The principles of attribution of a word to a certain part of speech have never been defined in traditional grammar, but it is clear that they are somewhat loosely associated with the meanings of the parts of speech listed before the semicolon in (12) and with the functions of those listed after it.

Whether as a result of early exposure to traditional grammar or not, native speakers of a language tend to agree with the accepted typical meanings of the parts of speech. Thus, nouns are typically associated with objects, verbs with acts, adjectives with qualities or attributes of things, adverbs with qualities or attributes of acts, numerals with numbers. Pronouns are characterized as only indicating to certain noun meanings rather than possessing them. Determiners, prepositions, and conjunctions are described in terms of their grammatical functions. Also, these three categories have a very limited membership in any language, and each can be easily listed. The same refers to the pronouns but not to the first six parts of speech listed in (12). In fact, there is a certain similarity between the dichotomy in the parts of speech, indicated by the placement of the semicolon in (12), and that between the lexical and grammatical morphemes. Like lexical morphemes, the first five parts of speech in (12) are sometimes labeled independent and the last three auxiliary, with the pronoun assigned to either or neither group.

The meaning-based classification into parts of speech is, however, rather unreliable. Thus, there are nouns that do not refer to objects but rather to acts (e.g., *writing*), qualities (e.g., *redness*), or numbers (e.g., *dozen*). To the extent that the parts of speech are part of the native speaker's competence, they should be defined formally, and the apparatus set up in the previous section makes it feasible for nouns, verbs, adjectives, and adverbs. We will need a definition of the paradigm first, as follows (cf. chapter 4, section 3).

(13) **Definition 3. Paradigm:** The paradigm of a word is the complete set of its forms.

Obviously, a word with only one form, such as *one, what, this, in,* or *and,* has a one-word paradigm. The paradigm of a typical noun, such as *boy,* contains four forms (14).

(14) { boy boys
boy's boys' }

Each form is a combination of the same lexical morpheme *boy* with a grammatical morpheme. With the exception of the very first form, the grammatical morpheme has the same pronunciation [z] but its meaning changes dramatically (and the three different spellings try to emphasize that). In the case of *boy,* it makes sense to postulate that it also has a meaningful grammatical morpheme, which is realized as no sound, that is, not pronounced. It is, in fact, the **zero morpheme,** whose meaning is clearly defined precisely by the absence of any sound after the lexical morpheme. The distribution of grammatical meanings in the paradigm of *boy* is shown in (15).

(15) { L + Sg L + Pl
L + PossSg L + PossPl }

Membership in the part of speech of noun can now be defined as follows:

(16) **Definition 4. Noun:** An English word that has the paradigm of (15) in part or in full is a noun.

Many English nouns are not supposed to have the possessive, reserved primarily for animate nouns, namely, animals and humans. Others do not have the plural form (and are referred to as *singularia tantum*). Still others lack the singular (*pluralia tantum*). These "defective" types of nouns are illustrated in (17.i–iii), respectively.

(17) (i) table, brick, page, line, preposition
(ii) honesty, sincerity, margarine, vinegar, wool
(iii) scissors, trousers

In (18–21) we have the same done for the English verb. (18) contains a typical verb paradigm. (19) presents it schematically, with the zero morpheme, /-s, -z, -ɪz/, /-t, -d, -ɪd/, and /-ɪŋ / expressing the four grammatical morphemes, respectively. (20) introduces the definition of the English verb. (21.i–iii) list examples of defective verbs, that is, those lacking the -*s* form in the present, the past, and the progressive aspect, respectively.

(18) $$\left\{\begin{array}{ll} \text{walk} & \text{walks} \\ \text{walked} & \text{walking} \end{array}\right\}$$

(19) $$\left\{\begin{array}{l} \text{L + PresNon-ThirSg} \\ \text{L + Past} \\ \text{L + PresThirSg} \\ \text{L + Prog} \end{array}\right\}$$

(20) **Definition 5. Verb:** An English word that has the paradigm of (19) in part or in full is a verb.

(21) (i) can, may, must
(ii) must
(iii) can, may, must

The verbs in (21) are known as the modal, or defective, verbs in English, precisely because of their incomplete paradigm. It should also be noted that the Past morpheme in English has a long though definitely limited list of exceptions, which contains the so-called irregular verbs. These verbs do have the past but do not form it by adding the /t, d, ɪd/ suffix as do *dressed, changed,* and *listed,* respectively. Instead, they have such forms as *ran, sang,* or even *went* for *go*. The irregular verbs also have a past participle form which, as is not the case for much more numerous regular verbs, is often distinct from the simple past (e.g., *wrote:written*), and because of that it is arguable that a fifth form, L + PastPart, should be added to (19).

The adjective is similarly served by (22.i–iv) and the adverbs by (23.i–iv). The positive degree of comparison for the adjectives is usually expressed by the zero morpheme, the comparative by /-ər/, and the superlative by /-ɪst/. For some adjectives, however, especially for the polysyllabic ones, Comp and Super are realized as *more* or *most,* respectively, preceding the positive form. This formation is obligatory for Comp and Super of the adjective. The positive form of the adverb often contains the grammatical morpheme /li/. The defective adjectives and adverbs do not have comparative and superlative forms.

(22) (i) {white whiter whitest}
(ii) {L + Pos L + Comp L + Super}
(iii) **Definition 6. Adjective:** An English word that has the paradigm of (22ii) in part or in full is an adjective.
(iv) unique

(23) (i) {slowly more slowly most slowly}
(ii) {L + Pos L + Comp L + Super}
(iii) **Definition 7. Adverb:** An English word that has the paradigm of (23.ii) in part or in full is an adverb.
(iv) uniquely

Because of the great similarity of (22.ii) and (23.ii), in many languages adjectives and adverbs cannot be distinguished as two parts of speech, and arguments for blending them in English as well are possible on grounds of their complimentary distribution: While adjectives modify only nouns, adverbs modify only verbs.

The paradigmatic approach to parts of speech (cf. chapter 4, section 3) does not work well for other parts of speech because their paradigms contain either very idiosyncratic forms or just one form without an identifying grammatical morpheme.

SECTION 4. INFLECTIONAL AND DERIVATIONAL MORPHEMES

Grammatical morphemes can be further divided into inflectional and derivational on the basis of their relation to the paradigm.

(24) (i) **Definition 8. Inflectional Morpheme:** A grammatical morpheme that forms a different form of the same word is inflectional.
(ii) **Definition 9. Derivational Morpheme:** A grammatical morpheme that forms a different word is derivational.

In other words, inflection remains within the same paradigm, while derivation always leaves it. All the morphemes mentioned in (14–15, 18–19, 22–23) are, therefore, inflectional. The much more numerous derivational morphemes are used for the formation of different words both within the same part of speech and—more typically—of different parts of speech, as in (25).

(25) **English Derivation:**
N—N: son:sonn**y**
N—V: beauty:beaut**ify**
N—Adj: book:book**ish**
V—N: write:writ**er**
V—V: do:**over**do
Adj—N: red:red**ness**
Adj—V: red:redd**en**
Adj—Adj: white:whit**ish**
Adj—Adv: free:free**ly**

In English, unlike in most other languages, a word may travel among different parts of speech with zero derivation, that is, without changing its form. The phenomenon is known as the **conversion** and is exemplified in (26).

(26) **Conversion in English:**
N—V: an impact:to impact
N—Adj: a stone:stone wall
V—N: to buy:a buy
Adj—N: poor:the poor
Adj—Adv: fast:fast

English emerges from this discussion as a language with a definite preference for suffixes over prefixes. Its inflection is exclusively suffixal and its derivation is predominantly so. Language in general emerges from this discussion as a nomenclature of types of words and of morphemes. The description of every particular language must include complete inventories of morphemes and words of every type. Clearly, however, language is much more than just words.

CHAPTER 7

Syntax

SECTION 1. PHRASE AND SENTENCE

Syntax is the next higher level of linguistic structure and it deals with entities which consist of words. The entities are the phrase, or word combination, and the sentence. The phrase usually consists of more than one word and the sentence is usually the combination of a few phrases, though exceptions are possible. (1.i) contains an example of a sentence whose phrases are listed in (1.ii); (1.iii) is a sentence which consists of one phrase, coinciding with itself (though it is, of course, possible to speak of one-word phrases, and this is what the formalism for generative grammar actually does—see section 3).

(1) (i) I am reading a book.
  (ii) reading a book, a book
  (iii) John snores.

As mentioned in chapter 4, section 1, in order to pair off sound sequences and meanings efficiently, language has to have a highly complex and sophisticated organizational component. In all languages, this responsibility is shared by morphology and syntax, and while the division of labor is not very straightforward or linear, it would be fair to say that the heavier the morphology of a language the lighter the syntax, and vice versa. In English, with its very simple paradigms (see chapter 6, section 3), practically free of noun declension (practically no cases) and with fairly light verb conjugation (practically no person differentiation of forms), one should expect, and does get, a heavy syntactic load.

The English fixed word order for an "ordinary," unemphatic, declarative sentence, Subject + Predicate + Object(s), clearly distinguishes the language from languages like Russian, Finnish, or German, whose word order is much freer than in English and whose morphology is typically much heavier. This word order also makes English a typical SVO (for **S**ubject, **V**erb, **O**bject) language, as opposed to languages like Japanese, which is clearly an SOV language. The word order is the only way to distinguish (2.i) from (2.ii) in English. In Russian, however, different word forms are involved in the equivalent sentences (2.iii) and (2.iv), respectively, and the word order is practically free, except for certain connotations, empathies, and emphases, sometimes associated with the less usual groupings.

(2) (i) The brother loves the sister.
(ii) The sister loves the brother.
(iii) Brat ljubit sestr**u**; Brat sestr**u** ljubit; Ljubit brat sestr**u**; Ljubit sestr**u** brat; Sestr**u** brat ljubit; Sestr**u** ljubit brat
(iv) Sestr**a** ljubit brat**a**; Sestr**a** brat**a** ljubit; Ljubit sestr**a** brat**a**; Ljubit brat**a** sestr**a**; Brat**a** sestr**a** ljubit; Brat**a** ljubit sestr**a**

While the word order is probably the most superficial manifestation of the kind of organization provided by syntax, it illustrates well the extremely high degree of selectiveness in language. It is popularly believed that language is "words." However, in no language can the words be just put together to produce a well-formed sentence. Thus, the five words in (1.i) can be arranged in 5! = 120 ways, only two of which (3.i) and (3.ii) are acceptable to all, and maybe two more (3.iii–iv) marginally so, the latter with a totally different meaning. In other words, in this example a language rejects up to 98% of the available options. Some of the rejected strings of the five words are listed in (4), and it is clear that each of them violates a syntactic rule; it follows that the well-formed sentences are those that abide by all the syntactical rules of the language.

(3) (i) = (1.i) I am reading a book
(ii) Am I reading a book?
(iii) A book I am reading
(iv) I am a reading book

(4) (i) *I a reading book am
(ii) *I am read a book
(iii) *I am reading book a
(iv) *I am reading a books

The asterisks in (4) are a typical linguistic convention to denote a deviant, non-well-formed, **ungrammatical** sentence. By contrast, a "good" sentence, such as (3.i–ii), is referred to as **grammatical.** As we will see in section 4, Chomsky made grammaticality the cornerstone of his syntactic theory.

The rules that are violated in (4), just as all the rules pertaining to (3.i–ii), must be known to native speakers because they abide by them. The problem is that this knowledge is "automatic" and unconscious—this is the syntactical competence of the native speaker, and an ordinary native speaker is unable, and he should not necessarily be able, to formulate the very rules he abides by. It is the task of the linguist to explicate those rules, and a modern syntactician tries to set up syntax as a sequence of formal rules.

SECTION 2. SYNTACTICAL ANALYSIS AND TREES

Each sentence can be analyzed syntactically by identifying all the phrases of which it consists and for each phrase, all the words that constitute it. Various formalisms and markings, including arrows, parentheses, and so on, have been used in syntactic analysis in the past but since their recent advent in American descriptive linguistics, tree diagrams, or simply trees, have been used widely in linguistics. (5.ii) is a typical tree for (5.i):

(5) (i) The boy kissed the girl

(ii)

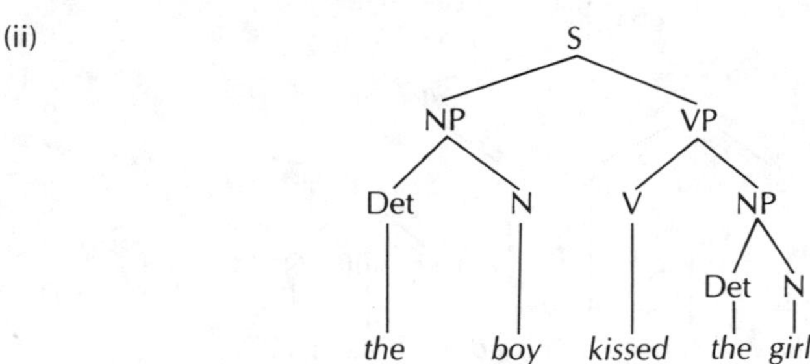

(S = sentence, NP = noun phrase, VP = verb phrase, Det = determiner, N = noun, V = verb)

Mathematically, a tree is a graph, and each graph consists of nodes and links. There are 14 nodes and 13 links, or edges, on (5.ii). Each link or sequence of links forms a path. A tree is a graph on which there is exactly one path between any two nodes. Thus, the path from S to the second occurrence of *the* on this tree is S to VP to NP to Det to *the*. A link from a higher node to a lower node is a downward link. A path consisting of downward links only is a downward path—the path from S to the second *the* is therefore downward, while the path from V to either NP is not.

A node is said to dominate another node if there is a downward path from the former to the latter; the dominated node is then a constituent of the dominating one. If the path consists of one link, the higher node is said to dominate the lower node immediately and the latter is then an immediate constituent of the higher node. Thus, the first NP on (5.ii) immediately dominates the first Det and the first N and dominates the first *the* and *boy*.

S, the highest node, naturally dominates all the other nodes on the tree. It is referred to as the initial symbol. The five italicized nodes in the bottom line dominate no other node. A node that does not dominate any other node is referred to as terminal, and the terminal nodes are usually words of the language in question.

Trees have been used pretty much in the same fashion by a number of grammatical approaches with different names, such as the immediate constituent grammar or phrase structure grammar. In the latter variety, they were incorporated into, and subsequently modified by, Chomsky's generative grammar (see section 3), which often referred to the tree of a sentence as its phrase-structure, or simply phrase, marker (PS-marker or P-marker, respectively).

In (6), there are examples of trees representing various expanded types of syntactic structure: adjectives in (6.i), adverbs in (6.ii), auxiliaries in (6.iii), prepositional phrases in (6.iv), and relative clauses in (6.v).

(6) (i)

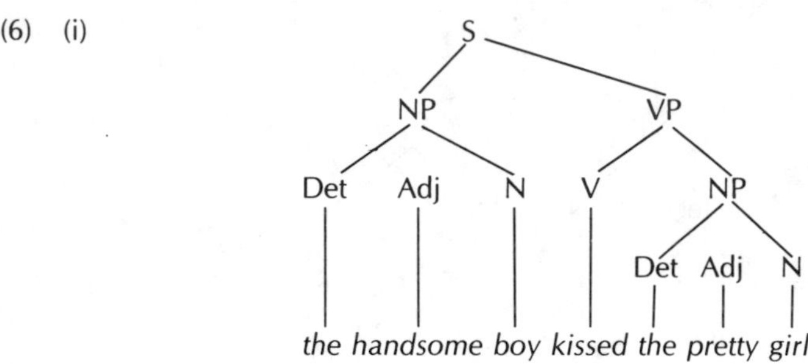

(ii)

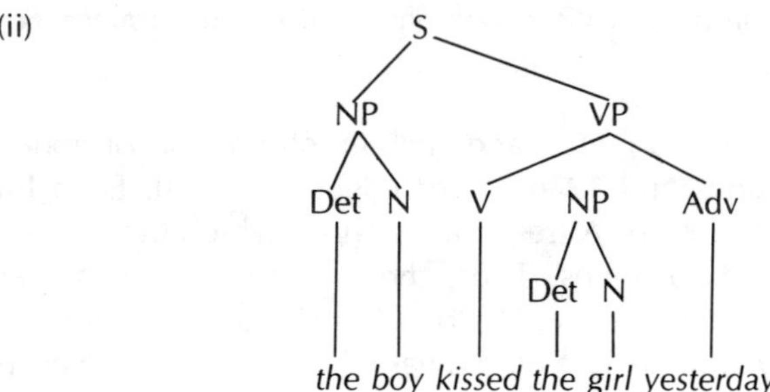

(iii)

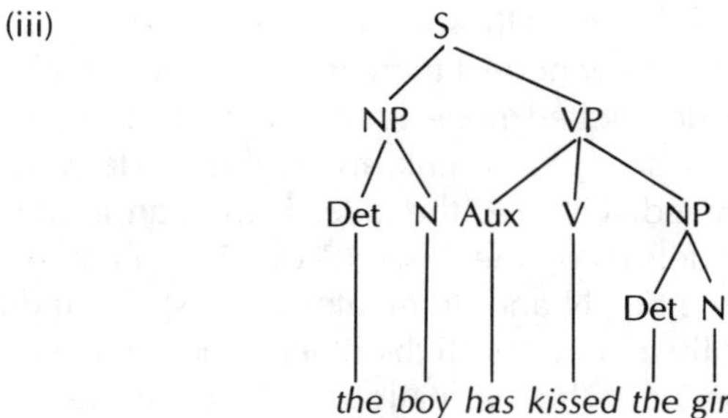

(iv)

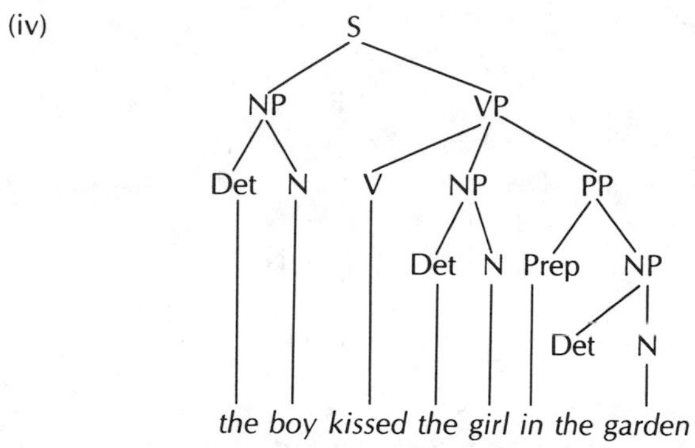

(v)

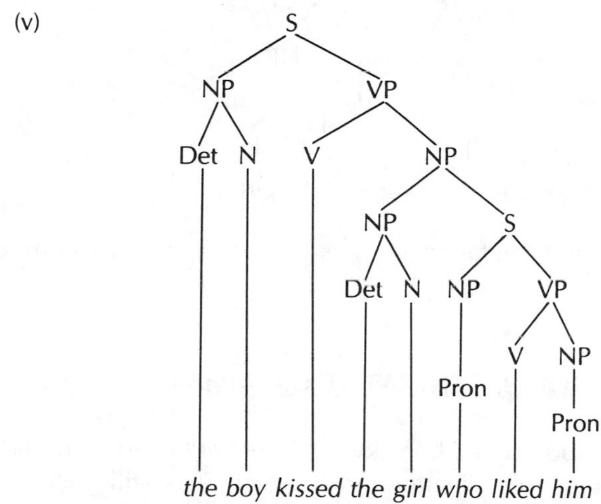

(Adj = adjective, Adv = adverb, Aux = auxiliary verb, PP = prepositional phrase, Prep = preposition, Pron = pronoun)

With the sentence like the one in (6.v) and especially with even more complicated sentences, the trees lose one major advantage they have, namely, their immediate and easy accessibility, the ability to "get" the syntactic structure of a sentence "at a glance." However, they face a much more serious problem with the so-called discontinuous constituents. Thus, the adverb in (7.i) can no longer be treated as part of the VP; even worse, the same applies to the auxiliary in (7.ii), which should, of course, belong to the VP and does so in the corresponding assertive sentence (6.iii).

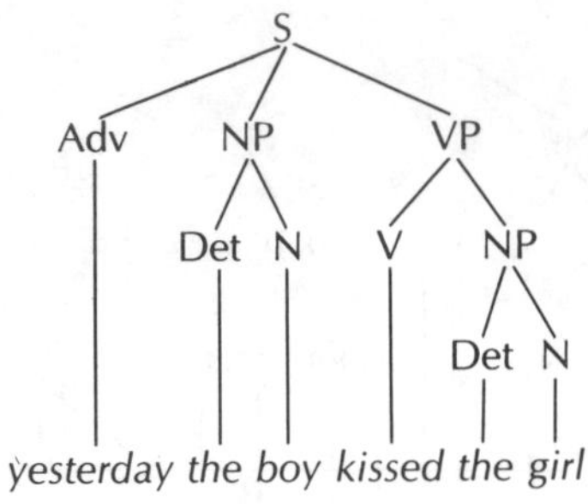

(ii)

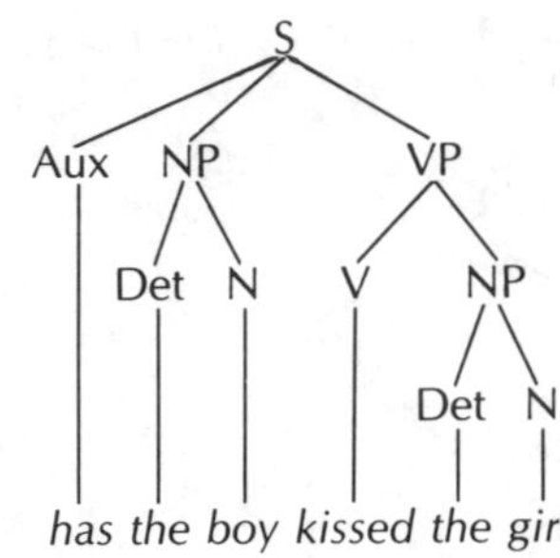

An alternative system of syntactic analysis was proposed by Chomsky in 1957.

SECTION 3. GENERATIVE GRAMMAR

The first innovation proposed by Chomsky in his *Syntactic Structures* (1957) was the replacement of tree diagramming, which was still used for illustrative purposes if convenient, by a logical-calculus type of mathematical notation, always involving a set of rules. Sets of rules organized according to a certain principle came to be referred to as generative grammars.

3.1. Basic Generative Grammars

Thus, (5.i) would be analyzed in the generative grammar by the set of six rules in (8).

(8) (i) S → NP + VP
(ii) VP → V + NP
(iii) NP → Det + N
(iv) V → *kissed*
(v) Det → *the*
(vi) N → *boy, girl*

Each rule in (8) is a **rewriting rule;** it rewrites its left part as its right part; it reads as 'rewrite X as Y,' that is, for (8.i), 'rewrite S as NP and VP'; or as 'X goes into Y,' that is, 'S goes into NP and VP.' The whole set of rules in (8) is a grammar that can *generate* (5.i). The term 'generation' is used here not in the sense of production but rather in the mathematical sense of analyzing. The process of generation of a sentence in a grammar is referred to as derivation. (9) is the line-by-line generation of sentence (5.i) in grammar (8). The initial symbolic S constitutes the first line; each next line is obtained purely mechanically by rewriting a symbol in the previous line with the help of an appropriate rule from (8).

(9)		
(i)	**S**	
(ii)	NP + **VP**	(8.i)
(iii)	**NP** + V + NP	(8.ii)
(iv)	Det + N + V + **NP**	(8.iii)
(v)	Det + N + **V** + Det + N	(8.iii)
(vi)	**Det** + N + *kissed* + Det + N	(8.iv)
(vii)	*the* + N + *kissed* + **Det** + N	(8.v)
(viii)	*the* + **N** + *kissed* + *the* + N	(8.v)
(ix)	*the* + *boy* + *kissed* + *the* + **N**	(8.vi)
(x)	*the* + *boy* + *kissed* + *the* + *girl*	(8.vi)

In (9), the numbers on the right of each line refer to the rewriting rule applied to the boldface symbol in the previous line to obtain this line. In (9.v, viii, x), the same rewriting rule is applied for the second time because the previous line contained a second occurrence of the symbol just rewritten. In case of multiple applications of a rule, a derivation proceeds one step at a time from the leftmost occurrence of the same symbol to its rightmost occurrence. (8.vi) provides an alternative: N can be rewritten both as *boy* and as *girl*. In order to generate (5.i), *boy* was selected in (9) for the leftmost occurrence of N and *girl* for the other one.

Different as they look, it turns out that tree (5.ii) and grammar (8) do a very similar job, analyzing (5.i). In fact, in terms of the phrase composition of the sentence and word composition of the phrases, the provided analysis is identical and so are the grammatical symbols used. Each node on (5.ii) is present in (8); whenever a node on the tree immediately dominates another node or other nodes, (8) contains a rule rewriting the dominant node as the dominated node(s), with a plus sign between the dominated nodes if there are more than one. The initial symbol constitutes the left part of the very first rule. The terminal nodes do not appear in the left part of any rule and therefore cannot be rewritten or, in other words, cannot dominate another symbol. The rules that have terminal nodes (i.e., words of the language in question) on their right parts are called the terminal rules.

A further similarity is that all the various extensions of (5.i) analyzed with the help of trees in (6.i–v) can be immediately accommodated by adding the appropriate rewriting rules, listed in (10.i–v), respectively, to (8).

(10) (i) NP → Det + Adj + N
Adj → *handsome, pretty*
(ii) VP → V + NP + Adv
Adv → *passionately*
(iii) VP → Aux + V + NP
Aux → *has*
(iv) VP → V + NP + PP
PP → Prep + NP
Prep → *in*
N → *garden*
(v) NP → NP + S
NP → Pron
Pron → *who, him*
V → *liked*

It is customary in generative grammar to combine all the rules with the same left part into one rule with multiple options. Parentheses are used for optional symbols, so that Det (Adj) N stands for two lines, Det + N and Det + Adj + N. Braces are used for multiple options. Plus signs are typically omitted around all the various brackets. (11) is a combination of (8) and (10), written in accordance with these technical conventions: New options are added to each rule in (8) from (10), and a few new rules, with the new left parts, are added from (10) as well.

(11) (i) S → NP + VP
(ii) VP → (Aux) V + NP (Adv) (PP)
(iii) PP → Prep + NP
(iv) $NP \rightarrow \begin{cases} \text{Det (Adj) N} \\ \text{Pron} \\ \text{NP + S} \end{cases}$
(v) Aux → *has*
(vi) V → *kissed*
(vii) Adv → *passionately, yesterday*
(viii) Prep → *in*
(ix) Det → *the*
(x) Adj → *handsome, pretty*
(xi) N → *boy, girl, garden*
(xii) Pron → *who, him*

Grammar (11) can now generate all the sentences in (5–6). In the case of each sentence, its derivation picks out those rules and options from (11) which lead to its generation. One grammar can thus generate a number of sentences. This was one significant difference between (5.ii) and (8): While the tree analyzed exactly one sentence, the grammar generated three other sentences, as in (12), along with that one sentence, thanks to the options in (8.ii).

(12) (i) = (5.i) The boy kissed the girl.
(ii) The boy kissed the boy.
(iii) The girl kissed the boy.
(iv) The girl kissed the girl.

In fact, many more sentences will be generated by (11) because each terminal rule in it is open in principle to all the members of the grammatical category in the right part of the rule. Formally, it is usually indicated, as in mathematics, by adding a comma and ellipsis points meaning "etc." after the last listed terminal symbol in the rule, so that (11) would in fact be presented as follows:

(13) (i) S → NP + VP
(ii) VP → (Aux) V + NP (Adv) (PP)
(iii) PP → Prep + NP
(iv) NP → { Det (Adj) N | Pron | NP + S }
(v) Aux → *has, . . .*
(vi) V → *kissed, . . .*
(vii) Adv → *passionately, yesterday, . . .*
(viii) Prep → *in, . . .*
(ix) Det → *the, . . .*
(x) Adj → *handsome, pretty, . . .*
(xi) N → *boy, girl, garden, . . .*
(xii) Pron → *who, him, . . .*

What the ellipsis points mean is that the same grammar will generate (5.i) with any verb in place of *kissed,* such as in (14.i); with any other determiner, as in (14.ii), any adverb, as in (14.iii); any adjective, as in (14.iv); any pronoun, as in (15.v), and so on.

(14) (i) The boy saw the girl.
(ii) A boy kissed that girl.
(iii) The boy kissed the girl ineptly.
(iv) The stupid boy kissed the ugly girl.
(v) The boy kissed her.

Thus (13) is capable of generating very many sentences. Transformation, a different kind of rule, increases this capacity manifold.

3.2. Transformational Grammar

Unlike the rewriting rules, **transformations** do not develop just one symbol into another or others. In fact, having just one symbol on the right is the sign of a rewriting rule. A transformation always has several symbols on the right because what it does is to transform the entire sentence structure into something else.

The basic idea behind transformations was initially to generate the simplest sentence structures with a minimum of rewriting rules and to have all the more complex structures derived from those with the help of transformations. Thus, given the fact that all the active sentences such as (15.i) are passivized in a similar fashion (15.ii), it turned out to be formally and conceptually simpler not to provide special rewriting rules for the generation of each passive sentence along with its active counterpart but rather to provide one general rule capable of passivizing any sentence. (18.i) is a simplified version of the passive transformation which transforms (15.i) into (15.ii) and many other active sentences into their passives. (18.ii) transforms (16.i) into (16.ii) and many other declarative sentences into interrogatives—it is a simplified version of the interrogative transformation. (18.iii), the simplified negative transformation, similarly transforms (17.i) and many other sentences into (17.ii) and the other corresponding sentences.

(15) (i) The boy kissed the girl.
(ii) The girl was kissed by the boy.

(16) (i) The boy kissed the girl.
(ii) Did the boy kiss the girl?

(17) (i) The boy kissed the girl.
(ii) The boy did not kiss the girl.

(18) (i) $NP_1 + V + NP_2 \Rightarrow NP_2 + \textit{be}^* + V^* + \textit{by} + NP_1$
(ii) $NP + V + NP \Rightarrow \textit{do}^* + NP + V^* + NP$
(iii) $NP + V + NP \Rightarrow NP + \textit{do}^* + \textit{not} + V + NP$

The asterisks in (18) mark the minor technical adjustments needed in the rules to make sure that all the verbs involved appear in the appropriate form (*was, did,* etc.). In fact, the examples of grammars in section 3.1 needed such minor adjustments here and there as well. There is no need to go into that much technical detail here and it will certainly suffice to say that it can be, and was, done pretty easily.

If the three transformations in (18) are added to a grammar like (13), it will be capable of generating the passive, interrogative, and negative counterpart of each sentence it could generate before. Transformations are typically listed at the end of the rule list, and the derivations of sentences that need transformations continue beyond the terminal line by applying one transformation at a time and stopping when the target sentence is generated. With the transformations added, (13) becomes a transformational generative grammar.

Generative grammars including transformations were called transformational generative grammars, or more frequently, transformational grammars. The adherents of this approach became known as the transformationalists, and it is fair to say that they clearly dominated American linguistics in the late 1960s and throughout the 1970s and that they probably still remain the most populous group among the linguists of the 1980s. Transformations could easily handle sentences with discontinuous constituents and just about any other "complication" in the syntactic structure. New transformations were postulated en masse to deal with various such complexities, and at the peak of transformationalism, some 300 standard transformations were in current use, and they were still counting!

However, the notion of transformation has itself undergone significant transformations since the naive approach of the late 1950s, somewhat simplistically introduced above. First, transformations expanded enormously so that just about every sentence was generated with the help of one or more of them while the idea of a 'nuclear sentence,' generated just by rewriting rules, was completely abandoned. At the same time, the strength of transformations was severely curtailed by abolishing some powerful types of transformations and imposing crippling constraints on the others. Much later, Chomsky eliminated transformations from his syntactical theory entirely.

However, the main contribution of transformations to linguistic theory has remained a most controversial claim that in the process of derivation of each sentence, the last pretransformational structure, called the **deep structure,** captures somehow the 'logical form' of the sentence, later distorted by the transformations, which ultimately produce the **surface structure** of the sentence. Thus, the transformational explanation of the fact that (19.i–ii) are virtually identical in form but different in meaning was that the deep structures of those two sentences included the radically different structures, such as (20.i–ii), respectively, and then the various transformations reduced the surface structures to the same form. Deep structures were also assigned a crucial role in the semantic component of transformational grammar (see chapter 8, section 2). It was this notion that brought about the irreconcilable differences in the transformationalist camp of the mid-1960s and has ultimately led to the decline of transformational grammar (see chapter 8, section 2.2).

(19) (i) John is eager to please.
(ii) John is easy to please.

(20) (i) John is eager—John pleases somebody.
(ii) John is easy—somebody pleases John.

3.3. Standard Theory

Besides the technical imperfections in the generative grammars above, all the examples have a serious built-in deficiency because of how the early version of transformational grammar—that of Chomsky's *Syntactic Structures* (1957) and the one presented simplistically above—was set up. Because every terminal rule had to list on the right all the members of the morphological category on the left, nonsensical sentences were generated by the grammars. Thus, in (13), because *garden* is treated as interchangeable with *boy* or *girl* by virtue of its being like the other two words a noun, a sentence like (21.i) will be generated by the grammar. Similarly, the grammar will generate sentences with the "wrong" verbs (21.ii), adjectives (21.iii), adverbs (21.iv), pronouns (21.v), and so on.

(21) (i) *The garden kissed the girl.
(ii) *The boy integrated the girl.
(iii) *The abstract boy kissed the nuclear girl.
(iv) *The boy kissed the girl falsely.
(v) *It kissed the girl.

In *Syntactic Structures* Chomsky seemed pleased with the fact that the famous sentence in (22) was generated by his grammar. In the years between 1957 and 1965, when he published his second major book, *Aspects of the Theory of Syntax,* he became increasingly unhappy about the fact that native speakers refused to treat that sentence as grammatical in any sense that was intuitively available to them. Chomsky also realized that the traditional grammar had been sensitive to the subcategories within the major morphological categories, such as nouns and verbs, the way his grammatical theory was not. In *Aspects* he undertook a major revision of transformational grammar and produced the late version of it that became known as standard theory.

(22) *Colorless green ideas sleep furiously.

Aspects is a book about one sentence, (23.i), that standard theory was supposed to be able to generate, and a refined mechanism was set up to do that, while at the same time preventing a sentence like (23.ii) or, for that matter, sentences like the ones in (21–22) from being generated.

(23) (i) Sincerity may frighten the boy.
(ii) *The boy may frighten sincerity.

Chomsky observed, following what had been known all along in the traditional grammars, that (23.ii) is meaningless because the verb *frighten* requires an animate object and *sincerity* is not animate. He realized that subcategories of nouns are involved here and set up a hierarchy of such subcategories, easily presentable in the form of a treelike chart, as in (24).

(24)

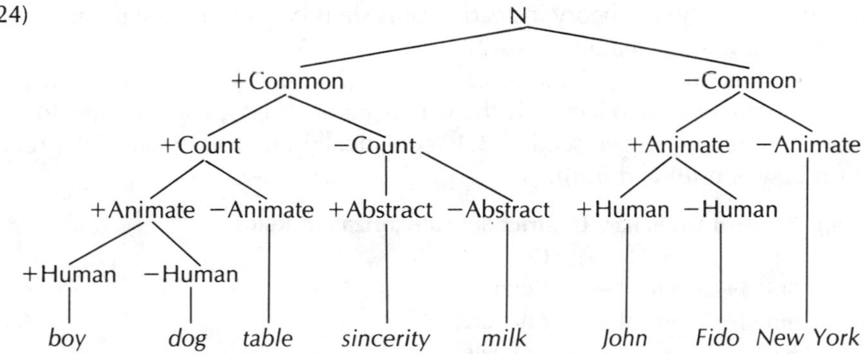

In (24), each path from N down to the examples in the bottom line corresponds to a feature combination assigned to the example at the end of the path. Thus, *boy* is characterized as [N, +Common, +Count, +Animate, +Human] and *sincerity* is [N, +Common, −Count, +Abstract]—listing N as the category first and enclosing the entire feature characteristic within square brackets are elements of the customarily accepted notation.

The subcategorization changed the nature of the terminal rules: No rule allowing the replacement of the sumbol N or V or any other symbol for a morphological category with any member of the corresponding category was any longer allowed. In other words, all the rules like (13.v–xii) were eliminated. A much more sophisticated mechanism was set up to account for noun subcategorization.

A transformational generative grammar now consisted of five parts, categorial rules, strict subcategorization rules, selection restriction rules, lexicon, and transformations. While the transformational component was modified significantly as well in standard theory, we will not deal with it here and will assume instead that the contents of section 3.2 pertain to standard theory. For this reason alone, transformations will be omitted from the grammar set up to generate (23.i).

The categorial rules of this grammar, (25), come closest to the early version (see section 3.1):

(25) **Standard Grammar: I. Categorial Rules**

(i) $S \rightarrow NP \frown VP$

(ii) $VP \rightarrow Aux \frown V \frown NP$

(iii) NP → (Det)N
(iv) Det → *the*
(v) Aux → M

(25.iv) is the only early-version-type terminal rule that survives, for reasons which will become clearer below, as will the meaning of (25.v). Arches are used in standard theory instead of plus signs because plus signs are used with the values of features (26–27).

The strict subcategorization rules, as in (26), are based on the chart in (24) and are related to it exactly the way a grammar is typically related to the corresponding tree (see section 3.1, specifically the discussion of the relation between (8) and 5.ii)).

(26) **Standard Grammar: II. Strict Subcategorization Rules**
(i) N → [±Common]
(ii) [+Common] → [±Count]
(iii) [−Common] → [±Animate]
(iv) [+Count] → [±Animate]
(v) [−Count] → [±Abstract]
(vi) [+Animate] → [±Human]

The selection restriction rules in (27) characterize verbs in terms of the subcategorial affiliation of the subjects and objects they take. The grammar is thus noun-biased: The nouns are subcategorized independently and the verbs indirectly in terms of the nouns with which they are compatible. The reverse approach is possible in principle, namely, characterizing the verbs independently and the nouns in terms of the verbs with which they are compatible. However, noun subcategorization is more established and more easily accessible in linguistics.

(27) **Standard Grammar: III. Selection Restriction Rules**
(i) V → [+Subject]/[N] Aux ____
(ii) V → [+[+Animate]Object]/ ____ (Det) [N, +Animate]

Unlike (25–26), which are context-free, the rules in (27) are context-bound, and what follows after the slash mark is the description of the context. The characterization of the context takes advantage of the direct word order in English, namely that the noun preceding the verb is its subject and the noun following the verb its object. The blank signifies the empty slot for the characterized verb. Therefore, (27.i) reads as follows: "If a verb occurs after a noun followed by an auxiliary, then characterize the verb as taking a subject." Since every English verb is preceded by a noun and every English verb, therefore, takes a subject, unlike some 'impersonal,' subjectless verbs in other languages (e.g., Russian), (27.i) characterizes the type of verb that is unrestricted as to its subject. Indeed, *frighten,* the verb it is being set up for, can take any subject. (27.ii) restricts the object; it reads as follows: "If a verb occurs before an animate noun (with an optional article in between), then characterize the verb as taking an animate object." Both of the rules are definitely geared toward *frighten,* but in fact they characterize separately any verb that can take any subject and any verb that can take an animate object. *Frighten* happens to be both.

The lexicon, as in (28), is the only part of the grammar that does not consist of rules. Instead, it contains a listing of all the words the grammar deals with. Each entry conforms to the same format consisting of two parts. The first part contains a complete phonological description of the word but we will simply let the spelling stand for that. The second part contains a feature characteristic for each word. Various brackets are used according to formal conventions.

(28) (i) (*boy,* [N, +Common, +Count, +Animate, +Human])
(ii) (*frighten,* [V, +Subject, +[+Animate]Object])
(iii) (*may,* [M])
(iv) (*sincerity,* [N, +Common, −Count, +Abstract])

May is characterized in the lexicon simply as a modal verb (M), a category which also includes *must, can,* and *ought. The* and the other determiners are introduced directly in the categorial rules because they are not affected by noun subcategorization.

In order to understand better how the lexicon and the rest of the grammar work, the derivation of (23.i) in the grammar (25–28) is given in (29–32):

(29)	(i)	S	
	(ii)	NP⌢VP	(25.i)
	(iii)	NP⌢Aux⌢V⌢NP	(25.ii)
	(iv)	N⌢Aux⌢V⌢NP	(25.iii–the no-determiner option)
	(v)	N⌢Aux⌢V⌢Det⌢N	(25.iii–the determiner option)
	(vi)	N⌢Aux⌢V⌢*the*⌢N	(25.iv)
	(vii)	N⌢M⌢V⌢*the*⌢N	(25.v)

The strict subcategorization rules use a slightly different formalism in the derivation (30): Instead of simple rewriting, the right parts of the rules (26) are added to the left parts, and the result always amounts to a complete downward path from N to a terminal node on (24). Each occurrence of N can be ultimately rewritten as any one of the eight paths on that chart. Naturally, we select the fourth path from left for the first N and the leftmost path for the second N.

(30)	(i)	[N, +Common, −Count, +Abstract]⌢M⌢V⌢*the*⌢N	(26.i—the plus option; ii—the minus option; v—the plus option)

(ii) [N, +Common, −Count, +Abstract]⁀M⁀V⁀the⁀[N, +Common, +Count, +Animate, +Human] (26.i–ii, iv, vi—the plus options)

The same additive formalism applies to the use of the selection restriction rules in derivation (31). V is simply replaced by a complete feature characteristic available in (27):

(31) [N, +Common, −Count, +Abstract]⁀M⁀[V, +Subject, +[+Animate]Object]⁀*the*⁀[N, +Common, +Count, +Animate, +Human] (27.i–ii)

At this point, the derivation completes the preterminal part, and now the lexicon has to be used. The use of the lexicon is carried out by the universal and language-independent **lexical insertion rule.** Since it is universal it does not need to be specified in any particular grammar. The lexical insertion rule replaces every feature characteristic in the last preterminal line of derivation (31) by any word in the lexicon with the same feature characteristic. In other words, if the second part of the entry in the lexicon fits the feature characteristic under consideration in the line, the lexical insertion rule replaces the feature characteristic in the line with the first part of the entry, that is, with the spelling of the word in our case. As in the notation in (29–31), the number on the right refers to the line of the lexicon inserted.

(32) (i) *sincerity*⁀M⁀[V, +Subject, +[+Animate]Object]⁀*the*⁀[N, +Common, +Count, +Animate, +Human] (28.iv)

(ii) *sincerity*⁀*may*⁀[V, +Subject, +[+Animate]Object]⁀*the*⁀[N, +Common, +Animate, +Human] (28.iii)

(iii) *sincerity*⁀*may*⁀*frighten*⁀*the*⁀[N, +Common, +Count, +Animate, +Human] (28.ii)

(iv) *sincerity*⁀*may*⁀*frighten*⁀*the*⁀*boy* (28.i)

When the arches are dropped, (32.iv) is (23.i) duly generated by the grammar. (23.ii), on the other hand, can no longer be generated by the grammar because the verb in that sentence will not meet the contextual requirement of (27.ii) since it is followed by an abstract and not an animate noun. In the process of derivation, the verb will have to be characterized as taking an abstract object (and the corresponding rule will have to be added for that purpose to (27). When the lexical insertion rule sets out to replace that new feature characteristic with a word, *frighten* will not fit and therefore will not be selected. A different verb, such as *appreciate,* will fit if it is contained in the lexicon because, unlike (23.ii), (33) is all right.

(33) The boy may appreciate sincerity.

In other words, *frighten* will be rejected by the grammar on the grounds of its incompatibility with *sincerity* as the object, which is exactly why the native speaker will reject it intuitively.

SECTION 4. GRAMMATICALITY AND LINGUISTIC THEORY

Transformational generative grammar, Chomsky's syntactic theory, is the best example of his theoretical standpoint, in particular on the important issue of the relation between formal theory and the native speaker's competence. The concept of grammaticality is the cornerstone of this theoretical position.

When formal methods were first introduced into linguistics by Chomsky's predecessors in American linguistics, they (primarily Bloomfield and his school) developed their "objective," formal methodology in order to exclude human intuition from the scope of linguistics as too unreliable and subjective from their point of view. This led to a variety of conceptual and practical difficulties.

Chomsky developed much further the mathematical basis of linguistic theory by moving it into the most sophisticated areas of contemporary mathematics. At the same time he restored the balance, lost by the descriptivists, between human intuition and the formal methodology and, by implication, between language as a human phenomenon and language as the object of scientific study.

He set up his transformational grammars as sets of rules that apply mechanically and generate symbols out of symbols. They comply to the ultimately formal paradigm of research known as the mechanical symbol-manipulation device. However, what this device is supposed to do is model the native speaker's competence by matching his output in some important respect.

Grammaticality is the respect to be matched in syntax. The native speaker is assumed to be able to tell a grammatical sentence from a nongrammatical sentence purely intuitively (see section 3.1). Transformational generative grammars possess a similar capacity: They generate some sentences and prevent others from generation. The goal of the entire transformational enterprise has been to set up a complete transformational generative grammar of a particular language and, ultimately, of all languages. **A complete transformational generative grammar of a language is the set of rules, such that each and every grammatical sentence of the language can be generated by a sequence of rules from the set and not a single ungrammatical sentence can.** In other words, if a sentence is grammatical it should be generated by such a grammar; if the sentence is ungrammatical it should not be generated by the grammar.

The relation between the formal syntactical theory and the native speaker, as set up by Chomsky, is summarized in (34). For any sentence, both the speaker and the grammar assess its grammaticality. The speaker passes a purely intuitive judgment and the grammar must match it formally.

(34)

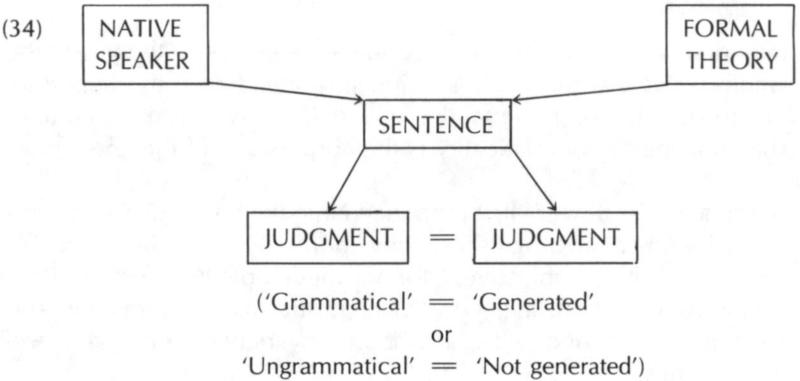

('Grammatical' = 'Generated'
or
'Ungrammatical' = 'Not generated')

The same model applies to the other levels of linguistic structure with grammaticality replaced by an appropriate feature from that level as the respect of the native competence to be matched.

This is an ideal and idealized model. In reality, grammaticality turns out to be a dubious concept because native speakers do not seem to have a clear sense of it and do not pass judgments as linguists would want them to. The concept of grammaticality associated with the early version of transformational grammar, according to which sentences like (21–22) were considered to be grammatical even if nonsensical, was particularly vulnerable on this count. In actual psycholinguistic experiments, native speakers uniformly assigned such sentences to the abnormal, deviant category along with the cases involving violations of purely syntactical rules, such as in (4). This was the most important reason why Chomsky had to revise transformational grammar, and the notion of grammaticality used in his standard theory came to include meaningfulness. The formula in (35) captures the transition from *Syntactic Structures* (1957) to *Aspects of the Theory of Syntax* (1965).

(35) $\text{Grammaticality}_{1965} = \text{Grammaticality}_{1957} + \text{Meaningfulness}$

SECTION 5. NON-TRANSFORMATIONAL SYNTAX

There is more to syntax than transformational grammar, but not that much. In opposition to Chomsky's syntax, a number of syntactical theories have been proposed, such as stratificational grammar, systemic grammar, relational grammar, $\bar{X}$ syntax, lexico-functional grammar, generalized phrase-structure grammar. Some are direct descendants of descriptivism and not really comparable to transformational grammar in terms of descriptive capacity and conceptual maturity. Others are largely notational variants of transformational grammar with different emphases.

The most standard charge against transformational grammar is that it does not use such 'notional' or 'relational' concepts as subject and predicate and prefers the related but distinct morphological categories, that is, parts of speech instead. The charge has been countered by transformationalists' assertions that it was easy but unnecessary to define the subject of a sentence as its leftmost NP and the predicate as its VP.

Lexico-functional grammar is one of the more influential grammatical proposals favoring relational concepts over morphological ones. However, in spite of the numerous protestations to the contrary, the grammar shares all the important premises with transformational grammar and is, for all practical purposes, its notational variant. In some such cases, the different notation may in fact turn out to be more accessible for, and digestible by, an adjacent area for a linguistic application to it.

The idea of language as rule-governed behavior and of linguistics as seeking to describe those rules is the basis of all modern syntax.

CHAPTER 8

Semantics

SECTION 1. SEMANTIC ENTITIES

Semantics differs from the linguistic disciplines discussed in the three previous chapters, namely, phonetics/phonology, morphology, and syntax, in an important respect. Those disciplines study the three hierarchically arranged levels of linguistic structure, such that the entities of each higher level consist of the entities (units) of the lower level. Instead, semantics deals with entities of different levels, as listed in (1), and it is responsible for the meaning of everything in language that has meaning. There is a wide range of meaningful language entities, from the morpheme, which is the minimal meaningful unit in language, up to the text, or discourse, which is in principle unlimited in length.

(1) **Meaningful Entities of Language:**
Text/Discourse
Paragraph
SENTENCE
Phrase
WORD
Morpheme

While in theory semantics does consider itself accountable for the meanings of all entities in (1), in reality it has been primarily concerned with the two capitalized in the list. From its inception in the 1880s through the 1950s, semantics dealt almost exclusively with word meaning. Since the 1960s, it has focused on sentence meaning. Recently there have been serious indications of an increased interest to paragraph meaning and even discourse meaning.

SECTION 2. WORD MEANING

2.1. Word Meaning: Elements

For the first 40 or so years of its existence, semantics handled almost exclusively the question of how words change their meanings. We will address this issue briefly in chapter 9, section 4. The synchronic study of word meaning began some time in the 1920s when people realized, apparently for the first time, that word meaning—and meaning in general—cannot be taken for granted, that is, simply assumed to be something words have. Instead, the immensely complex nature of word meaning started to emerge at the time, and many desperate attempts to define meaning were made.

A major breakthrough in the study of word meaning occurred in the 1930s when the idea of feature analysis, then new and exciting in phonology, penetrated semantics as well. It had been preceded somewhat by the research on **semantic fields,** each field being a group of words with contiguous meanings. Thus, the words in (2.i) all belong to the semantic field of kinship; the words in (2.ii) to color; the words in (2.iii) to the 'mental field.'

(2) (i) mother, father, daughter, son, aunt, uncle, niece, nephew
(ii) red, blue, green, white, gray, brown, black, pink
(iii) mind, idea, concept, thought, assumption, premise, reason

The analysis of various semantic fields by different authors may have pursued diverse goals but the very fact that those words belong to the same field is tantamount, in feature terms, to their sharing a semantic feature. In fact, the thesaurus, available in dictionary form for over a hundred years, is based on the principle of semantic fields. However, feature analysis was neither conscious nor explicit in that approach.

Feature analysis became both conscious and explicit with **componential analysis,** the analysis of word meaning into components. It was componential analysis that put forth for the first time the idea that word meaning was not just "there" but rather that it was a nonelementary and often rather complex aggregate of more primitive semantic units.

Semantic features that constituted word meaning were abstract constructs which did not coincide with the meanings of the morphemes constituting the word. There were no sequences of sounds corresponding to semantic features. Unlike phonetic features, they did not even correlate with acoustical or any other physical phenomena. They were 'pure meaning.'

The main idea of componential analysis was to reduce the enormous diversity of meanings in language to a manageable limited list of very basic and general features, such that the meaning of each and every word be assembled out of a few features from that list. The proponents of the approach thought in terms of at most a few hundred features to account for a few hundred thousand meanings. Some words lent themselves to componential anslysis readily, as indicated in (3).

(3) Word	Semantic Features
(i) *man*	(Physical Object) (Animate) (Human) (Male) (Adult)
(ii) *woman*	(Physical Object) (Animate) (Human) (Female) (Adult)

(iii)	*boy*	(Physical Object) (Animate) (Human) (Male) (Nonadult)
(iv)	*girl*	(Physical Object) (Animate) (Human) (Female) (Nonadult)

(Physical Object) is a very general feature that all tangible, spatiotemporal objects share, unlike abstractions, such as sincerity or love. People and animals are (Animate) in many languages including English. People are (Human) while animals are not. The difference between (Male) and (Female) and (Adult) and (Nonadult) is clearly illustrated in (3).

Logically, the simplest and most elegant type of feature is the **binary feature,** the feature which has exactly two values, '+' and '−,' or 'yes' and 'no.' All the features in (3) are, in fact, binary, and (3) can be represented in a different notation, (4), with plus and minus signs, typical at least for the later versions of componential analysis:

(4)	Word	Semantic Features
(i)	*man*	(+Physical Object) (+Animate) (+Human) (+Male) (+Adult)
(ii)	*woman*	(+Physical Object) (+Animate) (+Human) (−Male) (+Adult)
(iii)	*boy*	(+Physical Object) (+Animate) (+Human) (+Male) (−Adult)
(iv)	*girl*	(+Physical Object) (+Animate) (+Human) (−Male) (−Adult)

The meaning of *sincerity* will then include (−Physical Object); the meaning of *table* will include (−Animate); and the meaning of *dog* will include (−Human).

While one binary feature can distinguish two objects, two may distinguish four, three eight; in general, *n* binary objects may distinguish 2^n objects. A very small number of binary features can then distinguish an enormous number of objects. Thus, 20 binary features can distinguish over a million objects. The essence of componential analysis was to reduce the meanings of 500,000 or so words in a typical full-fledged natural language like English to such a number of features.

Again, some words lend themselves to the binary treatment beautifully. Three binary features can distinguish eight objects, and it takes exactly three semantic features to account for the meanings of the eight words in (2.i). The features are: sex (±Male); senior versus junior generation (±Senior); direct versus sideline relation (±Direct). The result is presented in the form of a simple table in (5).

What makes binary features so effective is that each of them divides all the meanings into two classes, each containing exactly half of the total, so that the members of one class have the feature (+) and the members of the other do not (−). This means that each feature should be applicable to every single meaning in the pool. This is exactly the case in (5), and each of the three features divides the pool of eight into four and four in its own, different way.

Unfortunately, such semantic fields as the terms of kinship in (2.i) and (5) are an exception rather than the rule in language—the words have clear,

(5) Word	Feature 1 (±Male)	Feature 2 (±Senior)	Feature 3 (±Direct)
father	+	+	+
uncle	+	+	−
son	+	−	+
nephew	+	−	−
mother	−	+	+
aunt	−	+	−
daughter	−	−	+
niece	−	−	−

distinct, discrete meanings and, consequently, there are enough binary features applicable to each word meaning. The words in (2.ii–iii) are more typical in that there is at best only one binary feature applicable to each word meaning, namely, (±Color) and (±Mental), respectively, and the remainder of each meaning requires a number of nonbinary features for its description, which makes the feature description much less economical.

Besides that, many meanings tend to be "fuzzy" rather than clearly delineated and separated from each other, and there are borderline cases which are not easily attributable to one single term; for instance, a color may be somewhere between green and blue.

Multiple attempts at componential analyses of various languages demonstrated that while an initial success with an exceptional semantic field or two is possible in terms of reducing many meanings to many fewer binary features, ultimately the number of necessary semantic features becomes comparable to the number of meanings to be described, and this was, of course, very inefficient. The reason is that word meanings typically contain very individual, idiosyncratic elements of meaning, for which a special semantic feature has to be postulated. Each such feature is applicable to a very limited number of word meanings, sometimes to just one, and thus lacks the generality and the quantitative power of the binary features in (5); if most semantic features are like that, it is obvious that very many of them are necessary to account for all the diverse meanings.

While the main ambition of componential analysis—to account for every word meaning in terms of a handful of semantic features—was defeated, the approach established a firm methodological tradition within semantics, and feature analysis remains the staple method in semantic descriptions though its theoretical foundations are entirely different (see section 3).

2.2. Word Meaning: Relations

Word meanings can enter into various relations with each other. At least three of these relations are well-known from traditional—and secondary-school—linguistics: synonymy, antonymy, and homonymy/polysemy.

Synonymy is the relation that links two or more words of a language whose meanings are identical or at least very similar:

(6) (i) freedom : liberty
(ii) buy : purchase
(iii) pretty : handsome

The identity of meaning is manifested in that synonyms are interchangeable, that is, they can replace each other in sentences, as in (7.i–ii), (7.iii–iv), and (7.v–vi), respectively, without changing the meaning.

(7) (i) Americans enjoy their freedom.
(ii) Americans enjoy their liberty.
(iii) I bought a car.
(iv) I purchased a car.
(v) This is a pretty view.
(vi) This is a handsome view.

In fact, however, languages do not tolerate complete duplication easily, and identical meanings are rare. Most synonyms are, therefore, incomplete; in other words, there are sentences in which one of the synonyms is appropriate and the other is not, and vice versa. Such sentences are called **diagnostic constructions.** Thus, (8.i–vi) contains the diagnostic constructions for *freedom, liberty, buy, purchase, pretty,* and *handsome,* respectively.

(8) (i) freedom fighter : *liberty fighter
(ii) taking liberties : *taking freedoms
(iii) I don't buy your premise : *I don't purchase your premise
(iv) I put all the purchases in one bag : ?I put all the buys in one bag
(v) pretty girl : *handsome girl
(vi) handsome warrior : *pretty warrior

The closer the synonyms are to each other, the harder it is to find a diagnostic construction. If everything else fails, one resorts to idioms, which are normally much more idiosyncratic than nonidiomatic expressions. To the extent one has to do that, the synonyms emerge as rather close. We had to do it in virtually each case in (8), which indicates that the synonyms in (6) are indeed close. In (8.iv), even a more "desperate" act was committed: Because *buy* seems to be able to replace *purchase* even in such idioms as *purchasing power* and *option to purchase,* we had to go to the noun version of the words and to discover there that *buy* as a noun is much more limited in usage.

In terms of componential analysis, complete synonyms must have exactly the same feature characteristics and incomplete synonyms must have heavily overlapping but partially distinct ones.

Antonymy is the relation linking two words with opposite meanings. At least three kinds of antonymy can be distinguished. The gradables (9.i) involve a scale, and the two antonyms mark the opposite poles of the scales. Such antonyms are called gradable because the intermediate points of the scale may be referred to and compared. Gradable antonyms are usually adjectives denoting a quality, and more or less of the quality can be possessed by objects; thus, the weather can be better or worse, the student can be brighter or less bright, and so on. The possibility of comparison along the scale is a clear indication that a given pair of antonyms is gradable. The complementaries involve a pair of words which are in an either/or relationship and no intermediate points are possible. The conversives, usually involving verbs and other words denoting actions, present the same phenomenon from the opposite points of view; for example, if John follows Bill thenBill precedes John, if Peter gives something to Paul then Paul takes it from Peter, and so on.

(9) (i) **Gradable Antonyms:** good : bad; bright : dumb; hot : cold
(ii) **Complementary Antonyms:** life : death; man : woman; win : lose
(iii) **Conversive Antonyms:** follow : precede; give : take; buy : sell

In terms of componential analysis, antonymy often involves a different value of a common feature, that is, a plus instead of a minus on a binary feature; thus, *man : woman; father : mother; actor : actress* are all complementary antonyms because the first member of each pair is (+Male) while the second is (−Male).

Both synonyms and antonyms can be local, or established as such in a particular discourse. In such a case, the relation holds only in this discourse and is invalid outside of it. Thus, if somebody utters something like (10.i), the words *linguist* and *neurotic* are established as local synonyms—one visible result of that would be that the former word, normally ungradable, could then be used gradably because the latter can. If (10.ii) is uttered, *Jewish* and *dumb* are established as local antonyms. Various biases, myths, stereotypes, and prejudices can often be reduced to phenomena of local synonymy and antonymy shared by a group of native speakers but not by all.

(10) (i) You are a linguist and, therefore, neurotic.
(ii) You are not Jewish—you are dumb!

Homonymy is the relation that holds between two words that satisfy all the conditions in (11). (12.i) contains an example. Two words may satisfy only two out of the three conditions in (11). If (11.i) is waived, the two words are not homonyms but rather **homophones** (12.ii). If (11.ii) is waived, the two words are **homographs** (12.iii). Finally, if (11.iii) is weakened by dropping the words *and unrelated,* the two words are not homonyms and they are not two separate words, either—instead, it is one word with related even if different meanings (12.iv). A word with a number of related meanings is polysemous, and the name of the phenomenon is **polysemy.**

(11) (i) same spelling
(ii) same pronunciation
(iii) different and unrelated meanings

(12) (i) *bear*$_1$ (N) 'animal' : *bear*$_2$ (V) 'give birth' : *bear*$_3$ (V) 'tolerate'
(ii) meat : meet : mete
(iii) *lead* (V) : *lead* (N) 'metal'
(iv) *go* 'move along,' 'leave,' 'proceed to an activity,' etc.

The dictionaries usually provide separate entires for homonyms and homographs (and, naturally, for homophones), numbering them similarly to (12.i) only for the former. There is usually one entry for a polysemous word, with the different meanings numbered within each entry. It would suffice to look at a page in any dictionary to see that very many words are polysemous.

Unlike synonyms and antonyms, homonyms do not normally share any semantic features—see (11.iii). In most cases, the phenomenon is the result of phonetic changes or borrowings rather than of any semantic processes. In some cases, however, one can suspect a connection at an earlier stage. Thus, *bear* 'carry' is usually lumped with *bear*$_2$ in (12.ii), apparently because the mother carries the fetus. In fact, some dictionaries put *bear*$_3$ there as well, thus presenting it as a metaphoric extension of *bear*$_2$. In that case, only the homonymy of *bear*$_1$ and *bear*$_2$/*bear*$_3$ is recognized. Whether to list two words as two homonyms or as two meanings of the same polysemous word depends ultimately on whether there is any easily accessible and widely recognized relation between the meanings, and opinions on that may of course vary.

Other relations between word meanings are known or can be easily postulated. Feature analysis itself induces a diversity of such relations on the basis of sharing features or even feature values.

SECTION 3. SENTENCE MEANING

Sentence meaning became the prime target of semantics only after syntax had reached a certain degree of sophistication and relative clarity. Two notions concerning relations between sentence meanings were, however, rather familiar—paraphrase relations between sentences are analogous to synonymy for words; ambiguity is the sentence-level counterpart of homonymy/polysemy.

The first formal theory of sentence meaning was based on transformational syntax. It was Katz and Fodor (1963), both of them Chomsky's associates at the time at MIT, who introduced the semantic component into transformational grammar, which along with the central syntactical component and the phonological component developed by Chomsky and Halle constituted the complete standard theory of Chomsky's *Aspects of the Theory of Syntax* (1957; see chapter 7, section 3.3). The formal function of the semantic component was defined by Katz and Fodor as the semantic interpretation of the deep structures (see chapter 7, section 3.2) generated by the base of the syntactical component, as shown on the chart of standard theory, in (13).

3.1. Semantic Theory

The theoretical position of Katz and Fodor in semantics is a direct extrapolation of Chomsky's views in syntax, and their semantic theory is a direct spinoff of his concept of linguistic theory. As explained in chapter 7, section 4, for Chomsky, formal linguistic theory models, or matches, the native speaker's competence. This is the only raison d'être, function, and justification of the formal rules.

Katz and Fodor's formal semantic theory attempts to match the native speaker's semantic competence. Obviously, this competence includes primarily the ability to understand sentences. Katz and Fodor (1963) distinguish the following components within semantic competence:

(14) (i) determining the number of meanings of a sentence and the content of each meaning;
(ii) detecting semantic anomalies;
(iii) establishing paraphrase relations between sentences;
(iv) detecting every other semantic property or relation.

(14.iv) is, of course, the proverbial wastebasket category, and we will ignore it as, in fact, did Katz and Fodor themselves. (14.i) and (14.iii) deal with two well-known relations between sentence meanings, namely **ambiguity** and **paraphrase,** respectively. (15.i) is at least three-way ambiguous (*bill* as a sum of money, a part of a bird's anatomy, or a legal document); (15.ii) is two-way ambiguous; (15.iii) is a paraphrase of one of the two meanings of (15.ii); (15.iv) is a paraphrase of the other meaning of (15.ii), and the native speaker is believed to be able to establish all of this purely intuitively.

(15) (i) The bill is large.
(ii) Flying planes can be dangerous.
(iii) There are situations in which flying planes are dangerous.
(iv) There are situations in which flying planes is dangerous.

Incidentally, the ambiguity in (15.i–ii) is of two different kinds. In (15.i) it is due to the homonymy/polysemy of *bill*. In (15.ii), there are no such

(13)

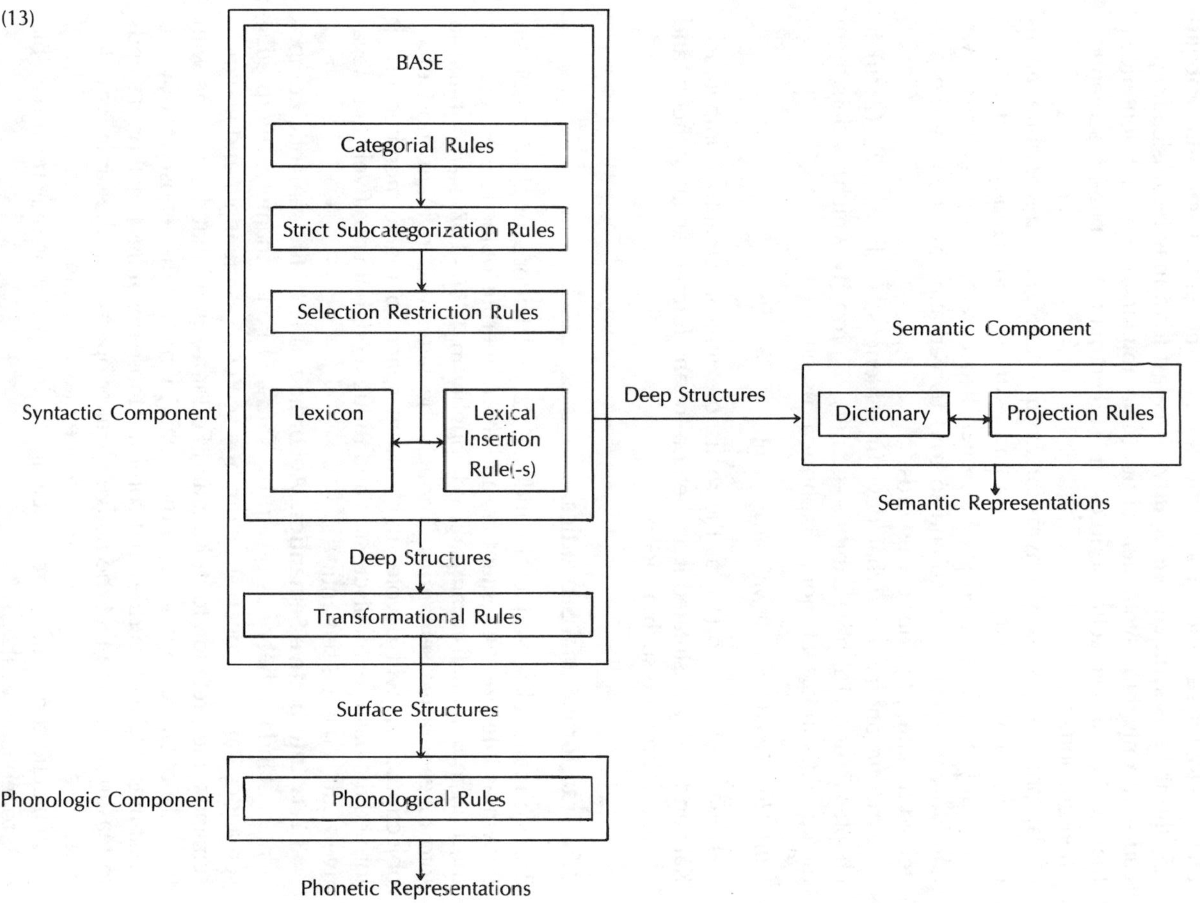

Syntactic Component
BASE
Categorial Rules
Strict Subcategorization Rules
Selection Restriction Rules
Lexicon
Lexical Insertion Rule(-s)
Deep Structures
Transformational Rules
Surface Structures
Phonologic Component
Phonological Rules
Phonetic Representations
Deep Structures
Semantic Component
Dictionary
Projection Rules
Semantic Representations

words, and the ambiguity is due to the possibility of two different semantic analyses for the sentence. The former kind of ambiguity is **semantic ambiguity;** the latter is **syntactic ambiguity.** This last term may be misleading because the only thing syntactical about the ambiguity of any such sentence is that it has a syntactic source—it still remains a purely semantical phenomenon.

Paraphrases, just as synonyms for word meaning, are never quite identical; still, native speakers use paraphrases freely and happily. In fact, just about any act of reported speech, even if accurate, is a paraphrase—we hardly ever repeat what so-and-so told us verbatim, we convey the perceived meaning "in our own words."

Semantic anomaly is what deviant sentences, such as (22), (23.ii) in chapter 7, and (16) here exhibit—namely, a property which renders them meaningless in casual, nonmetaphorical usage.

(16) He painted the wall with silent paint.

Having established (14) as the realistic extent of semantic competence, Katz and Fodor postulated it as the goal of any formal semantic theory and set out to propose such a theory.

3.2. Transformational Semantics

Transformational semantics includes Katz and Fodor's original proposal, known as **interpretive semantics,** and the numerous objections to it within the transformationalist camp raised roughly in 1966–1971, amounting in toto to **generative semantics.** Though the latter was right in most of its objections, we will devote much more space to the former because it formed the basis for all discussion and influenced, both positively and negatively, all sentence semantics.

3.2.1. Interpretive Semantics. According to (13), the semantic component of standard theory as set up by Katz and Fodor, namely, interpretive semantics, takes the deep structure of a sentence as the input and assigns a semantic interpretation to it. Katz and Fodor assumed that this is done with the help of two components, a dictionary, which is the repository of word meanings, and a set of rules that combine those meanings together. It stands to reason to assume that the native speaker operates in the same way: If a word meaning is unknown, the sentence may not be interpreted correctly; if the syntactic connections are not clear, the interpretation may be impossible or erroneous as well.

Katz and Fodor's **dictionary** is a formalized version of a typical English–English dictionary, in which every entry is standardized according to a set of principles. In fact, they borrowed all of their examples from one such dictionary, *The Shorter Oxford English Dictionary,* and never bothered to treat the material critically. What mattered for them was not how words are defined or what entries were considered appropriate but rather how their dictionary would handle various phenomena. The examples below should be taken with this very clearly in mind.

Each dictionary entry consists of the lexical item to which the entry is assigned, one syntactic marker, one or more **semantic markers,** one **semantic** distinguisher, and, for some entries, one **selection restriction,** which may be a logical combination of semantic markers. The first three are illustrated in (17), in which *bachelor* is, of course, the lexical item, N represents the syntactic part of the entry, the items in parentheses are semantic markers, and the terminal elements in square brackets are distinguishers, while each numbered combination of items corresponds to one meaning of the entry.

(17) *bachelor* N (i) (Human) (Male) [Who has never married]
(ii) (Human) (Male) [Young knight serving under the standard of another knight]
(iii) (Human) [Who has the first academic degree]
(iv) (Animal) (Male) [Young fur seal when without a mate at breeding time]

This is, of course, componential analysis, but with a difference. The semantic markers are set up to capture only the most general part of the meaning of each entry. Each semantic marker is postulated only if it is widely applicable to other entries. The meaning of each entry is described in terms of as many markers as are applicable to it while the balance of the meaning is assigned to the distinguisher which can be characterized in any arbitrary fashion, including the way the word is defined in a regular dictionary. The advantage of this version of componential analysis is that the number of semantic markers may remain small. The disadvantage is that the theory is set up to ignore the distinguishers and to operate with only a limited set of markers. Thus, the most significant part of the meaning will be ignored by the theory: In (17.i), for instance, the part of the meaning captured by the theory coincides with the meaning of *man* (cf. (4.i)), while the distinguisher expressing the important part of the meaning is ignored. The theory (along with the componential analysis) gains in feasibility but loses in semantic accuracy.

The difference between the semantic markers and distinguishers is thus meant to be the difference between what is general and what is idiosyncratic in the meaning, respectively. The semantic markers represent that part of the meaning of an item on which the whole semantic theory is based and with the help of which all the semantic relations are expressed. If some piece of information is put within a distinguisher it will be ignored by the theory altogether—the theory cannot see, and does not look, inside the distinguisher's square brackets. Nor will the distinguisher be part of any semantic relations; for instance, no ambiguity can be resolved and no paraphrase relation between some two sentences established on the basis of the information in the distinguisher. This provides an important clue about how to distribute semantic information between markers and distinguishers: If a certain semantic property that one wants one's theory to account for can be stated in terms of a certain semantic feature, the latter should be assigned the status of a semantic marker. Thus, for instance, the speaker would take (18) for an almost unambiguous sentence.

(18) The old bachelor died.

In this sentence, the first meaning of (17.i) will be perceived as the most probable meaning of *bachelor* but (17.iii) cannot be excluded either. The other two meanings (17.ii,iv) are impossible, because the semantic element 'young' is implied by (17.ii,iv) and contradicts the meaning of *old* in the sentence. However, if 'young' is hidden within a distinguisher, as in (17.ii,iv), the theory will have to ignore it and will continue to treat the sentence as four-way ambiguous. Then the theory will not match the intuition of the native speaker and, therefore, not model his semantic competence. To correct the situation, one must transfer 'young' from the distinguisher to the marker status, as in (19):

(19) *bachelor* N (i) (Human) (Male) [Who has never married]
(ii) (Human) (Male) (Young) [Knight serving under the standard of another knight]
(iii) (Human) [Who has the first academic degree]
(iv) (Animal) (Male) (Young) [Fur seal when without a mate at breeding time]

In this example, Katz and Fodor (1963) also seem to miss another similar point. There is nothing in (19) to suggest that the speaker would classify (20) as odd, which he would. This means that the semantic marker (Adult) should be added to the human part (19.i–iii) of the entry. Thus, the speakers' reaction to anomaly must also be reflected in the systematic, or, semantic-marker, part of the entry.

(20) Her two-year-old son is a bachelor.

Traditional dictionaries also frequently contain information about cooccurrence of words, for example, the italicized parts of (21), which is part of an entry for *honest* in *The Shorter Oxford English Dictionary*.

(21) ". . . 3. *of persons:* of good moral character, virtuous, upright. . . *of women:* chaste, virtuous . . ."

Katz and Fodor capture the same information in their selection restrictions. Selection restrictions appear at the end of some dictionary entries—adjectives and adverbs, primarily—in angle brackets, and they are expressed in terms of semantic markers, because of the important role assigned to them in the projection rules. The corresponding part of Katz and Fodor's dictionary entry for *honest* is (22).

(22) *honest* Adj (Evaluative) (Moral) [Innocent of illicit sexual intercourse] ⟨(Human) & (Female)⟩

The formalized dictionary is thus the first part of the semantic component (see (13)). The **projection rules** constitute the second and last part of it. The projection rules operate on two inputs. The first one is the set of entries, with all of their meanings, for each of the words constituting the sentence, and this input is provided by the dictionary. The second input is the deep structure of the sentence provided by the syntactic component.

The projection rules operate on the tree diagram representing the deep structure of the sentence. They start from the very bottom of the tree and look for any two words dominated by a common node and combine the entries for these words into one common entry, depending primarily on the type of syntactic substructure involved and on the selection restrictions, if any, in the entries. They repeat this operation until the combined entry (or entries if the sentence is ambiguous) is (are) calculated for the entire sentence.

Katz and Fodor analyzed one example of a sentence (23.i). They represented its deep structure, coinciding in this simplified version with its structural description, as (23.ii).

(23) (i) The man hit the colorful ball.

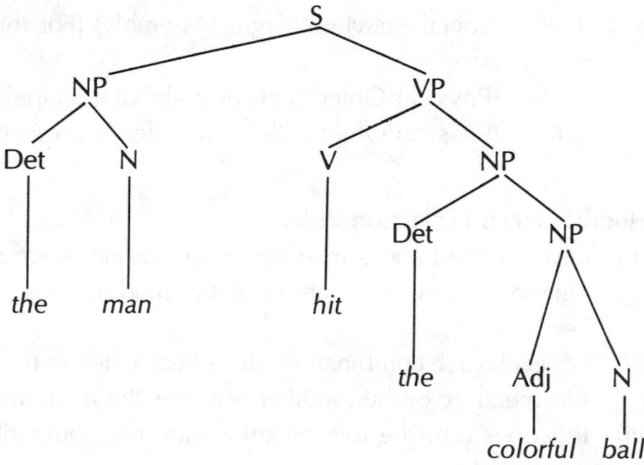

The first thing to do is to make an inventory of all the syntactic substructures represented in (23.ii). There are four, namely, the determiner-head construction realized twice (*the* + *man; the* + *colorful ball*); the modifier-head construction (*colorful* + *ball*); the verb-object construction (*hit* + *the colorful ball*); and the subject-verb construction (*the man* + *hit the colorful ball*). Generally, there is a very limited inventory of possible syntactic substructures in a language, and each of them is served by its own projection rule.

One can begin the process with any two nodes on the tree of the sentence whose grammatical categories are dominated by a common node. In other words, any substructure of type (24), in which *D* and *E* are words, will do. There are two possible beginnings for the process in (24), *the* and *man* or *colorful* and *ball*. Following Katz and Fodor, we will begin with the latter, which requires the modifier-head projection rule.

(24)

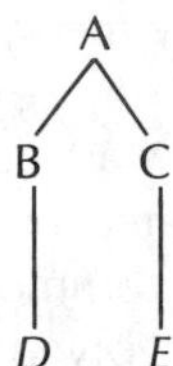

Let (25) and (26) stand for the entries for *colorful* and *ball,* and respectively, and (27) be the modifier-head projection rule.

(25) *colorful* Adj (i) (Color) [Abounding in contrast or variety of bright colors]⟨(Physical Object) V (Social activity)⟩
(ii) (Evaluative) [Having distinctive character, vividness, or picturesqueness]⟨(Aesthetic Object) V (Social Activity)⟩

(26) *ball* N (i) (Social Activity) (Large) (Assembly) [For the purpose of social dancing]
(ii) (Physical Object) [Having globular shape]
(iii) (Physical Object) [Solid missile for projection by engine of war]

(27) **Modifier-Head Projection Rule:**
(i) Given a head and a modifier, observe one by one all the possible combinations of every meaning of the modifier with every meaning of the head.
(ii) For each such combination, first check whether the selection restriction of this meaning of the modifier matches the meaning of the head.
(iii) If it does not, the two meanings are not compatible and are not to be combined.

(iv) If the match is there, combine the two meanings in question in the following way. First write down the dominant grammatical node as the syntactic marker of the new combined entry, then write down all the semantic markers of the head followed by those of the modifier (if they share some markers these should be listed only once). Next write down the semantic distinguisher of the modifier in its square brackets followed by that of the head in its square brackets and put in another pair of square brackets to enclose both of the distinguishers.

The selection restriction in (25.ii) blocks the combination of this meaning with (26.ii–iii)—informally, it corresponds to the intuitive feeling the native speaker is supposed to have about the incompatibility of the figurative meaning of *colorful* with the physical meanings of *ball*. Therefore, the result is the set of only four (out of the possible six) combined meanings (28):

(28) *colorful ball* NP
(i) (Social Activity) (Large) (Assembly) (Color) [[Abounding in contrast or variety of bright colors] [For the purpose of social dancing]]
(ii) (Physical Object) (Color) [[Abounding in contrast or variety of bright colors] [Having globular shape]]
(iii) (Physical Object) (Color) [[Abounding in contrast or variety of bright colors] [Solid missile for projection by engine of war]]
(iv) (Social Activity) (Large) (Assembly) (Evaluative) [[Having distinctive character, vividness, or picturesqueness] [For the purpose of social dancing]]

At the next stage, the new entry *colorful ball* is combined with *the,* whose simplified entry is given in (29). The determiner-head projection rule is even simpler than the modifier-head projection rule. Both are essentially instructions to rewrite the two combined entries together in a certain order. In this case, the determiner-head projection rule will simply add the sole semantic marker of *the* before each of the four meanings in (28). The new combined entry *the colorful ball* preserves then the four-way ambiguity of (29).

(29) *the* Det (Definite)

The entries for verbs are generally somewhat more complicated in structure than (25–26). Besides the usual markers and distinguishers, they contain two special semantic markers with an empty slot in each. The empty slot may be preceded by another semantic marker putting a restriction on the type of noun the verb can take as a subject or an object. Thus, the simplified entry for *hit* may look like (30).

(30) *hit* Vtr (i) (Action) (Physical) (Collision) (Subject: (Physical Object) ____) (Object: (Physical Object) ____) [To come in contact forcefully]
(ii) (Action) (Physical) (Arrival) (Subject: (Human) ____) (Object: (Social Activity) ____) [To come upon]

(30.i) describes *hit* in that meaning as requiring physical object for both subject and object; (30.ii) requires a human subject and a social-activity object. The effect of (30) is similar to that produced by selection restriction rules in the syntactic component of standard theory (see (27) in chapter 7).

The verb-object projection rule takes the entry of the noun phrase immediately following a transitive verb and tries to insert each of the meanings, one by one, into the empty slot of the Object marker. If there is an inside semantic marker in the Object marker and the meaning under consideration does not contain it, the insertion is blocked and the combination of this meaning of the object with this meaning of the verb is blocked. Thus, the physical meaning of *hit* (30.i) is compatible with only two meanings of *the colorful ball* (28.ii–iii), and the other meaning of *hit* (30.ii) is compatible with only the other two meanings of *the colorful ball* (30.i,iv). As a result, the new combined entry *hit the colorful ball* remains four-way ambiguous.

What is still to be done is first to combine *the* and *man* (31) with the help of the already familiar head-determiner rule and then to insert the result in the Subject marker of the verb within the entry for *hit the colorful ball*. Since (Human) implies (Physical Object), *the man* is compatible with all the four meanings of *hit the colorful ball*.

(31) *man* N (Human) (Male) (Adult)

The final result, the semantic interpretation of (23.i), is the set of four combinations of markers and distinguishers. If the native speaker does indeed discern in the sentence the four meanings which can be loosely paraphrased as (32), then the formal semantic interpretation assigned to the sentence by the theory matches the native speaker's semantic competence.

(32) (i) The man got to a dance characterized by bright colors.
(ii) The man struck a brightly painted globular-shaped object.
(iii) The man struck a brightly colored globular-shaped artillery shell.
(iv) The man got to a memorable dance.

3.2.2. Generative Semantics. Katz and Fodor's interpretive semantics was seminal not only because it was the first formal semantic theory proposed in linguistics and the first transformational theory of semantics, but more important, because it made very significant and explicit claims. Thus, it defined the scope of semantic competence for the theory to match for the first time. It established unambiguously the format of semantic theory as consisting of a dictionary and a set of rules combining the meanings of the words together (later, this became known as the principle of **compositionality,** and the approach based on this principle has been referred to as **compositional semantics**). It introduced partial componential analysis, coupled with a claim that a semantic theory can be based on the most general elements of word meaning captured by a handful of features and that it can ignore the rest of the meaning.

The claims Katz and Fodor put forward were so clearly stated that, somewhat paradoxically but not at all unexpectedly, they caused a great deal of opposition. Semanticists seemed to understand their proposal well and to reject many of their claims. In fact, the late 1960s–early 1970s were completely dominated by a bitter controversy between interpretive semantics and what became known as **generative semantics,** collectively and somewhat diversely proposed by an influential group of early transformationalists, such as Ross, G. Lakoff, McCawley, Fillmore, and Postal. (Postal had earlier contributed a great deal to interpretive semantics by coauthoring with Katz an influential book, *An Integrated Theory of Linguistic Descriptions* (1964), which revised the concept of transformation to make transformational syntax compatible with Katz and Fodor's transformational semantics. The revisions were fully endorsed by Chomsky and incorporated into standard theory in his *Aspects* (1965).)

Proposing a much less detailed and, from their point of view, streamlined scheme for linguistic theory, represented in (33), the generative semanticists attacked interpretive semantics on a number of formal and organizational issues, as in (34), and the main point of contention was the notion of deep structure.

(33)

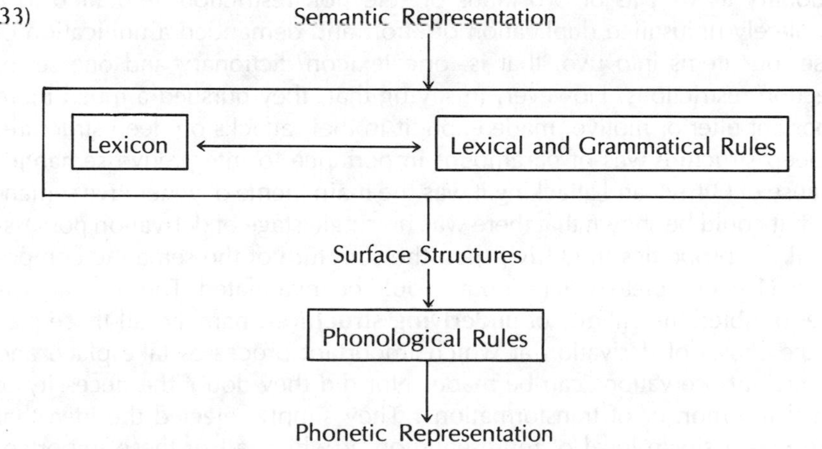

(34) **Interpretive-Semantics Claims Attacked by Generative Semantics:**

(i) Deep structure constitutes the input to the semantic component, and therefore transformations applied to deep structure in the process of further derivation of a sentence do not change meaning (see (13)).

(ii) There is a lexicon within the syntactic component of standard theory and a dictionary within its semantic component (see (28) in chapter 7 and (13)).

(iii) There are selection restrictions both within the base of the syntactic component of standard theory and within certain dictionary entries in the semantic component (see (27) in chapter 7 and (25)).

(iv) There exists a derivational stage, called deep structure, such that it serves as the boundary between syntax and semantics, as represented in (13), that all the lexical insertion occurs before it (see chapter 7, section 3.3, especially the discussion before (32)), and that all transformations are applied after it, as in (13).

While Katz and Postal freed the syntactic component from those transformations which obviously violated (34.i), many scholars refused to accept that a useful notion of transformations not affecting meaning could be possible. Chomsky conceded this claim by the late 1960s and introduced an **extended standard theory,** in which some transformations do affect meaning. The dotted line in (13) reflects this claim, and, with the dotted line made solid, (13) becomes the outlay of that new theory. Katz never conceded that point and remained the minority of one in this respect in the tiny interpretive camp.

(34.ii–iii) pertain to the question of neatness and elegance in linguistic theory. Katz's opponents felt that the existence of a lexicon along with a dictionary as well as of two kinds of selection restriction amounted to a completely unjustified duplication of effort and demanded a unification of those four items into two, that is, one lexicon/dictionary and one set of selection restrictions. However, in saying that, they pursued a much more important ulterior motive, made explicit in their attacks on deep structure.

Deep structure was of paramount importance to interpretive semantics because of (34.iv), and attacking it was the main theme of generative semantics. If it could be shown that there was no single stage of derivation possessing all the properties in (34.iv), then the structure of the semantic component in (13), complete with its input, would be invalidated. The generativists never doubted the validity of **underlying structures,** namely, all those presurface stages of derivation at which important processes take place and significant observations can be made. Nor did they doubt the necessity of lexical insertion or of transformations. They simply rejected the idea that there was a single level of representation at which all of these important events cooccurred.

The generativists' objections, formulated by Lakoff (1971a) and indirectly but more convincingly by Postal (1971), ran along the same lines, namely, that there are words so semantically complex that they can only be inserted into derivation by a transformation. Lakoff used the word *dissuade*, analyzed as a complex combination of a negation with *persuade*, while Postal justified a semantic analysis of one meaning of the verb *remind* as *perceive* + *similar*. If these claims were true, then the applications of the lexical insertion rule had to be interspersed with transformations, and there was no stage separating the two, as deep structure was claimed to do.

If deep structure could be invalidated, that supported the generativists' main claim, namely, that syntax and semantics were inseparable, nonautonomous from each other, and, of course, the arguments against the duplication of effort implicit in (34.ii–iii) were offered for the same purpose.

(33) can be interpreted as a less clear and detailed variant of (13), with some rules reversed, if one "reads" (13) beginning with the output of the semantic component and, "backward" through that component into the base of the syntactic component, then on to transformations and into and through the phonological component. In fact, in the last major statement in the interpretive-generative battle, Katz (1971) did make a forceful attempt to present generative semantics as an inferior notational variant of interpretive semantics. The two approaches did share all the principal transformational premises, both philosophical and methodological. The generativists never questioned Katz and Fodor's dictionary-cum-rules view of semantics or, perhaps until the very last moment and even then very tentatively, their definition of the scope of semantic theory. The controversy about the autonomy or nonautonomy of syntax and semantics hinged largely on a logical fallacy on the part of the generativists: They assumed that if, as they claimed, syntactical and semantical rules had to be used alternately rather than separately, then the syntactic and semantic components were also one component. No proof of this assumption was ever offered, nor did it seem clear that the assumption was made consciously.

In spite of that, generative semantics made an enormous contribution to semantics because of the way polemics was conducted there. The customary way to falsify an interpretive claim was to challenge interpretive semantics with a particular problem of semantic description in the English language and to claim that interpretive semantics could not handle the phenomena in question well because of the falsity of the attacked claim. A generative-semantics description was then offered, and as a result, generative semantics left behind a host of first-rate semantic descriptions, much emulated subsequently, and it established a high standard in the business to which its successors have tried to live up ever since.

The most serious problem in generative semantics, which turned out to be fatal for it, was the inability to conceive of a format for semantic representation. Katz and Fodor's partial componential analysis in their semantic interpretations was rejected by the generativists for a number of reasons, and their attempts to turn to logic and to represent meaning in terms of simple predicate calculus proved to be naive and inconsequential. In the process of doing that, some of the generativists began to feel that they were trying to squeeze natural language, a very complex phenomenon, into the Procrustean bed of a very primitive mathematical framework. They became increasingly sensitive to those elements of meaning which resisted such treatments, namely, emotive connotations, noncasual and metaphorical usage, contextual inferences, and so on. After Katz put in his forceful claim that there was not much difference between the warring camps, it was realized in the generative one that they were no longer happy about the shared claims either. A rejection of the entire transformational paradigm and of the formal approach to language in general began to loom larger and larger, and generative semantics disintegrated. The important writings of that period by the former generativists went somewhat beyond the scope of semantic theory as postulated by Katz and Fodor (see (14)) and led eventually to the development of contextual and pragmatic semantics (see sections 4–5).

SECTION 4. CONTEXTUAL SEMANTICS

Both interpretive semantics and generative semantics dealt with the meaning of the individual sentence not only in the sense of not handling such larger entities as the paragraph but also in the sense of analyzing each sentence totally separately from any adjacent sentence. Recently, semanticists have been trying to accommodate within semantic theory the fact that the meaning of a sentence almost always depends on that of the adjacent sentences and other elements of the context. Contextual semantics is emerging now as a more mature and realistic approach to meaning.

4.1. Katz and Fodor's Sentence in Isolation

One of the central and most controversial claims Katz and Fodor made was never attacked by the generativists or anybody else till Raskin (1977). Katz and Fodor refused to make their theory accountable for the meaning of any sentence in any context and made the meaning of the sentence in isolation the sole object of any semantic theory. They argued that exclusively on grounds of feasibility.

Taking (14) for the lower bound of the scope of any semantic theory, that is, for the absolute minimum of what semantic theory must deliver, they set up the goal of accounting for the meaning of any sentence in any context as the unattainable upper bound of semantic theory. Such an upper bound, they assumed, would be a theory which would account for the manner in which different contexts determine how an utterance is understood. This hypothetical theory could be thought of as a function taking as its arguments the sentence, its grammatical description, its semantic interpretation (the set of possible meanings), and an abstract characterization of the context, and could have as its value one or more or no meanings out of the possible set of meanings the sentence has, depending on the situation in which the sentence is uttered.

A certain context would then select an appropriate meaning (or meanings) out of the set of all possible meanings of the sentence. Thus, the context in which it is clear that some hunters were shot would disambiguate (35.i) as (35.ii), while the context in which the hunters' marksmanship is discussed would disambiguate (35.i) as (35.iii).

(35) (i) The shooting of the hunters was terrible.
(ii) Somebody shot the hunters and that was terrible.
(iii) The hunters shot terribly.

The situation of an intellectual talk will probably deprive (36.i) of the meaning (36.ii) but will not disambiguate between (36.iii) and(36.iv):

(36) (i) He follows Marx.
(ii) He dogs the footsteps of Groucho.
(iii) He is a disciple of Karl's.
(iv) He postdates Karl.

The situation of being uttered in the daytime will render (37) odd and deprive it of any meaning:

(37) This is the happiest night of my life.

In order to construct a complete theory of contexts it would be necessary, Katz and Fodor argued, to describe all the knowledge the speakers have about the world and, moreover, to pattern, structuralize, and formalize it, as seems to follow from Katz and Fodor's analysis of the reasons why the sentences in (38–42), similar as they are within each example, are understood differently by different speakers:

(38) (i) Our store sells horse shoes.
(ii) Our store sells alligator shoes.

(39) (i) Should we take Junior back to the zoo?
(ii) Should we take the lion back to the zoo?
(iii) Should we take the bus back to the zoo?

(40) (i) Can I put the wallpaper on?
(ii) Can I put the coat on?

(41) (i) Joe jumped higher than the Empire State Building.
(ii) Joe jumped higher than you.

(42) (i) Black cats are unlucky.
(ii) People who break mirrors are unlucky.

The theory would have to take into account such diverse pieces of information about the world that are available to the native speakers of American English as the fact that horses "wear" shoes while alligators do not, but it is alligator skin and not horse skin that human shoes are made of (38); that Junior might want to visit the zoo again, the lion might need to be returned to the zoo where it lives, and the bus can be used as a means of transportation to the zoo, where the speaker already was earlier (39); that wallpaper is glued onto the wall while a coat is a garment people wear (40); that the Empire State Building cannot jump while humans generally can (41); that black cats bring bad luck while people who break mirrors experience bad luck (42). It seemed obvious to Katz and Fodor that such a theory of contexts, no matter in which way one might try to conceive it, is unattainable, and hence the upper bound of semantics is also unattainable.

This position is indefensible. First, a semantic theory of the sentence in isolation interprets many sentences that are never ambiguous in real discourse as ambiguous. Thus, the only way interpretive semantics can handle (38–41) is to present the sentences within each example as having all the meanings illustrated in it. In other words, both (38.i) and (38.ii) are interpreted as having both of the alternative meanings—the meaning of wearing shoes and the meaning of shoes made out of the animals' skin. This fallacy led to the fact that interpretive semantics had to spend most of its effort on disambiguating the sentences that were not ambiguous in the first place. This contributed greatly to the widespread misperception of the theory as exclusively a disambiguation technique.

Second and most crucial, in establishing itself as a theory of the meaning of the sentence in isolation, interpretive semantics abandoned the general goal of matching the native speaker's competence simply because what the native speaker has is the ability to interpret each sentence in any context. A theory that cannot do that in principle cannot be a close enough approximation of semantic competence. Moreover, it can also be demonstrated (see Raskin 1977) that the native speaker never interprets a sentence in isolation and is unable, in principle, to do so naturally.

Third, while accommodating all we know about the world within a formal semantic theory does not seem to be a feasible project, it does not at all make the sentence in isolation the only possible object for semantics. There is a wide gap between the meaning of the sentence in isolation and the meaning of any sentence in any context. What Katz and Fodor claimed, for all practical purposes, was that only the ability to interpret sentence meaning in isolation is of a linguistic nature while contextual meaning derives from our knowledge of the world. It does make perfect sense to differentiate between **linguistic knowledge** and **encyclopedic knowledge** (see Raskin 1985a, 1985b); however, the boundary should not be drawn where Katz and Fodor saw it—otherwise, as argued above, the entire semantic competence of the native speaker would be excluded from matching.

4.2. Contextual Semantics and Scripts

One promising way to make meaning more context-sensitive and thus to approximate much better native semantic competence is to replace the ordinary dictionary entries with **scripts.**

Formally, scripts are graphs of a somewhat more complicated nature than the syntactic trees, one major difference being that there are multiple paths from nodes to nodes in the scripts but a single path in a tree. What these graphs stand for is structured chunks of semantic information about a particular phenomenon. Thus, the script for EAT will not only relate the action to the act of ingestion and to the mouth—and this is the limit to which a typical ordinary dictionary will go—but also associate it with the notions of edible and inedible, of meals and their frequencies, of tables and utensils, and so on. An informal representation of the script for DOCTOR will probably look like (43):

(43) DOCTOR
Subject: [+Human] [+Adult]
Activity: 〉 Study medicine
= Receive patients: patient comes or doctor visits
doctor listens to complaints
doctor examines patient
= Cure disease: doctor diagnoses disease
doctor prescribes treatment
Place: 〉 Medical School
= Hospital or doctor's office
Time: 〉 Many years
= Every day
= Immediately
Condition: Physical contact
(〉 and = stand for 'past' and 'present,' respectively.)

Such linguistic scripts of 'common sense' are an integral part of the native speakers' competence. Without them, such ordinary sentences as (44–45) cannot be fully comprehended and the difference of meaning within each pair cannot be accounted for:

(44) (i) John was a dime short and had to do without milk.
(ii) John was a dime short and had to do without family.

(45) (i) John tried to eat his hamburger with a spoon but did not succeed.
(ii) John tried to eat his hamburger with a fork and a knife but did not succeed.

(44.i) makes perfect sense to the native speaker because his or her script for *money* would contain information about the fact that money is used to buy a commodity and the amount of money, which makes it possible to acquire a commodity, should be not lower than the price of the commodity. The script for *milk* will make it a commodity. There is no such script for *family,* though, and accordingly, the native speaker will correctly perceive (44.ii) as odd. The ordinary dictionary entries, however, as well as the dictionary/lexicon entries associated with the precontextual formal theories, contain no information linking *milk* with *money* or *family* with *money*. What follows from this is that theories based on such dictionary entries will treat (44.i–ii) as equally meaningful, which is counterintuitive and, therefore, inadequate.

Similarly, John's failures in (45.i–ii) are very different, from the native speaker's point of view. In (45.i), his or her scripts for *hamburger* and *spoon* would contain enough information for figuring out the most obvious reason for the failure: Spoons are used with pourable stuffs and hamburger is not pourable. No such script information is available for (45.ii), and the reason for the failure is unclear. Once again, no information on pourability is contained in an ordinary dictionary entry for either *hamburger* or *spoon,* and consequently a semantic theory based on such entries will be insensitive to the difference between (45.i) and (45.ii).

In these simple examples, the scripts proved to be sensitive to different parts of the same sentence. Similarly, they provide links with the other sentences of the same text, and the absence of such links makes semantic interpretation incomplete. Needless to say, the structure of the scripts and the volume of information they are assigned present a challenging theoretical and practical problem. The links between the nodes, which correspond to semantic associations between words, are not all the same, and which of them should be evoked in a given situation has to be determined by general strategy. A theory of contextual semantics is thus more complex than a noncontextual theory (one example of such a theory, script-based semantics, is described briefly in Raskin 1981, 1985c, and in more detail in Raskin 1984, chapter 3, and Raskin 1986b). Nothing short of a contextual theory, however, can come close to matching native semantic competence.

It is also important to include in the scripts only the linguistic information possessed by the native speaker. It is true that our understanding of the sentence may profit from some encyclopedic information which happens to be available, and there is certainly nothing wrong with that (see also sections 5.2.2 and 5.2.5). However, it is the linguistic information proper that ensures the minimally full and universally accessible level of comprehension.

SECTION 5. PRAGMATICS

In the process of accounting for the context of a sentence, a contextual semantic theory has to calculate a few kinds of semantic information which are often listed under pragmatics. Pragmatics is perceived as a separate discipline by those who still perceive semantics as noncontextual. Contextual semantics is impossible without the pragmatic phenomena and, therefore, pragmatics is incorporated into it.

5.1. Ideal Pragmatics

Pragmatics in its current linguistic meaning should not be confused with the American pragmatic philosophy. The linguistic meaning of the term is derived from Charles Morris's concept of the pragmatic plane of sign systems introduced by him in the later 1940s. Unlike the syntactic and semantic aspects, pragmatics reflected the individual user–related side of the signs. Pragmatics as a linguistic discipline should thus incorporate all the aspects of language study that are sensitive to user variation. In other words, every linguistic phenomenon that is independent of the idealized treatment of each speech community as homogeneous (see chapter 9, section 1) should be part of pragmatics. That would then include sociolinguistics and dialectology.

In fact, however, pragmatics is being currently perceived not as full-fledged **user-sensitive linguistics** but rather as the study of contextual meaning for the idealized native speaker. In other words, pragmatics as perceived exactly as contextual semantics. Even more narrowly, pragmatics is being done as a standard collection of a handful of topics, selected in all probability on such tenuous grounds as feasibility and even fashionability.

5.2. Practical Pragmatics

The standard agenda for pragmatics includes presupposition, speech acts, and implicature. Semantic recursion and inference will be added to this minimum list here.

5.2.1. Presupposition. The notion of **presupposition** was initially introduced into linguistic theory to denote one of those statements which should be true or to describe a state of affairs which should have taken place prior to the utterance of a certain sentence. Defined in purely logical terms, the presupposition of a sentence should be true in order for the sentence itself to be either true or false; for example for (46.i) or its negation, (46.ii), to be either true or false, their common presupposition, (47), must be true. In general, as immediately follows from the logical definition of presuppositions a sentence and its negation share the same presupposition(s).

(46) (i) I meant to insult him.
(ii) I did not mean to insult him.

(47) I insulted him.

Negation can, therefore, be used as a diagnostic test for this **logical presupposition:** Take a sentence, negate it; if something remains from the content in spite of the negation it is a good candidate for presupposition.

A much broader and somewhat looser notion of presupposition is known as **pragmatic presupposition.** Lakoff's (1971b) pragmatic presupposition includes various conditions that should be satisfied in order for the sentence to be 'appropriate,' including such individual factors as subjective assumptions and personal beliefs of the speakers. Thus, according to him, the well-formedness (or, for that matter, the truth, the appropriateness, or the aptness) of any sentence in (48) depends on whether the speaker believes that the corresponding condition for each of them in (49) is satisfied.

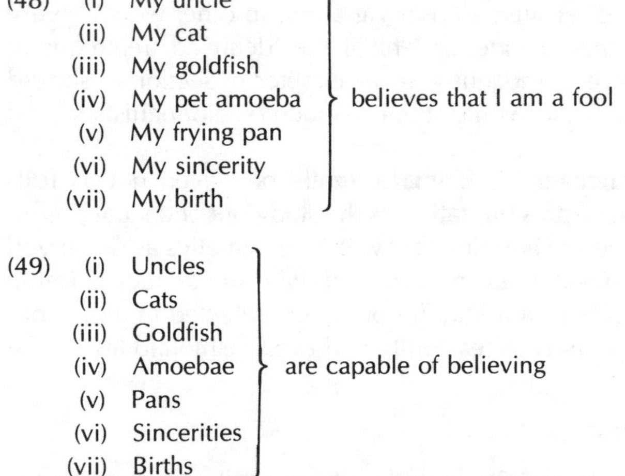

(48) (i) My uncle
(ii) My cat
(iii) My goldfish
(iv) My pet amoeba
(v) My frying pan
(vi) My sincerity
(vii) My birth
believes that I am a fool
(49) (i) Uncles
(ii) Cats
(iii) Goldfish
(iv) Amoebae
(v) Pans
(vi) Sincerities
(vii) Births
are capable of believing

It seems most useful to use a general and "neutral" notion of presupposition and to understand it as a set of conditions that should obtain in order for a sentence to be comprehended fully (cf. Raskin 1978a).

5.2.2. Semantic Recursion. The notion of **semantic recursion** provides a somewhat different perspective on the conditions that have to be met for the sentence to be understood correctly. It relates these conditions to certain elements of the sentence, presents a taxonomy of those elements and constructs a near-algorithm for discovering those conditions (see Raskin 1968, 1978a, for a more detailed account of semantic recursion).

According to this view, the meaning of each sentence is considered to depend on at least two additional factors, besides its own constituents and the way they are combined:

(50) (i) the degree of understanding of the previous discourse (if any);
(ii) the quantity of pertinent information the hearer possesses.

It can be safely assumed that the greater (50.i–ii) are purely quantitatively, the more fully the sentence is comprehended. This means that there is a whole spectrum of partial comprehension for most ordinary sentences. Most sentences require one or more operations of semantic recursion to obtain the additional semantic information necessary for their complete comprehension and not contained in the sentences themselves. The operations of semantic recursion that may be performed, in various combinations, with respect to a given sentence may be represented as follows:

(51) (i) distinguishing all the non-self-sufficient elements of the sentence, that is, words that refer to something outside the sentence;
(ii) relating the sentence to the previous sentence in the discourse, which has already been interpreted;
(iii) relating the sentence to the pertinent information not contained in the previous discourse.

The elements of the sentence mentioned in (51.i) are called the **semantic recursion triggers** of the sentence. (51.ii) is, of course, the principle that renders the approach recursive in the mathematical sense: First, the first sentence of the discourse is interpreted semantically; then, the next sentence is interpreted in the same way but this time the complete information obtained in the previous cycle with regard to the first sentence is taken into account as well; and so on. The pertinent information mentioned in (51.iii) will include various elements of the hearer's linguistic and encyclopedic knowledge of the world, such as common sense, logical models, evaluative scales, accepted patterns of humor.

In terms of semantic recursion, sentences form a continuous scale with two poles. On one pole of the scale there are those sentences that contain no recursion triggers whatsoever—their meaning follows immediately from that of the lexical items of which they consist and that of the ways in which they are combined. Such sentences are quite special and rare, and they are termed 'nonindexical' (Bar-Hillel 1954:359), 'eternal' (Quine 1960:191ff) or 'noncircumstantial' (see Raskin 1979a). Most sentences require some semantic recursion, but on the other pole of the scale there are sentences that cannot be comprehended correctly at all by anybody who is not familiar with the previous discourse and/or does not share the previous experience with the speaker/writer. Those sentences are likely to contain factual or literary allusions, nonuniversal associations and conventions, 'coded messages,' taboos, and so on. The examples of (52) illustrate the two poles and a case in between. (52.i) is a classic example of a nonindexical, nonrecursive sentence. (52.iii) is a maximally recursive sentence from a Russian novel. The sentence will not be comprehended by those unfamiliar with the preceding part of the novel, where the peculiar expression was used in a context which determined its highly idiosyncratic, euphemistic meaning, namely 'to make love.' The reader not in the know will see that the heroes are spending a night in a house, not at all on a train, and will therefore fail to interpret (52.iii), perfectly meaningful to him otherwise, in a context that rules out any meaning. (52.ii) is a typical recursive sentence which can be understood partially without any semantic recursion and fully with semantic recursion (see below).

(52) (i) Ice floats on water.
(ii) Watch your speed—we are.
(iii) That night they jumped off the train again.

Brushing aside the somewhat dubious grammaticality of the popular Indiana road sign in (52.ii), we can analyze it from the point of view of semantic recursion. At least four out of the five words are semantic recursion triggers:

(53) (i) *watch:* Watching here means making sure from time to time that you are not exceeding a certain speed—it does not mean looking at the speedometer all the time.
(ii) *your:* The message is addressed to automobile and motorcycle drivers, not to pedestrians, joggers, cows, car passengers, helicopter pilots, UFOs, and so on.
(iii) *speed:* There is a federal speed limit and any violation of that law is, in theory, punishable.
(iv) *we:* The law is enforced by the police, and *we* must stand for some representatives of this body detailed to a certain sector of the assigned area at a certain time.

It is clear that a representative of a different civilization who happens to understand English but not to be familiar with (53), will grasp only the semi-empty meaning of (52.ii) loosely paraphrased here as (54):

(54) Somebody is urged to become engaged in visual inspection of a certain feature of a motion though some other people are saying that they are doing it already themselves.

(53.ii,iv) are typical examples of grammatical triggers, words that always trigger semantic recursion by virtue of their belonging to a certain grammatical category. Pronouns have always been known as words that 'indicate' rather than 'mean,' and finding an 'antecedent,' the reference of each pronoun, is essential for the comprehension of a sentence containing them. (53.i,iii) are examples of a more complex kind of semantic recursion—here words are recursive because of their individual meaning and its relation to the context.

5.2.3. Speech Act. The concept of **speech acts** was first proposed by Austin (1962) and later developed into a speech act theory by Searle (1969). The purpose of the theory is to capture the function that the sentences perform in discourse.

According to Searle, every utterance, or speech act, consist of two parts, the **propositional act** and the **illocutionary act.** The propositional act expresses the proposition, which in its turn consists of a **reference** and a **predicate,** in other words, of what or whom the sentence is about and what it says about that object, person, phenomenon. The illocutionary act characterizes the utterance as an assertion, a question, a command, a request, a threat, a promise, a greeting, an apology, or any other item from a long list of possible illocutions. Thus, in (55), all three sentences have the same propositional content. The identical propositions have *Sam* for the reference and *smoking habitually* for the predicate. However, the illocutionary acts are all different. (55.i) is an assertion; (55.ii), a question; (55.iii), a request, command, or order.

(55) (i) Sam smokes habitually.
(ii) Does Sam smoke habitually?
(iii) Sam, smoke habitually.

Searle's purpose was to recognize the illocution in each case by postulating a set of necessary and sufficient conditions for each kind of speech act. As an example for detailed analysis, he selected the speech act of PROMISE. The conditions he discovered were such that whenever a promise is made all these conditions obtain and, conversely, whenever these conditions obtain the resulting speech act is a promise (see (56)). The conditions are listed in a much shortened and simplified version in (57). In Searle's version, they are preceded by a couple of conditions that hold for all speech acts and ensure that normal communication be possible and that each utterance contain a proposition. The conditions hold between the speaker (S) of the utterance (U), containing a proposition (p), and its hearer (H); the proposition predicates an act (A).

(56) SPEECH ACT OF PROMISE ⟷ SET OF CONDITIONS

(57) **Necessary and Sufficient Conditions for the Speech Act of PROMISE:**
- (i) p in U predicates a future act A of S.
- (ii) H would prefer S's doing A to S's not doing A, and S believes that H feels that way.
- (iii) It is not obvious to either S or H that S will do A in the normal course of events.
- (iv) S intends to do A and places himself under an obligation to do A.
- (v) S conveys (iv) to H by virtue of their shared understanding of the meaning of U.

Conditions (56) should make perfect sense. One cannot promise anything by referring to the past or present (56.i), and when the word *promise* is used this way it does not convey the illocution of promise (58.i). One does not promise to do what the other definitely does not want one to do (57.ii)—thus, (58.ii) is usually a threat rather than a promise. A promise must involve a special effort (56.iii), and this is why (58.iii) cannot be a serious promise; a serious interpretation of the sentence is, however, possible if *promise* is interpreted as having the same nonpromising meaning, close to that of *swear* as in (58.i). (57.iv) was referred to by Searle as the sincerity condition, and such insincere promises as (58.iv) were excluded by him from consideration; obviously, dropping (57.iv) will include insincere promises in the set of situations determined by (57).

(58)
- (i) I promise I never came near her.
- (ii) I will kill you!
- (iii) I promise that the sun will rise tomorrow morning.
- (iv) I promise that I will change my personality entirely by this afternoon.

If such sets of conditions are assigned to each speech act, sentences could be characterized as to their functions after the conditions are checked. It should be noted that no linguistic procedures have been proposed for assessing the conditions, nor was the linguistic nature of those conditions claimed. In fact, speech act theory was not proposed as a linguistic theory at all—it emerged in the totally different paradigm of the philosophy of language and it is not really compatible with the research paradigm of contemporary formal linguistics. However, it does capture a meaning-related property of sentences and, therefore, has attracted semanticists.

In a later development, Searle came even closer to linguistic semantics when he became interested in **indirect speech acts** (see (59)), speech acts that seem to be of one kind on the surface but in fact belong to another kind (see Searle 1975). Thus, (59.i) is a direct speech act of interrogation (or, simply, a question) but, indirectly, it is a request, equivalent to the direct speech act of request in (59.ii):

(59) (i) Can you pass me the salt?
(ii) Pass me the salt.

Linguists Gordon and Lakoff (1975) postulated the existence of a special kind of linguistic rules, **conversational postulates,** which are internalized by the native speaker. One such conversational postulate, (60.i) in their simple predicate-calculus formalism, "translated" here into plain English as (60.ii), transforms (59.i) into (59.ii).

(60) (i) ASK(*a*,*b*,CAN(*b*,*Q*))*→REQUEST(*a*,*b*,*Q*)
(ii) When *a* (the speaker) asks *b* (the hearer) whether *b* can do *Q* (in this particular case, pass the salt) and does not happen to mean it literally (hence the asterisk), what he actually means is that he requests the hearer to do it.

Obviously, conversational postulates have to be postulated for all such cases, and whether it is feasible or not, they clearly constitute a legitimate kind of semantic information available to the native speaker who will, indeed, interpret (59.i) as (59.ii) unless some very strong clues to the contrary are present in the discourse.

5.2.4. Implicature. (59) is also an example of **implicature.** Introduced by another philosopher of language, Grice (1975), the concept encompasses the use of sentences not in their literal or conventional meaning. Thus, under appropriate circumstances, (61.i) may be used to mean that John is an idiot, (61.ii) that the meeting should be adjourned, and (61.iii) that the hearer(s) should shut the window. The appropriate circumstances are exemplified in (62.i–iii), respectively.

(61) (i) John is a real genius, isn't he?
(ii) This issue should be studied in detail.
(iii) It is cold in here.

(62) (i) John just made a fool of himself in front of the speaker and hearer(s) and left.
(ii) It is close to dinnertime, and the meeting has lasted for a long time when somebody introduces a new item for discussion; however, nobody wants to be the one to suggest that the meeting be adjourned.
(iii) The duke and his butler enter the library and the window is open; the duke is the speaker.

Grice's main idea was that the meaning actually intended by the speaker can supercede and even squeeze out the proper meaning of the sentence, given the right context, and that the speaker manages to convey the intended meaning to the hearer. Grice maintained that what he called **bona**

fide communication, the fact-conveying mode of speaking, free of lying, jokes, playacting, and so on, is determined by a cooperative principle. The essence of the cooperative principle is that the speaker tells the truth, the hearer recognizes his intention and therefore believes what is said. What follows from this is that if something goes wrong, the hearer gives the speaker the benefit of the doubt and attempts to get the intended meaning at all costs before finally giving up and assuming that the speaker is not communicating in good faith or is incompetent.

When nothing goes wrong, bona fide communication is ruled by Grice's four maxims (63).

(63) **Grice's Four Maxims of Bona Fide Communication:**
- (i) Quantity: Relate exactly as much information as necessary.
- (ii) Quality: Say only what you believe to be true.
- (iii) Relation: Speak to the point.
- (iv) Manner: Be succinct.

However, the speaker can violate one or more of the maxims and still remain in bona fide communication if he or she does it deliberately, signals the violation to the hearer(s), and the hearer(s) can decipher the meaning intended as a result of this violation.

Thus, for instance, when you are standing on Regent Street in London and somebody asks you (64.i), it is ridiculous to respond (64.ii), which would be in strict accordance with (63.i); instead, (64.iii), a clear violation of the maxim of quantity and possibly of the maxim of relation, is fully in order.

(64)
- (i) How far is it to Piccadilly Circus by cab?
- (ii) Fifteen seconds.
- (iii) You don't need a cab—there it is, just a hundred yards down the street.

In the lyrics of a Cole Porter song, (65.i), a blatant violation of (63.ii) will be easily interpreted along the lines of (65.ii):

(65)
- (i) You're the cream in my coffee.
- (ii) You make my life better as cream improves coffee.

(66.ii), a clear violation of (63.iii) when uttered in immediate response to (66.i), will easily and unmistakably signal to the hearer something like (66.iii):

(66)
- (i) I think that Hilda is a real pain. She is utterly incompetent. She slows us all down and messes whatever she is assigned to do.
- (ii) Oh yes, it is pretty hot for October.
- (iii) Hilda or somebody else who should not hear (i) is near.

And finally, (67.ii), an obvious violation of (63.iv) if uttered in response to (67.i), is deciphered—as experiments show—surprisingly accurately as (67.iii):

(67) (i) What were John and Mary doing in the library?
(ii) Well, they were not reading books.
(iii) John and Mary were doing something improper and involving romance but certainly not making love on the desk; in all probability, they were kissing or petting heavily.

Because implicatures abound in everyday discourse, the mechanism of their functioning is important for linguistics to understand. Each implicature also demonstrates clearly the crucial role context can play in modifying the meaning of the sentence and, consequently, the ultimate inadequacy of a context-free semantic theory, such as interpretive or generative semantics.

5.2.5. Inference. Whatever the hearer can derive from the speaker's utterance and the context is referred to as **inference.** Along with entailment, a statement immediately following from another statement, inference includes presupposition because it can be also inferred from an initial statement. Thus, if (68.i) is the initial statement and (68.ii–iii) are its entailment and presupposition, respectively, both are inferences.

(68) (i) John and Mary are married (to each other).
(ii) It is likely that John and Mary live together.
(iii) John and Mary are adults.

Inferences may be probable as well. Thus, (69) presents probable inferences of (68.i), and the probabilities may vary from case to case:

(69) (i) John and Mary make love (to each other) regularly.
(ii) John and Mary have children.
(iii) John and Mary share all they own.
(iv) John and Mary have made love at least once.

While linguistic semantics has not yet paid much intention to inference, probable inference, or entailment, the importance of this phenomenon is becoming very clear in linguistic applications. In writing, inferences must be taken into account and tightly controlled—otherwise the coherence of the text is jeopardized (see chapter 13, section 3, and chapter 14, section 4.1.2). In natural language processing, it turns out that it is very hard to program the computer to be limited and selective in its inferencing and to obtain only those inferences that are evoked in and are helpful for the discourse. Native speakers do it constantly and easily, and therefore selective inferencing is an important ability for formal semantic theory to match.

Language emerges from this discussion as a very complex tool for conveying very complex meaning.

CHAPTER 9

Language Variation

SECTION 1. IDEALIZATION OF LINGUISTIC REALITY

Linguistics is the study of language. Language manifests itself as a large number of natural languages, such as English, Russian, Hebrew, Chinese, or Hanunoo. Each natural language is spoken by a number of people, and all of them use it slightly differently.

The individual language of each native speaker is called the **idiolect.** Similar idiolects constitute a **dialect.** Each language is a complex aggregate of dialects, **regional, social,** and **professional** (cf. chapter 4, section 2). What, then, is a particular natural language? What is it that a linguist describes when dealing with English syntax, or Russian morphology, or Hebrew phonology? The object of such a study is some generalized concept of the particular language, not any particular dialect or idiolect.

At the very beginning of his *Aspects of the Theory of Syntax,* Chomsky makes a significant disclaimer—he admits that the book deals with a "homogeneous speaker-hearer community" (1965:3). Such an admission is rare—usually linguists do exactly the same without seeming to be aware of it. A homogeneous speech community is a fiction; quite simply, it does not exist. Do linguists deal with a fiction then? This is exactly what a famous French linguist claimed a couple of generations ago (see Vendryès 1923). But what is the alternative? Should a linguist aspire to describe every one of the 400 million or so English idiolects instead of the English language as a whole? There are very few idiolects worth describing in their complexity: an idiolect with an interesting speech defect, the idiolect of a child acquiring language, the idiolect of a multilingual speaker. The study of an individual idiolect will be exactly as time- and labor-consuming and present exactly the same conceptual and methodological problems as the study of the "whole language."

Declaring a natural language a total fiction seems to be counterintuitive or at least in contradiction to what we are trained to believe. Surely, English exists, does it not? Is not English simply the common part of all English idiolects? This is indeed something one would want to assume. The problem is that all English idiolects intersect on a very small common part, which would not be viable as a language. If one compares the highly technical dialect of, say, nuclear physics and the fuzzy dialect of American drug-infested counterculture, the intersection will probably consist of not much more than the auxiliary words and a few major verbs and nouns. The truth of the matter is that each language is, in fact, a large diversity of sublanguages. Surprisingly, this aspect of linguistics is seriously underexplored (see, however, Raskin 1971, 1974, and Kittredge and Lehrberger 1982—the latter includes a brief summary of Raskin 1971).

In spite of all diversity, however, two representatives of the most remote dialects of English will still perceive each other as native speakers of the same language, and much more communication will be possible between them than between one of them and a monolingual speaker of a foreign language. It is true that a particular language does not have the same status of an empirical phenomenon as an idiolect—nobody speaks English per se, just an idiolect of it. However, English does exist as an entity in the minds of its speakers—it is clearly a sociological, cultural, philosophical, and perhaps a psychological phenomenon, and this does justify its treatment as a linguistic phenomenon as well. What will make it a linguistic phenomenon is an act of conscious and deliberate idealization along the lines of Chomsky's admission quoted above. To make linguistics feasible as the study of language in general and of individual natural languages in particular, most of linguistics assumes that there are no differences between the native competences within the same speech community.

This idealization certainly underlies chapters 5–8. It is typically rejected in dialectology and sociolinguistics. However, even there, the same idealization is applied to a speech subcommunity. In other words, within the same dialect, be it regional and, therefore, an object of study by dialectology, or social and studied by sociology, it is assumed that there are no distinctions between the native speakers of the same dialects. No linguistic discipline does, or can afford to—or should, for that matter—study the idiolect.

SECTION 2. DIALECTOLOGY

Dialectology is the study of regional dialects (cf. chapter 1, section 3.3). In principle, such a study should consist of the complete set of complete descriptions of each dialect of the language. In reality, it is often different.

Dialects are not totally distinct and independent. They intersect in various combinations. They are rarely 'pure' but instead, they 'interfere' with each other a great deal. Most native speakers tend to be bidialectal or even multidialectal. In the United States, for instance, where the population is highly mobile geographically and socially, it is common for a person to leave his or her hometown with its dialect, go to college in a different area and pick up (at least elements of) another dialect, marry the speaker of a third dialect, move again, and raise children in a different place as speakers of still another dialect.

The mental map, as it were, of a native speaker of American English contains a vague concept of the southern dialect and perhaps of a New England dialect. The "Texan dialect" is often comically imitated in the media. People may believe that English is "funny" as spoken in New York City.

In fact, dialects can be characterized best as an aggregate of particular properties that may be different in other dialects. Thus, Coca-Cola is *soda* in some dialects and *pop* in others, *he do* is fine in some dialects but not in others, the pronunciation of *wash* as [warš] is accepted in some dialects but not in others. Each such feature can be discovered or not discovered in a certain region. If it is discovered, a point may be put on the map. When a line joining all such adjacent points is drawn, it usually turns out that all the points on the line mark places where people talk like that as well. A line marking the spread of a certain linguistic phenomenon in regional dialects is called an **isogloss,** and each dialect is then a set of isoglosses. Dialects are thus characterized by a sliding scale of constantly varying combinations of isoglosses. This is a much more economical approach to dialectology than comparing the complete descriptions of each dialect, not only because some of those are not available and those that are may have not been executed in exactly the same way or at the same level of quality, but, more important, because there will be many elements in those descriptions that will be exactly the same and the comparison will consist of the search for variations. A map of isoglosses captures all of them more economically. The dialectological atlases for various languages and regions are usually precisely this: maps with isoglosses and their explanations.

SECTION 3. THE STANDARD DIALECT

Another popular perception concerning English dialects is that they are all deviations from the proper way to speak the language. The proper way in the United States is **Standard American English (SAE;** cf. chapter 1, section 3.3), but this is a dialect nobody really speaks. This dialect is the manifestation of the fictional language "as a whole," discussed in section 1. Some people come close to this fiction in their performance, and it is desirable to acquire for upward social mobility. Therefore, for most people the standard is a second or a third dialect, which they acquire as a result of deliberate efforts, comparable in its nature to the study of a foreign language though much easier in execution. It was widely rumored, for instance, that candidate Jimmy Carter took phonetic lessons prior to his 1976 presidential campaign to make his pronunciation less "Dixie," and he did indeed speak much less regionally than the rest of his family.

For generations, the standard has been used by teachers and pop grammarians (the term used by linguists very pejoratively for those who assume the task of policing contemporary language use without a proper linguistic background), for putting nonstandard dialects down as aberrant and inferior. For at least two or three generations now, linguistics has stayed away entirely from making any recommendations about language use and has simply recorded and described dialects without passing any judgment. This is a basically healthy attitude; however, the relations between the standard and nonstandard dialects deserve a proper linguistic treatment—the alternative is pop grammarianism, and Messrs. Simon, Newman, and Mitchell will continue to reign supreme.

Linguists are correct in ridiculing and repudiating the judgments passed on dialects from the point of view of the standard, because dialects are more real than the standard and because every consistent dialect is just as legitimate as any other. They are not right, however, in refusing to elucidate the role of the standard in society (see section 5).

In terms of its specific isoglosses, the choice of a certain dialect or even a concoction of dialects as the standard is, of course, arbitrary, and the standard is certainly not "better." Once it is chosen, however, the standard dialect plays the role no other dialect has. It is the standard that is used as the common language of the multidialectal community and that acquires, rightly or wrongly, the status of the national language. It is the standard dialect that is sought and emulated, that has the highest social value, that becomes the language of literature and of the media. It is the standard dialect that forms the basis of all the writing courses, and the necessity of this arrangement should be made very clear to instructors and students in these courses and to the community at large. It should also be made clear that instructors will not make their students succeed in the task of learning to write in a different dialect unless they are familiar with the students' dialect(s) and are capable of explaining 'formulae of transition' to the standard. Needless to say, ignoring or, worse, berating the students' dialect, especially a **radical dialect,** that is, a dialect exhibiting significant differences from the standard (the opposite term is **moderate dialect**), will be a clear sign of linguistic ignorance and prejudice on the part of the instructors (cf. *The Ann Arbor Case* 1979). The situation is further complicated by the fact that the standard dialect is constantly changing with the rest of the language (see section 5).

SECTION 4. LANGUAGE CHANGE

Languages change with time. The change is gradual in the sense that there is and should be no gap between any two subsequent generations—they do understand each other and can communicate successfully, and this is essential for continuity in society. On the other hand, changes are introduced constantly, and over the lifetime of a few generations the cumulative effect may be substantial. Grandchildren often feel that their grandparents talk differently but the difference between Shakespeare's English and, say, modern American English is so pronounced that the identity of language is called into question.

Language changes are usually more dramatic at the times of social and political cataclysms, such as wars, revolutions, and political reorganizations. Changes are especially noticeable when a speech community is separated into two parts as a result of such an event, and the contacts between those parts are disrupted for a few generations. In each of the two communities, normal changes then continue to occur but they are not the same, and the distance between the languages of these speech communities steadily increases. Thus, for instance, some 300 years ago, when the Russians first annexed the corner of the Baltic coast between what is now Estonia to the west and Finland to the north, the difference between Estonian and Finnish, two sibling languages, was barely even dialectal—the languages were essentially the same. Now they are certainly different languages. Similarly, the Russian revolution of 1917 separated some 3 million emigrés from the rest of the population, and only half a century later, Russians abroad already spoke and wrote a dialect of Russian clearly distinct from Soviet Russian.

The reason for continuous changes is clear enough—it is primarily the desire to express one's thoughts better and, vying for attention, innovatively. It is not at all accidental that the most conspicuous and usually short-lived innovations occur with youngsters, in their grade school and high school slangs. Those change considerably every 5 to 10 years, if not sooner, so that even older siblings sometimes have trouble following the younger ones' conversations. What is less clear is the direction of the changes. Native speakers do seem to prize economy, and explanations of changes in terms of 'simplicity' or 'laziness' are common. It is indeed true that morphological cases, for instance, are much likelier to disappear than to be introduced into a language that has none. Languages without cases and other well-developed paradigms may be perceived as easier to learn; however, the prepositional structures which take the place of the cases are not at all conceptually simpler or easier to maintain. Besides, in phonology, for instance, the substitution of one sound with another can hardly ever be convincingly explained in terms of economy. It is quite common for one language to change, say, /ε/ into /o/ while another language is busily replacing /o/ with /ε/ at the same time—and both changes cannot be treated as economical in terms of articulations or some other parameters.

Some languages tend to change less and others more, even in comparable social and political environments. Languages that change less over long periods of time are perceived as 'archaic.' This is usually measured loosely and impressionistically as the degree of deviation from some earlier stage in the history of the language. Thus, if the common ancestor for some two sibling languages is known or can be reconstructed with the methods of **comparative linguistics,** each of the siblings can be compared to the ancestor and measured in terms of common structural elements. It will emerge, for instance, from such a comparison of Arabic and Hebrew with their common source that Arabic is more archaic than Hebrew because it has kept much more of the original complex Semitic verb structure as well as more of its ancient pronunciation than has Hebrew—and this despite the fact that Arabic has been alive for all this time and Hebrew was reduced in status to the sacred language for centuries at a time. Similarly, Lithuanian is very archaic in comparison to its sibling Latvian, its Slavic cousins, and its Germanic and Romance second cousins in that it shares certain structural qualities of Sanskrit, a recorded ancient Indo-European language believed to be an immediate descendant of Proto-Indo-European, the common ancestor of all Indo-European languages. Like dialects, extremely nonarchaic, "runaway" languages can be characterized as radical.

Within the same language, certain levels of linguistic structure are more susceptible to change and others are more conservative. It is the higher levels that submit to change easily, not the lower ones. Most conspicuous and rapid changes are lexico-semantical and concern words. The least frequent changes concern the phonology of a language.

4.1. Lexico-Semantical Change

The two lexical changes mentioned briefly in chapter 4, section 2, concern neologisms and archaisms. **Neologisms** are new words which did not exist before. **Archaisms** are dead words which exist no longer. Semantic changes involve changes in meaning of existing words.

4.1.1. Neologisms. New words can be introduced as a result of the processes listed and described in (1.i–ix) and illustrated in (2.i–ix), respectively:

(1) **Processes of Neologism Formation:**

- (i) Coinage: Creating a new word "from scratch"
- (ii) Acronymization: Reducing a word or—more usually—a phrase to the initial letters or syllables
- (iii) Compounding: Gluing two or (rarely) more words together
- (iv) Derivation: Adding a productive derivational morpheme to a lexical morpheme with which it was not used before
- (v) Back-Formation: Removing a derivational morpheme from an existing word for the first time

(vi) Commonalization: Using proper names as common
(vii) Blending: Combining elements of two words
(viii) Clippings: Using one syllable for the entire word
(ix) Borrowing: Appropriating a foreign word with its meaning

(2) (i) nylon, byte, teflon
(ii) USA, UN, NOW
(iii) software, overall, spoonfeed
(iv) diskette, uglify, diagonalize
(v) enthuse, televise, ept
(vi) kleenex, jumbo, quisling
(vii) motel, smog, thinsulate
(viii) gas, math, grad
(ix) chutzpa, chef, taco

4.1.2. Archaisms. Archaisms are words that disappear from languages and are no longer understood by contemporary native speakers (3.i). Some words are semi-dead, as it were, and are used in restricted contexts, religious for (3.ii), for example.

(3) (i) *beseem* 'to suit'; *wherefore* 'why'
(ii) *thou* 'you singular'

4.1.3. Semantic Change. Semantic changes are often of a purely historical nature—an object or phenomenon disappears or fades from focus and the word is transferred to its replacement (4.i), often keeping the old meaning as well. More usually, however, semantic changes are caused by linguistic reasons proper resulting primarily from similarities or contiguities of meaning. One standard process is the narrowing of word meaning (4.ii); the other is broadening (4.iii); and the third and most numerous category includes shifts or transfers of meaning (4.iv):

(4) (i) *car* 'horse-ridden carriage' 〉 'railroad car' 〉 'automobile';
hardware 'tools, etc.' 〉 'computer'
(ii) *meat* 'food' 〉 'meat'
(iii) *dog* 'hound' 〉 'dog'
(iv) *make love* 'court' 〉 'have intercourse';
sex 'gender' 〉 'sexual activity';
silly 'happy' 〉 'dumb'

4.2. Syntactical Change

Syntax is much less susceptible to change than is word meaning, and examples are scarce in any language. In the last century, English acquired a syntactical rule that forbade double negation. It was no longer possible to use (5.i), and (5.ii) was used instead; (5.i) remains, however, common to many nonstandard dialects.

(5) (i) I do not know nothing.
(ii) I do not know anything.

At a certain stage of its development, English acquired a much more rigid word order than before. Also, at a certain time, English started forming questions with the auxiliary word *do* from sentences with no auxiliary in the declarative form, and sentences like (6.i) were replaced by sentences like (6.ii):

(6) (i) Know you . . . ?
(ii) Do you know . . . ?

All of these are major changes affecting hundreds and thousands of sentences, and languages have them very infrequently.

4.3. Morphological Change

Just like syntactic changes, morphological changes are usually very infrequent and massive in scale. At a certain time, English lost almost all of its noun case system and replaced the cases with prepositional phrases. The possessive case is the only remnant of the once powerful noun case system. Here as well, the tendency is to lose rather than acquire forms. However, it would be naive to assume that the form loss always means simplification. Some examples of ongoing morphological changes of a lesser scope are mentioned in section 5.

Another example of morphological change is **morphological redistribution.** The three examples in (7) seem to have very similar morphemic structure, except that (7.iii) clearly fails condition (2.iii) in chapter 6, section 1, because the meaning of the word is not at all the "sum" of the meanings of *under* and *stand*. The same condition is clearly met by (7.i), while (7.ii) floats somewhere in between the two in the sense that some speakers may still relate the assumption of financial liability in insurance with the now extinct tradition of having the underwriters sign the policy at the very bottom, under everything else.

(7) (i) underlie
(ii) underwrite
(iii) understand

To the extent that the semantic links between (7.ii–iii) and the meanings of their morphemes are lost, the morphological structure of the word is 'redistributed,' and in these cases, a two-morpheme word becomes one-morpheme.

4.4. Phonological Change

Phonological changes are the least frequent of them all and, of course, even a tiny change affects thousands of words. Massive phonological changes usually involve whole natural classes. Thus, the Great Vowel Shift in Middle English between 1400 and 1600 affected every single long vowel and is largely responsible for the disastrous orthography of English (cf. chapter 5, section 2), because while the pronunciation changed, the spelling did not, and it still reflects accurately the pronunciation of half a millennium ago (see (8)).

(8) **The Great Vowel Shift:**
- (i) [i:] > [ay] : mice
- (ii) [e:] > [i] : geese
- (iii) [ɛ:] > [e] : steak
- (iv) [u:] > [aw] : mouse
- (v) [o:] > [u] : goose
- (vi) [ɔ:] > [o] : spoke
- (vii) [a:] > [e] : make

The reason all of these changes occurred together is that each individual changes creates an imbalance in the phonological system, and the latter adjusts itself by carrying out some other changes until the balance is restored. This is the reason for the stronger resistance of phonology, morphology, and syntax to change than that of vocabulary. The first three form simpler and tighter structures than vocabulary does. However, even with semantic changes, accompanying changes are always necessary. Thus, when the change in (4.ii) occurred, another word had to take over the abandoned meaning of *meat,* and *food* did.

There are, however, phonological changes of an easier and more limited kind. Thus, the change involving the loss of distinction between /ɪ/ and /ɛ/ before nasals, as in (19.i), is of a recent nature and is now almost completed in American English, seemingly without any chain reaction on the part of the other vowels. One reason is that the separate existence of the two involved phonemes is still maintained by a large enough number of minimal pairs, such as in (9.ii), for a large enough group of speakers.

On the other hand, a few Midwestern American dialects have lost the distinction between /ɔ/ and /a/ (see (10.i)), except when they precede /r/ (see (10.ii)); if [ɔr] and [ar] are treated as diphthongs, then even these minimal pairs will disappear, and one phoneme will replace /ɔ/ and /a/ in the phonological system of such dialects. Because this change, unlike the previous one, affects the list of phonemes, it does not irradiate as easily and painlessly as the previous one. Both changes, when and if they penetrate the standard dialect, will lead to the emergence of a few pairs of homonyms, not numerous enough, however, to create a serious problem.

(9) (i) bin = Ben; pin = pen
(ii) bit ≠ bet; six ≠ sex

(10) (i) caught = cot
(ii) core ≠ car

SECTION 5. THE "SHIFTING" STANDARD

It is clear that the standard dialect in a language has to be very moderate if not outright conservative to fulfill the linking, unifying function for which it is singled out. However, it cannot resist a change if the latter permeates all the dialects of a language. If a change occurs within the lifetime of one generation it may cause a great deal of frustration. For many speakers and writers, the rules of the standard language are set in concrete, as it were, and these people refuse to modify them. The situation does create problems for teachers who may not know which usage to prescribe to their students. Grammar books and dictionaries are usually at least a generation behind and cannot settle the issue.

A few examples of ongoing changes attacked by pop grammarians are listed in (11). Another two which seem to be ignored by them are listed in (12).

(11) (i) *hopefully* 'full of hope' ⟩ 'I/we hope that . . .'
(ii) *whom* ⟩ *who* as in 'Who did you see there?'
(iii) *-ae, -i* ⟩ *-s* as in *formulas, syllabuses*
(iv) *me* ⟩ *I* in 'It is I'

(12) (i) *where* ⟩ *where at* as in 'Where's he at?'
(ii) Neg + *anymore* as in 'I do not do this anymore' ⟩ Pos + *anymore* as in 'I do do this anymore'

Linguistics can and should contribute to this not the prescriptive rules but the criteria that will help to decide whether the change is for real or is an accidental aberration which will fade away. The most reliable criteria are two:

(13) **Criteria for Assessment of Ongoing Changes:**
(i) **Statistical:** What percentage of the population and how many dialects are already affected by the change?
(ii) **Structural:** Does the change fit into the system of the language, or in other words, is there an analogous phenomenon?

(13.ii) is more important than (13.i) because native speakers are unconsciously sensitive to the structure of their language and consequently, at least for the most part, will not easily accept a counterstructural change. What this means is that if the change is statistically prevalent, chances are that it is perceived as structurally valid.

Out of the changes in (11), (11.i–ii) are statistically dominant already; (11.iii) is going strong; (11.iv) is probably only halfway there. Structurally, the "objectionable" usage of *hopefully* is analogous to that of *regretfully* or *remorsefully,* and those are not usually attacked by pop grammarians. *Whom* is one of the last casualties of the decline of the case system and cannot be saved. The case still exists with some pronouns but the use of *me* for *I* and vice versa threatens that as well (see below). The possessive case is being weakened first by the expansion of its scope from only animate and some proper nouns, as in (14.i), to practically all nouns, possibly with the exception of [+Abstract], as in (14.ii), and, second, by the growing frequency and acceptance of the adjective use of nouns, as in (14.iii).

(14) (i) the boy's toy, the cat's toy, New York's population, the *Queen Elizabeth*'s outbound voyage
(ii) the table's leg, the milk's freshness, *the sincerity's quality
(iii) the table leg, the Jones house, the Purdue team

(11.iii) is certainly structurally sound because it leads to the liquidation of some exceptions to the otherwise very regular rule of noun pluralization (see chapter 6, section 2) and is thus a further step in the process of anglicization of borrowings. The early stages of this process are usually rejected, and sorrowfully lamented, as the decline of learning and scholarship.

(11.iv) is more complicated. The original rule was that *I* was used as the subject and *me* otherwise. This rule kept (15.i) from becoming (15.ii). On the other hand, in many languages with cases, including Middle English, the accusative case of a predicative, that is, a nominal complement of the verb *to be,* coincides in form with the nominative case used as the subject. This last argument is hardly applicable, so (15.i) should still be correct under the rule. The problem is that as a result of **hypercorrection** native speakers whose (15.i) was corrected by pop grammarians to (15.ii) (and the speakers no longer understood why) started saying (15.iv) instead of (15.iii), and there is no case-related excuse for that. All this clearly spells out only one thing, which always explains the phenomena of hypercorrection as well, namely, that the native speaker no longer has any feel for, or sense of, the category of case in English at all, and the distinction between *I* and *me* is the next casualty down the line.

(15) (i) It is me.
(ii) It is I.
(iii) for Jack and me
(iv) for Jack and I

(12.i) is interesting because the change introduces a form rather than lose it, which is more typical. The opposition of *where* and *where at* is semantically motivated because it differentiates between the directional meaning of *where* (16.i) and its locational meaning (16.ii). Many languages use different interrogative words for these two meanings, but the real question is whether this distinction is indeed essential or redundant for English, because the directional or locational meaning is usually expressed unambiguously by the verb. The statistical proliferation of the change clearly depends on the speaker's intuition.

(12.ii) probably emerged as an extension of (17.i) to (17.ii) to (17.iii), and finally to (17.iv), with the reversal of the meaning. To the extent that *anymore* expresses a meaning not expressed by any other English word, the change is legitimate. To the extent that this meaning remains vague, it is not. The change does seem to be on the decline in the sense of not really making it to the standard dialect.

(16) (i) Where are you going?
(ii) Where are you?

(17) (i) I do not love you anymore.
(ii) It is not true that I love you anymore.
(iii) It is false that I love you anymore.
(iv) I love you anymore.

The negation is distanced from *anymore* in the transition from (17.i) to (17.ii), hidden in *false* = 'not true' in (17.iii), and dropped altogether in (17.iv) to produce either a strange paraphrase of (18.i) or an objection to the presupposed accusation of (18.ii).

(18) (i) I love you now.
(ii) You do not love me anymore!

The criteria in (13) are probably the closest linguistics can reliably approach the matters of prescription involved in maintaining the standard dialect. The criteria provide a sound basis for making an informed guess about the form to use and for realizing that no firm rule may be possible for the dilemma at the moment.

This is also the closest anybody can come to prescription because no grounds other than linguistical can dictate the choice. What follows is that pop grammarians' admonitions are usually groundless and should be—and almost invariably are—ignored by native speakers.

Language emerges from this discussion as a complex, changing, and continuous phenomenon whose variations have a clear social weight.

This chapter completes the basic introduction to linguistics begun in chapter 4. Chapter 10 looks at state-of-the-art linguistics in relation to rhetoric and composition.

CHAPTER 10

Linguistics for Rhetoric and Composition

This chapter is a response to chapters 1–3 and it is broadly based on the introduction to linguistics in chapters 4–9. The purpose here is to review briefly the linguistic concepts and phenomena pertaining to the issues of rhetoric and composition surveyed in chapters 1–3. Naturally, treated by linguistics, these issues have to be grouped differently in some cases, so numerous cross-references have to be used.

Unlike in chapters 4–9, where the foundations of the relevant linguistic concepts reviewed here were introduced, the emphasis will be on the state-of-the-art versions and the most recent research. The exposition will be brief because the actual application of linguistics to certain rhetorical issues will be the focus of the subsequent chapters. The exposition will also have to be much less elementary than in chapters 4–9 but definitely accessible to the reader who has absorbed the preceding chapters.

SECTION 1. THE WORD

1.1. Diction

The choice of a word to express a thought is a complex process, and linguistics does not claim a monopoly to it. Thus, it is clear that the impulse to convey certain information starts as a content to express. This content and its representation in the mind is what the generative semanticists tried to capture with their notion of **semantic representation** (see chapter 8, section 3.2.2). Their desire to represent this content as a logical function of predicate-calculus formulae is quite understandable. Can we not assume that when we want to say something we usually have certain things in mind and we mean to say something about those things? Can we not then take those things for references and what we want to say about them for predicates (cf. chapter 8, section 5.2.3)? If so, the next step is simple: Make the predicates into functions, the references into arguments, and your formula is ready. Thus, for instance, if I want to tell you something like (1.i), *house* is a reference, *white* is a predicate, and (1.ii) is the formula (with the possessive element omitted for the sake of simplicity). However, instead of uttering (1.i), I can produce any of the utterances in (2). In (2.i–ii), *white* and *house* are both in the predicate and in (2.iii), *white* is part of the reference and *house* is part of the predicate, so the simplified formula for (2.iii) will be the reverse of (1.ii)—see (2.iv).

(1) (i) My house is white.
(ii) WHITE (house)

(2) (i) I live in a white house.
(ii) I have a white house.
(iii) The white structure is my house.
(iv) HOUSE (white)

Now, it is clear that some of the sentences above are more appropriate in a certain context and others are less so. However, even in a given context, there are multiple variants for expressing the same thought, and linguistics has no firm rules to offer here. Besides, it is crucial to understand that linguistics is primarily responsible for **casual language,** the everyday, ordinary expression of thought, as opposed to **noncasual language,** such as the language of literature, poetry, military orders, computer technology, and other special-purpose sublanguages, which fulfill other requirements besides simple well-formedness. Thus, rhetoric and composition deal with well-written texts rather than simply well-formed ones. The former constitute a subset of the latter, and while linguistics is solely responsible for the latter, it cannot reach for the former and still remain a formal, rigorous discipline (see chapter 15, section 2). The choice of a word for a well-written text may be different from that for just a well-formed text, but even for the latter the mechanism is not fully known.

Every word can be characterized by the properties listed in (3), and all of this information is stored in the mind of native speakers who know the word. The lexicon of an adequate linguistic theory will provide for all of them as well (cf. chapter 8, section 4).

(3) (i) the phonological composition of the word, complete with the allophone assignment for each phoneme (See chapter 5, section 3.)
(ii) the syntactic valences of the word, that is, the complete information on how the word is combined with others in a sentence (This information assigns the word to one of the parts of speech—see chapter 6, section 3; also, it contains information similar to that about the verbs in the selection restriction rules of standard theory—see chapter 7, section 3.)
(iii) the semantic information about the word, including all the possible meanings (See chapter 8, section 2.2.)
(iv) the semantic connotations, that is, the accompanying emotive and other scale-related meanings, leading to various inferences (See chapter 8, section 5.2.5.)

The writer's **competence-related** errors occur if one or more of the parts in (3) are missing or incomplete. Thus, the use of *forfilling* for *fulfilling* and *coulternate* for *cultivate* in (1) in chapter 1 is made possible by the fact that (3.i) is vague and incomplete for the writer—it is characteristic that more phonological elements are recalled correctly close to the stress and fewer for the unstressed parts.

The complete or partial absence of (3.ii) results in assigning a word to the wrong part of speech, as in *supervise* for *supervisor* or *stagnant* for *stagnate* (see (4) in chapter 1), as well as using a word in an inappropriate syntactic structure, as in *maladjusted environment* (chapter 1, section 1.1.6). Characteristically, more errors occur with those parts of syntactical information that have to be memorized rather than understood: Thus, the prepositions that are perceived as used in their logical meaning, such as the directional ones in *out of the window* and *to the left,* are hardly ever misused, but the other ones, which are used in more abstract meanings, can be distorted (see chapter 1, section 1.1.4).

Incompleteness of (3.iii) is most often expressed when the writer retains one salient feature of the meaning and ignores the others and when the competing meanings of a polysemous word are ignored. The former results in expressions like *life fulfilling with happiness,* in which the word *fulfill* is engaged for its element of *filling,* falsely reinforced by the association of the word with *happiness*. The latter results in uncontrolled ambiguities, such as *Reagan, Bush ready for fall* in the headline of the 1980 post-convention issue of a student newspaper. In that example, the failure to capitalize *fall* (cf. chapter 1, section 3.1) makes it possible to think of *fall* referring to failure rather than to one of the seasons and the inexperienced copy writer and editor overlooked that.

Ignoring the inference-related connotations of (3.iv) leads to redundancies, such as *heavy in weight* (see chapter 1, section 1.1.5), and also to inappropriate stylistic usages.

It is typical for inexperienced writers to make errors they will not normally make in their speech. There is a conceptual difference here. Native speakers feel competent in their everyday speech. In writing, however, they believe they must have competence because they write in their native tongue, but in fact they do not have it because more often than not they perform in a different dialect. In the similar situation of a foreign language, similar errors will occur in both the oral and the written form. However, nonnative speakers tend to navigate much more cautiously and rely more on those words for which (3) is complete in their minds than on those that remain **semi-empty words** for them. Native speakers (and writers) are much bolder with such words because they are likelier to presume the completeness (or at least sufficiency) of their knowledge of them while in fact the opposite is true.

We will ignore here and elsewhere the **performance-related** errors with diction, which occur when the writer "has it right" in his mind but makes an error all the same because of a lapse of attention or memory or a similar temporary contingency.

1.2. Usage Errors

As in the previous discussion, only competence-related usage errors are discussed here. In other words, usage errors are perceived as systematic reflections of discrepancies between the writer's idiolect and the dialect it represents, on the one hand, and the standard dialect, on the other (see chapter 9, section 3).

1.2.1. Agreement Errors. Many agreement errors (cf. chapter 1, section 2.1.1) are dialectal in the regional sense. There are quite a few American dialects that ignore the morpheme PresThirSg (see chapter 6, section 2) or the number of the verbs. A writer speaking this dialect is often unable to avoid the errors in his writing as well.

Other agreement errors reflect an ongoing change. Thus, the move toward nonsexist language has excluded the generic *he* in such sentences as (4.i) and led to the increasing acceptance of (4.ii) in spite of the obvious lack of agreement in number between *everyone,* which is grammatically Sg, and *their,* which is syntactically and semantically Pl (cf. (6) in chapter 1).

(4) (i) Everyone should bring his notebook tomorrow.
(ii) Everyone should bring their notebooks tomorrow.

The proliferation of Pl after the construction *there is* is a typical indication that the speakers are losing their sensitivity to its singularity as opposed to *there are,* while the standard dialect still insists on the distinction. A similar phenomenon involves such expressions as *a lot,* whose singularity tends to be increasingly ignored, making (5.ii) more acceptable than the once solely normative (5.i).

(5) (i) A lot of people attends the show.
(ii) A lot of people attend the show.

These phenomena and also the growing tendency to make the verb agree with the last noun if there are more than one in the subject (as in *Jack and Jill is* instead of *Jack and Jill are*) are (not *is*!) indicative of a growing discrepancy between live dialects and the standard dialect concerning the grammatical number (cf. chapter 9, section 5).

1.2.2. Double Negatives. The use of double negatives (cf. chapter 1, section 2.1.2), unacceptable in the standard dialect, is the result of a situation in which many nonstandard dialects did not follow the example of the standard one in assuming a recent syntactic change (cf. chapter 9, section

4.2). Quite logically, the admissible nonnegative use of the double negative in the standard dialect (6.i), paraphrased as (6.ii), is not acceptable in those nonstandard dialects.

(6) (i) I do not know nothing.
(ii) It is not true that I do not know anything.

SECTION 2. THE SENTENCE

Formally, the sentence is sometimes defined as the text between two periods, or between the beginning of the entire text and the first period. The definition is not error-proof because periods may occur after acronyms, as a decimal point, and as part of various formulae and special notations. Syntactically, the sentence can be recognized as the main verb with all of its syntactical valences filled. Thus, if a verb requires a subject and an object, and only one of them is present in a string of words, that string is not a sentence (7.ii–iii). Similarly, if the verb requires more slots to be filled and not all of them are there, the result is not a sentence either (8.ii–vii).

(7) (i) John loves Mary.
(ii) *loves Mary
(iii) *John loves

(8) (i) John reminds Mary of Bill.
(ii) *reminds Mary of Bill
(iii) *John reminds of Bill
(iv) *John reminds Mary (in the "similarity" meaning)
(v) *John reminds
(vi) *reminds Mary
(vii) *reminds of Bill

Verbless strings of words can serve as elliptic constructions (see section 2.1.1.1) under certain specific circumstances, as in (9.i), but are generally unacceptable. Sentences without subjects are acceptable only if they are elliptic (9.ii) or imperative (9.iii).

(9) (i) A pleasant morning. Bill gets up early. . . .
(ii) A nice car. Starts every time.
(iii) Shut the door!

In (9.i), *it is* is omitted as a permissible stylistic device. In (9.ii), the missing subject of the second sentence is immediately reconstructed from the previous sentence, and a mechanism similar to semantic recursion (see chapter 8, section 5.2.2) can take care of that. In (9.iii), the subject *you* is standardly (and grammatically) assumed and omitted.

2.1. Grammar and Syntax

The phenomena discussed in this section are typically referred to as 'syntactical' in rhetoric and composition though linguistically they often go beyond syntax proper.

2.1.1. Sentence Boundaries. There are two possibilities of errors concerning sentence boundaries (cf. chapter 2, section 1.1), namely, to draw the boundary too soon—to have an incomplete sentence—or to draw it too late—to have too much between the periods. **Fragments** are of the former kind, **comma splices** of the latter, and **fused sentences** are often a combination of the two.

2.1.1.1. Fragments. As a competence-related error, a fragment can occur only if the writer's competence does not include the complete syntactical information for each verb or the notion that the verb should be there as a rule and, if it is, it must have a subject.

The notion of ellipsis is part of linguistic competence as well, and it is based on the principle that whatever is omitted should be immediately recoverable from the context. There are also the stylistic rules for using ellipsis that go beyond the purely linguistic rules, but those will not be addressed here.

Errors may also occur because the writer lacks the print-code competence (see chapter 1, section 3.1, and chapter 2, section 1.1), for example, the proper use of the period, or as a result of performance aberrations. Linguistics cannot be directly useful for either kind.

2.1.1.2. Comma Splices: A Taste of Text Linguistics. It used to be said in the transformational grammar literature of the 1960s that any sequence of sentences can be presented as one sentence, with semicolons instead of periods, or with commas, for that matter, and therefore transformational grammar could be perceived as a text grammar, not simply as a sentence grammar. The claim has never been followed up there, nor was there any use for making it within that school of thought. Whether the claim is true or false, remains, however, a crucial question for **text linguistics.**

Text linguistics was first proposed (see van Dijk 1972, and references cited there) as a simple and straightforward extension of sentence linguistics to the study of the paragraph and of the entire discourse (the alternative term for text linguistics within linguistics is **discourse analysis;** in communication, however, discourse analysis usually involves what linguists refer to as **conversational strategies,** namely, the patterns and structures in dialogues).

The early attempts to pursue this idea fizzled out primarily because much of what was working reasonably well within the sentence could not be extrapolated to larger units. Thus, for instance, the semantics of the sentence was acontextual at the time and could not be taken beyond the sentential boundaries. It also turned out that the sentences within the paragraph were held together by elements of the extralinguistic context rather than by anything in the text itself.

Over the last decade, text linguistics has evolved into two major directions. The first one remains within linguistics and handles the connectives between sentences, such as the ones listed in (10) (cf. chapter 3, section 3). Obviously, those numerous sentences that do not contain any element of (10) are left out of such studies. The other direction is interdisciplinary and attempts to discover the extralinguistic connectives and other elements of paragraph structure and to elicit help from the adjacent disciplines, which seem to be responsible for some of these elements. The disciplines in question may include anthropology, sociology, psychology, and philosophy, especially the theory of actions.

(10) **Typical Sentential Connectives:** meanwhile, in the meantime, at the same time, similarly, first/second/third/ . . . , thus, therefore, for this/that reason, accordingly, . . .

The study of the paragraph by text linguistics should aim at something like the **discourse structure of the paragraph** (see Reichman 1985, and Tucker, Nirenburg, and Raskin 1985), a graph with sentences for nodes and discourse relations between sentences (but see below) for links. Thus, the paragraph in (11.i) can be roughly presented as (11.ii).

(11) (i) John did not like Mary. He hated parties. He had an exam the next day. Because of all that, he declined Mary's invitation to her birthday party.

(ii)

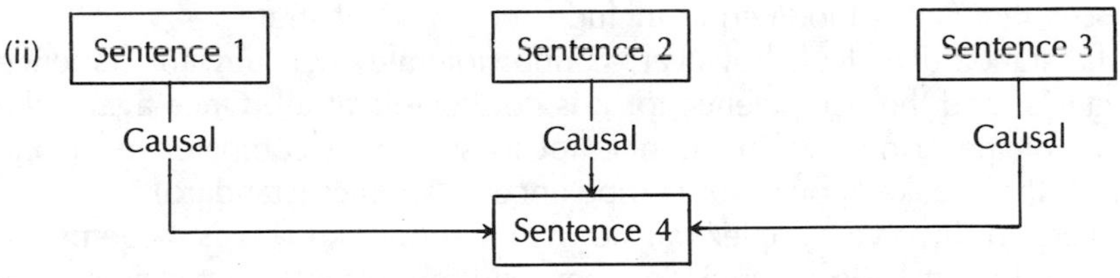

Obviously, the discourse structure will change if we rewrite (11.i) with comma splices as (12):

(12) John did not like Mary, he hated parties, he had an exam the next day, because of all that, he declined Mary's invitation to her birthday party.

The change, however, is due entirely to the decision, made surreptitiously in (11.ii) and in most of the literature on the subject, to make sentences the atoms of discourse structure. A strong argument can be offered in favor of drawing connecting links between clauses, including those within the same sentence. If that is done, can it be argued that no difference exists between (11.i) and (12), or—to strengthen the case—between (11.i) and (12) with improved punctuation, say, with a dash instead of the third comma? If that happens to be the case, then no competence-related argument against comma splices can be offered, and it becomes entirely the matter of print-code-related and stylistic conventions.

2.1.1.3. Fused Sentences. As a combination of the two deviations from the proper sentence boundaries, fused sentences may be caused by defective competence. However, they are usually mentioned in linguistics as typical performance-related violations of rules contained in the speaker's or writer's competence (see chapter 2, section 1.1) and caused by accidental, nonsystematic, and nonlinguistic factors (see also below).

2.1.2. Problems Within Sentences. Blurred patterns, various types of **consolidation errors,** and **inversions** (see chapter 2, section 1.2) may all be caused by the absence of a certain rule from the writer's competence. In most cases, however, just as with fused sentences above, the root of the problem seems to be in the confusion of the written and oral dialects, that is, ultimately of the writer's own dialect, which is and should remain oral, with the standard language, which is and should remain written.

As a result of the limitations of our short-term memory or because of any other related circumstance, speakers often change plans in the middle of sentences, leaving parts of them incomplete, fusing the beginning with a new plan, splicing their oral commas, and so on. The short-term memory (or whatever else it is) of hearers, however, is just as overburdened, and in a similar move, hearers usually manage to keep track of a speaker's sentence. The fact that he can get away with such sentences constitutes a very strong reinforcement for the speaker. In fact, it can be argued, that as a result his oral competence is modified to include such deviant strategies.

The standard dialect, however, cannot tolerate such deviant sentence structures, and the competence for it is not flexible at all. Once again, the source of the errors lies in the attempt to substitute competence in one dialect (the speaker's own) for competence in another (standard).

Inversions involve complex transformational rules known as **movements.** Many oral dialects do not include them, and movement-affected sentences are perceived as weird and nonnative. The inclusion of most of them in the standard dialect makes it necessary to add a whole new block of competence to the mind of the writer. Without this addition, writers are likely to repeat the moved element in the sentence anyway (cf. (15) in chapter 2), and this constitutes many errors. Typically, nonproficient nonnative speakers, who also lack this block of competence, make exactly the same errors.

Sentences like (16.i) in chapter 2, in which the direct order in an interrogative subordinate clause is replaced with the standard inverted order, which the clause would have had as an independent sentence, also testify to the absence of movement from the native competence. Examples of this are so prevalent that the standard dialect may soon change its position on this issue (cf. chapter 9, section 5).

2.2. Meaning and Syntax: Speaker Intention

Many syntactic constructions are subject to constraints which make them meaningful or resolve ambiguity. When these constraints are not part of the writer's competence, problems of comprehension occur. As a rule this happens when the constructions themselves are not part of the writer's idiolect and have to be acquired in the process of acquisition of the standard dialect. However, even before such acquisition takes place, an inexperienced writer has a mechanism at his disposal that makes it possible for him to use such semifamiliar constructions in his writing to his own—but not his reader's—satisfaction. The mechanism is based on Grice's notion of **speaker intention.**

In his work immediately preceding and leading to the concept of implicature (see chapter 8, section 5.2.4), Grice (1957) distinguished between three possible meanings of the verb *to mean* as illustrated by the following three examples:

(13) (i) Clouds usually mean rain. (mean_N for 'natural meaning')
(ii) This sentence means that . . .
(iii) By uttering this sentence, the speaker means that . . . (mean_{NN} for 'nonnatural meaning')

For Grice, both the natural and the nonnatural meanings—(13.i) and (13.iii), respectively—are permissible uses of *mean*. (13.ii), however, is not. In other words, Grice denies the property of having meaning to any linguistic entity until it is actually uttered, and then it means exactly and solely what the speaker intends it to mean. This is the exact reverse of Katz and Fodor's (1963) position concerning the meaning of the sentence in isolation (see chapter 8, section 4). They refused to consider the contextual modification of sentence meaning, while Grice denies any meaning to a sentence outside a context and claims that the context fully determines sentence meaning. Grice's position is just as counterintuitive as Katz and Fodor's—he seems to ignore entirely the fact that the speaker's intention to convey certain information determines the choice of a suitable vehicle for this information, namely of a certain sentence or a sequence of sentences, and this choice is made on the basis of the meaning that the sentence possesses and that is known to the speaker.

It is definitely true, however, that the speaker's intention may add some new elements of meaning to the sentence meaning. The realization of this intention and the full comprehension of the meaning by the hearer or hearers depends on the speaker's success in taking the existing context into account and creating new contextual elements for the uttered sentence to be interpreted correctly. Thus, (14.i) (cf. (61.i) in chapter 8) will be interpreted literally and not as (14.ii) unless the speaker is sure that he and the hearer share some evidence of the opposite perception, such as foolish behavior, a stupid statement, a flunked test, or something else of this kind.

(14) (i) John is a real genius, isn't he?
(ii) John is dumb.

What happens with semifamiliar syntactic constructions, of whose built-in constraints the inexperienced writer is innocent, is that the writer's intention, clear only to him at the very best, clings, as it were, to a deviant use of the construction and makes him believe that the sentence does mean what he wants it to mean.

2.2.1. Dangling and Misplaced Modifiers. The simple participle constructions are often misused, as in (15.i) (cf. (15.i) in chapter 2) because the coreferential constraint is violated in them. By contrast, (15.ii) is fine because the subject of the participle and the subject of the main clause are coreferential (cf. (15.iii) and (15.v)) the way the subject of the participle (see (15.iv)) and the subject of the main clause (see (15.v)) in (15.i) are not.

(15) (i) Hiking all afternoon, my legs felt tired.
(ii) Hiking all afternoon, I felt tired.
(iii) I hiked.
(iv) legs felt
(v) I felt

This is further complicated by the continuing though rapidly decreasing acceptability in Standard American English of absolute participle constructions with their own subjects, distinct from the subject of the other clause, as in (16).

(16) (i) Winter having come so soon, we lost the sunflowers.
(ii) Mary having married George, John remained single.

Since the writer's competence does not have either of the two constructions actively, and his prior passive perception of them renders them semifamiliar, the constraint of coreferentiality of the two subjects or, alternatively, of their explicit presence is violated, and the speaker's intention bridges the gap and "makes up" for the deviance.

The same fate is shared by elliptical clauses with omitted subjects, such as (17.i = (18.ii) in chapter 2), which is an inadmissible ellipsis of the perfectly correct sentence in (17.ii = (18.iii) in chapter 2). By itself, (17.i) is not inadmissible though it is somewhat unlikely to occur; but its meaning is distinct from that of (17.ii), because (17.i) is a correct ellipsis of (17.iii), not of (17.ii). These examples show even more clearly than in the case of participle constructions that the competence for the standard dialect should contain a subject-deletion transformation, which works only on coreferential sentences such as (18) omitting *she was* from (18.i) and yielding the correct sentence in (18.ii) (cf. (18.i) in chapter 2).

(17) (i) When only seven, her father changed jobs.
(ii) When she was only seven, her father changed jobs.
(iii) When he was only seven, her father changed jobs.

(18) (i) When she was only seven, she started to write novels.
(ii) When only seven, she started to write novels.

The position of any modifier in the sentence is important for its correct interpretation. If there is any doubt about its attribution to a head in the sentence and a different analysis is possible, the sentence will be unintentionally ambiguous, and the speaker will lose control over which of the meanings will be perceived by the hearer. If the modifier is analyzed as belonging to a head other than that intended by the speaker, the wrong or absurd meaning will be conveyed as a result. Thus, the use of one adjective with two conjoined nouns (19.i) is inherently ambiguous as to whether just the first of the nouns or both of them constitute the head, and to resolve the ambiguity of a sentence with such constructions, such as (19.ii), the speaker and hearer must possess some common knowledge, for instance (19.iii), which excludes all but one of the meanings, the one intended by the speaker. Short of that, ambiguity uncontrolled by the speaker will remain.

(19) (i) old men and women
(ii) Old men and women will be inoculated first.
(iii) It is known that two groups, old men and women of all ages, are particularly susceptible to the disease.

The situation is further complicated by the fact that the native speakers always perceive sentences in a context, real or imaginary, and have a hard time breaking out of the context to discern an alternative meaning. Because of that, the writers of uncontrolled ambiguities often get away with them when the readers just happen to perceive the sentences in the intended meanings and to remain oblivious to the unintended ones.

The wrong placement of a modifier, for example, as belonging to the wrong head or where two or more heads can "compete" for it, if competence-related, clearly indicates that such constructions are not part of the writer's idiolectal competence.

2.2.2. Ambiguous Reference. The correct use of pronouns and other grammatical semantic recursion triggers (see chapter 8, section 5.2.2) depends on the immediate and unrivaled accessibility of the antecedent to the hearer. Short of that, the sentence will not be interpreted at all or at least not correctly (cf. chapter 2, section 2.2). The same principles that pertain to the placement of modifiers are abided by here: The antecedent should be either the closest of all to the pronoun in the same or adjacent sentence or the only one around that is suitable morphologically, in gender for instance, or semantically.

The generic use of *you* as in (22) in chapter 2, is often complicated by the presence of the regular, personal, second person, singular or plural use of the pronoun, which comes into conflict with other personal pronouns in the same sentence as in chapter 1, section 2.2.1. It can also be interchanged with *one* in a stylistically inadmissible way.

Very close to the pronoun-antecedent situation is the intentionally coreferential use of two nouns that cannot be coreferential, such as *art* and *level* in chapter 2, section 2.2.

2.3. Style and Syntax: Limitations of Linguistics

Stylistics is an area of research adjacent to but distinct from linguistics. Linguistics is applicable to stylistics along the same lines as it is to rhetoric and composition, namely, a linguistic application is valid only if a linguistic correlate to an important stylistic property can be found. There is no doubt that linguistics is immensely applicable to stylistics. However, it is primarily stylistics that should deal with the style-related issues of rhetoric and composition, and linguistics can be involved in that only via stylistics. A few comments somewhat independent of stylistics will, however, be made here.

A consistent style may be studied by linguistics as a sublanguage (see chapter 9, section 1). As any sublanguage, it will be characterized, among other things, by an inventory of syntactical constructions. Any deviation from this inventory will be perceived as the use of a different style. What linguistics cannot control, however, is the choice of a style appropriate for a purpose or a situation. These choices exist outside of linguistics and determine the status of any stylistic sublanguage as **noncasual language,** or **language for special purposes.**

The various stylistic phenomena do, of course, have their linguistic correlates. Thus, **variety** calls for a complete use and alternation of the syntactic constructions from the inventory of the style while **conciseness and clarity** call for nonduplication of syntactical and semantical elements. **Emphasis** involves a much more complex and interesting semantic notion of inference, and its use has to be regulated according to the intended meaning, which includes the intended inference. Thus, sentences (8.ii–vi) in chapter 5, with the different words emphasized, infer sentences (9.i–v) in chapter 5, respectively, and it is the emphasis that makes each of these different inferences possible in each case.

SECTION 3. DISCOURSE

3.1. "Natural Rhetoric?"

Much of the discussion on discourse in rhetoric and composition hinges around those aspects of it which fall, just as stylistics, within noncasual language and language for special purpose. Linguistics can address the prescribed modes of discourse or format of essays only inasmuch as the native competence of an unsophisticated, untrained, and possibly illiterate speaker also contains these elements, and there is not much evidence of that. It would, however, be an interesting linguistic application to rhetoric and composition if a set of linguistic properties could be proven to correlate with each expository mode. An exploration of the "natural rhetoric" stored in the mind of the native speaker and not imposed on him by rhetorical scholarship or tradition is, undoubtedly, a very worthy subject of investigation both for rhetoric and composition and for semantics. It would be similar to the study of natural logic in contemporary semantic theory (see Lakoff 1972; McCawley 1972). On the other hand, to the extent that it is imposed on the writer by extralinguistic conventions, the possibilities of rigorous linguistic applications to this part of rhetoric and composition seem to be limited (see chapter 15, sections 2 and 4).

Linguistics can contribute a number of concepts and ideas primarily to the subject of coherence and cohesion. Some of these concepts have been mentioned before (see especially chapter 8, section 5 and section 2.1.1.2 on discourse structure) and they will be further explored in chapter 13. In this section, we will deal briefly with two new areas in semantics which bear on discourse and which begin to penetrate research in rhetoric and composition, namely the 'given-new contract' and script-based semantics.

3.2. Given-New

These terms refer to a new form of an eighty-year-old linguistic theory which emerged from Prague even before the formation of the Prague Linguistic Circle but which is true to the spirit of the linguistic approach formulated there. The theory of the 'actual articulation of the sentence,' or—as it is referred to more frequently—of the **functional perspective of the sentence** was formulated by Mathesius (see, for instance, Mathesius 1947).

The theory is based on a simple and clearly intuitively appealing idea that in each sentence there is something already supposed to be known to the hearer or reader and something supposed to be unknown to him. The original terms for these concepts were 'thema' and 'rhema,' or 'theme' and 'rheme'; however, such pairs as 'topic' and 'content,' 'topic' and 'focus,' 'presupposition' and 'focus,' 'old' and 'new,' and, finally and most recently, 'given' and 'new,' have also been used (see Chomsky 1971; Clark and Clark 1977; Prince 1981). Thus, in (20.i), *he* is definitely given while *was a teacher* is new. Generally, personal pronouns, definite noun phrases and other anaphoric, or semantically recursive, elements of the sentence are given, while predicates and indefinite noun phrases are usually new. Thus, in (20.ii), *the room* is given and *is small* is new. In (20.iii), however, both *the man* and *the room* are given, and it is *came into* which is new. *A man came into* is new in (20.iv).

The same graphic sentence can be analyzed into given and new differently in a different context. Thus, *George* (and *the room*) in (21.i) will be given if the sentence is uttered in the same context in which its emphatic paraphrase (21.ii) is appropriate, that is, when the discourse or the situational context of the utterance have already brought George to our attention. On the other hand, *George* will be new in the context appropriate for the emphatic (21.iii), that is, when it is just the room that has been mentioned in the previous discourse or established by the situation.

(20) (i) He was a teacher.
(ii) The room is small.
(iii) The man came into the room.
(iv) A man came into the room.

(21) (i) George came into the room.
(ii) What George did was come into the room.
(iii) It was George who came into the room.

The definite and indefinite articles in English and other languages are clearly recognized in the framework of this theory as powerful means of focus control in the sentence. Those languages that lack articles—Russian, Latin, or Czech, for instance—typically use word order for the same purpose; they must, of course, be free-word-order languages (see chapter 7, section 1) then, which they are. Thus, (20.iii) and (20.iv) are translated into Russian as (22.i) and (22.ii), respectively, and the translations represent a regroupment of four identical words, which correspond to the English words minus the articles; the glossary is provided in (22.iii).

(22) (i) Čelovek vošel v komnatu
(ii) V komnatu vošel čelovek
(iii) *čelovek* 'man'; *vošel* 'came (in)'; *v* '(in)to'; *komnatu* 'room'

Every new semantic theory has tried its hand at functional perspective but the problem of determining what is given and what is new has escaped every one of them, and the reason for that is, of course, that functional perspective is determined by the context of the sentence. It follows then that only contextual semantics can handle the given-new contract. In fact, it actually subsumes it.

3.3. Script-Based Semantics

The script-based semantic theory (see Raskin 1981, 1984, 1985c, 1986b) is the first full-fledged formal theory of contextual semantics, and its main concept, the **script,** subsumes the other pragmatic notions discussed in chapter 8, section 5. Scripts are briefly mentioned and exemplified in chapter 8, section 4. What follows is a brief self-contained exposition of the theory in its entirety.

The script-based semantic theory consists of a lexicon and a set of combinatorial rules.

The lexicon is a repository of all semantic information associated with lexical items. In order to make it possible to account for the meaning of every sentence in every context, the lexical entry for each item has to contain more information and to be more specific than the entries required and enabled by any acontextual formal semantic theory. This does not mean that, among them, all the lexical entries in the script-based lexicon contain more semantic information than the lexicon in any other theory or, in other words, that a deeper penetration into the semantic texture of language is necessarily required. What it means is that more connections between various concepts have to be included explicitly in each lexical item.

Formally, this is accommodated by postulating the lexical entry for each lexical item, and in fact for each separate meaning of each item, as a graph with semantic nodes and mostly unlabeled but directed and distance-measured links between them. A typical lexical entry includes a node for the item in question and a "round" of adjacent nodes. Some of the nodes may correspond to other lexical items, others to semantic features or properties that are not expressed by any lexical items, and still others to functional syntactic concepts (see Raskin 1984 for detailed examples).

In fact, all the lexical entries of a language are interrelated and make up one continuous graph. Each domain of this graph may be referred to as a script. It is obvious then that scripts may be "smaller" or "larger." The former usually correspond to one lexical entry.

In practice, however, it is often convenient to present the scripts that constitute lexical entries in a discrete and simplified way, as in (23) for the verb *to love*.

(23) LOVE Vtr
Subject: Human, Adult, Sex **x**
Object: Human, Adult, Sex $\bar{\mathbf{x}}$

Activity: State
Attitude
Good
Extreme degree
Limited to the object
Presupposing: KNOW
Presupposed by: SEXUAL INTERCOURSE

In the graph, the combinations of semantic features under Subject and Object above correspond, of course, to words like *man* and *woman* and those whose meanings include the meanings of *man* and *woman*. One link leads then from the node LOVE to SUBJECT and then branches out to MAN and WOMAN and another link from LOVE to OBJECT and then also branches out to MAN and WOMAN. Another link leads from LOVE to STATE, from STATE to ATTITUDE, from ATTITUDE to GOOD, and from GOOD one link goes to EXTREME DEGREE and another to EXCLUSIVE, with a back link from EXCLUSIVE to OBJECT. Still another link leads from LOVE to PRESUPPOSITION to KNOW. A different link comes to LOVE from PRESUPPOSITION and to that node from SEXUAL INTERCOURSE.

Many of the listed nodes correspond to lexical items, and the lexical entries for those items are domains of the graph which partially overlap with the one for *love*. The node for EXTREME DEGREE, however, may correspond to other actual words, such as *very,* which does not necessarily have a separate node of the same order in the graph.

It is obvious that such nodes as SUBJECT, OBJECT, and PRESUPPOSITION have numerous outgoing and incoming links, which connect different pairs of words. In order to avoid confusion with the pairings, a technical problem concerning the formal structure of the graph has to be solved. One simple solution is to index the corresponding incoming and outgoing links within each pair. Another involves a more complex topological reality and leads to a multidimensional graph, and there is nothing wrong with that.

The entry in (23) corresponds to only one possible meaning of the verb *to love*. At least two others are possible between the given pair of Subject and Object, roughly 'to hold dear' and 'to make love.' Each of these has a similarly organized entry. Some of these and other meanings of *love* are possible between other subjects and objects, such as nonhuman animates and inanimates.

The shorter links in the graph correspond to closer semantic ties, and the longer links to more remote ties. Since the graph is continuous, every node is connected to every other node, so that in principle there is a semantic tie between any two items but in reality most of them are insignificant. This situation has a strong intuitive appeal in the sense that we perceive language to be exactly that way.

The combinatorial rules combine the lexical entries; calculate their compatible combinations and reject the incompatible ones; disambiguate among the compatible interpretations if they can; establish absolute and probable presuppositions; and make absolute and probable inferences.

Thus, in processing (24), combinatorial rules reject the meanings of *love* that are incompatible with the given pair of subjects (after filling in the antecedents for *I* and *you* with the help of a basically syntactical, though not totally asemantical procedure) and fail to disambiguate between sexual love and holding dear, but since the latter meaning is included in the former, the rules proceed to establish the common presuppositions and inferences for these meanings as absolute and those related only to sexual love as probable. The absolute presuppositions include the existence of both John and Mary and the fact that he knew her prior to making the utterance. An absolute inference is that John intended that whoever could hear him would know that he loved Mary; that he intended Mary to know that is a highly probable inference. A probable presupposition is that John and Mary are adult humans of opposite sexes. A probable inference is that John desires sexual intercourse with Mary.

(24) "I love you," John said to Mary.

If (24) continues, more information becomes available for the combinatorial rules to disambiguate (24) and to make some presuppositions and inferences more absolute. We will not go into the possible consequences of the established procedure for text linguistics here. We are also omitting some of the other functions of combinatorial rules in the theory.

The theory as outlined above consists of two complex components. Both the lexicon and the combinatorial rules should be formally defined entities, and between the two of them, they should provide a formal match for the meaning of each sentence in each context as perceived by the native speaker. It is claimed here that nothing short of the properties utlined above is a semantic theory.

The fact of the matter is that in perceiving (23) or (24) the native speaker can do all the things the lexicon and the combinatorial rules are assigned to do. If we fail to calculate the presuppositions and inferences, for instance, the output of the semantic description based on the theory will not match the semantic competence of the native speaker of the language in question. If we fail to disambiguate a sentence, which is unambiguous in the discourse—and this is basically what Katz and Fodor (1963) proposed to do—the match is not there either.

The native speaker actually disambiguates rather radically, albeit unconsciously, and takes risks doing that. Many native speakers lack the ability to discern ambiguity in most cases. Thus, in the case of (24), most native speakers will perceive the sexual meaning of *love* as the obvious one. It pays, therefore, especially in the practical semantic descriptions associated with the theory, to mark certain scripts as most probable and to let the combinatorial rules disambiguate even when there is no absolute certainty. In this case, they should be able to backtrack to the next most probable script if some adverse information comes up, for example, if John and Mary turn out to be brother and sister, five and three years of age, respectively. (It is, of course, possible for sexual love to hold between two unusual subjects and objects, but it will be perceived as nonnormative exactly because of its deviation from the script in the lexicon.)

The situation is further complicated by the fact that the native speaker may be able to do more by way of disambiguating, presupposing, and inferring than the theory is capable of, if he uses his nonlinguistic knowledge of the world to do that. We will not discuss here the most important question of the boundary between linguistic and encyclopedic knowledge (see Raskin 1985a, 1985b) but will simply provide an example of nonlinguistic inference. If, for instance, the hearer of (24) happens to have observed John and Mary in the process of lovemaking, he will be able to disambiguate between sexual love and holding dear immediately and absolutely. This kind of encyclopedic knowledge is not common, and therefore, another hearer, who knows nothing about the two protagonists, will not be able to disambiguate in the same way. The pieces of common encyclopedic knowledge are harder to distinguish from linguistic knowledge.

On the other hand, an association of (24) with *marriage* as a probable development or an accompanying state can be inferred linguistically, simply because, in the graph, SEXUAL INTERCOURSE will be linked closely to MARRIAGE.

Script-based semantics seems to hold more promise for rhetoric and composition and for other linguistic applications than do other parts of linguistic theory and practice (see Raskin 1986a for more discussion).

CHAPTER 11

Linguistic Analysis of Errors

SECTION 1. DICTION ERRORS

As stated in Chapter 1, diction errors occur when language users attempt to use words they know imperfectly and thus are often indications of the error-maker's efforts to expand his or her vocabulary. Though often the intuitions and greater knowledge of language of a writing teacher or error analyst can provide explanations for specific diction errors, linguistics, which tries to account systematically for native language users' intuition (or competence), offers more general and generalizable explanations of the sources of such errors. For the most part, semantics, with its broad responsibility for everything in language that has meaning (see chapter 8, section 1), is the branch of linguistics that is most helpful in the analysis of diction problems, but as we shall see, phonology, not usually associated with meaning-related problems, has a role in the analysis also. Phonologically based errors include the failure to distinguish phonological differences, the confusion of phonologically similar and rhyming words, the association of the right meaning with the wrong word, and the belief that a non-word or an incorrect word exists and is a legitimate lexical option.

Phonology offers a better explanation than semantics for one fairly frequent category of diction error, the use of words that share sound but not meaning with the correct word for the context. An example cited in chapter 1, section 1.1.2, the substitution of *pacific* for *specific,* illustrates this error. In terms of meaning, the words share only a grammatical morpheme, the suffix *-ic* which identifies them both as adjectives, and this similarity is too little to explain their frequent confusion. Instead, this similarity simply contributes to the phonological similarity of the words, which is responsible for *pacific* being used in place of *specific* (the opposite substitution does not occur). While it is possible that *pacific* is simply a transcription error, the error is reinforced by the fact that the word rhymes with the correct word. Further, since the writer is likely to know that the word *pacific* is a legitimate word, he may not detect the error as he proofreads his work.

The phonological element is certainly at play in the creation of non-words like those mentioned in (1) in chapter 1 and listed again here.

(1) (i) forfilling
(ii) coulternate
(iii) subcepticle

Each of these non-words bears a phonological resemblance to the word intended (*fulfilling, cultivate, susceptible*); none, however, is a legitimate, meaning-conveying word in English. Thus, as was suggested in chapter 1, it seems likely that the users of each of these non-words relied upon what they heard, or thought they heard, in the speech of others when they chose to use the particular word in question here. In addition, the writer's choice was probably based on context, since each non-word is used in an appropriate context for the correct word.

Phonological similarity also plays a role in the creation of word blends like *notrocious,* apparently a blend of *atrocious* and *notorious*. And again, the context in which *notrocious* appeared, (2), suggests that the writer is aware of the meaning she wishes to convey.

(2) An individual may find that placing capital letters in the right place is an easy task, while word division is notrocious.

What distinguishes this error linguistically from the kinds of non-words discussed above is that in this case it is possible to discover semantic as well as phonological similarities between *notrocious* and the words from which it is derived. For example, in terms of Katz and Fodor's interpretive semantics (see chapter 8, section 3.2.1), *notorious, atrocious,* and *notrocious* share the syntactic marker Adj, indicated by their shared grammatical morpheme *-ious*. The key semantic feature shared by the two legitimate words is (Wicked) or (−Good). (*The Oxford English Dictionary* includes 'heinously wicked' as a definition of *atrocious* and "used attributively with designations . . . which imply evil or wickedness" for *notorious*.) Though *wicked* itself would not be appropriate here, its undesirable connotations are what the student writer has appropriated for her own word. Both words also share what Katz and Fodor (1963) refer to as selection restrictions; that is, they can both be used to refer to persons or actions. The shared syntactic and semantic markers, selection restrictions, and phonology of *atrocious* and *notorious* combine in the student's word *notrocious*. One unshared semantic feature is (Well-known), which is an important part of the meaning of *notorious* but not part of the meaning of *atrocious*. *Notrocious* is, however, used in a context that implies that (Well-known) is part of its intended meaning. Thus far we have examined diction errors that can be analyzed in terms of phonology alone or phonology and semantics together. But phonological similarity does not play a role in all diction errors, many of which are the result of a failure to recognize the breadth or the limits of the meaning of a particular word. The failure to recognize the breadth of meaning often results in redundancy, while the error referred to in chapter 1, section 1.1.6, as 'inappropriate context' can be traced to a misunderstanding of the limits on the meaning and thus the use of a word.

Isolated words cannot be redundant. Rather, redundancy is the result of using words that mean the same as words already being used in a phrase or sentence, as (3) illustrates.

(3) blue in color

The redundancy here can be explained by the fact that *blue* contains the semantic feature (Color), and as long as the word is being used literally, the phrase *in color* simply repeats meaning that the word *blue* already conveys. (When words are used metaphorically, semantic features may change. When the word *blue* is used to mean sad or depressed, it no longer conveys its typical meaning.) Thus (3) conveys more information than is necessary: The meaning of *blue* is broad enough to encompass *in color* and to render its use unnecessary. Redundancy can also occur if a language user fails to recognize the meaning contained in a grammatical morpheme. In (4), the prefix *re-* means *back,* so the word *back* is redundant.

(4) return back

In a sense, using a word in an inappropriate context is the opposite of redundancy. Redundancy suggests that the language user is not aware of how much a word means; not aware, that is, of all that the word conveys. A phrase like (5) suggests that the language user does not understand the limits to the meaning of a word and thus employs it in contexts that are inappropriate.

(5) maladjusted environment

The problem with (5) is that the adjective *maladjusted* and the noun it attempts to modify, *environment,* are incompatible semantically (see chapter 8, section 2.1). The semantic restriction of *maladjusted* is (+Animate). (It might also be argued that (+Human) is an essential feature of *maladjusted,* but the word is used, perhaps metaphorically, in conjunction with animals, especially domestic pets.) The meaning of *environment,* on the other hand, includes the feature (−Animate); in other words, *maladjusted* requires the noun it modifies to have the feature (+Animate), while *environment* has the feature (−Animate).

Semantic features also offer an approach to analyzing errors like those in (6).

(6) (i) There was a large amount of cars in the parking lot.
(ii) We saw less pigeons as we left the city behind.

(7) (i) There was a large number of cars in the parking lot.
(ii) We saw fewer pigeons as we left the city behind.

As was suggested in chapter 1, section 1.1, (6.i) is incorrect because the word *amount* is not used to refer to countable objects. (6.ii) is incorrect for the same reason: *less* is not used to modify countable nouns. The correct versions, (7.i–ii), differ only in the fact that words that refer to or modify countable nouns are used. Semantic analysis would suggest that, first, the nouns *cars* and *pigeons* both include the semantic feature (+Count). But the selection restrictions of *amount* and *less* dictate that these words are to be used only with nouns with the feature (−Count). Words like *number* and *fewer,* on the other hand, are semantically restricted in the opposite way: They are used only to refer to (+Count) nouns.

It might be argued that the preceding analyses tell us little more than what common sense (or intuition or linguistic competence) tells us—that diction errors are the result of phonological and semantic confusion. We would have to agree, and our agreement would emphasize a point that is central to this book: Linguistics models and explains the competence of native speakers. It is an attempt to formulate rules that explain what native speakers as a group know about their language. But it is exactly by formulating such rules that linguistics can provide the means to analyze errors that occur because linguistic performance does not match linguistic competence. Linguistics places each error precisely in terms of specific features of specific linguistic entities and provides significant generalizations leading to the discovery of useful rules.

SECTION 2. SPELLING AND USAGE ERRORS

Although spelling is a print-code, not a linguistic, phenomenon (see chapter 1, section 3.1, and chapter 5, section 1.1.1), linguistics can shed light on and predict why certain kinds of misspellings occur. Most generally, we can recognize that English orthography, frozen since the fifteenth century, does not reflect the phonetic changes which have occurred over the centuries. Thus, letters that are now silent, such as the *k* in *knight,* were at one time pronounced. Furthermore, the fact that conventional spelling allows more than one spelling for a sound, a fact illustrated by the IPA presented in (3) in chapter 5, demonstrates the near impossibility of trying to base spelling on phonetics alone. But many writers depend on phonetics to guide their spelling of unfamiliar words, often settling on the most obvious spelling for an unknown word.

Phonetics, phonology, and, to a lesser extent, morphology can provide insight into why certain kinds of spelling errors occur more frequently than others. The IPA, for example, demonstrates that the sound represented by the symbol [ay] can be exemplified in English spelling by words such as *b**i**te*, *f**igh**t*, and ***ai**sle*. The identical pronunciation of *ite* and *ight* provides a phonetic explanation for the common misspellings (mentioned in chapter 1, section 3.1) of *lite* for *light* and *nite* for *night*. Similarly, the sound [u] can be represented not only by the letter *u*, but also by *ou*. This phonetic identity is responsible for such shortcut misspellings as *thru* for *through*. A final example explains the common misspelling of *could've*—the contraction of *could* and *have*—as *could of*. The phoneme /v/ can be spelled not only by the letter *v*, but also, and particularly in this example, by the letter *f*, as in the word *of*. Interestingly, phrases like *could of* and *would of* are often interpreted as diction errors or variants attributed to dialect differences, but an understanding of the phonetic identity underlying the error would lead one to recognize it as a mistake in spelling.

The absence of some sounds from some dialects offers another explanation for why some people make certain kinds of spelling errors. If, as was suggested in chapter 5, section 2.1, some dialects do not distinguish [w] from [ʍ], confusion of words such as *weather* and *whether* as well as the misspelling of these words as *wheather* or *wether*, becomes more understandable. Speakers who do not hear a distinction between these phonemes or who do not distinguish them in their speech will have difficulty making the distinction when they attempt to spell words that as far as they can tell contain identical sounds. The phonological rule (27) in chapter 5 applies here as well. The syncretism that results when two phonemes are pronounced similarly, as may occur with the phonemes /t/ and /d/, can (as pointed out in chapter 5, section 3.4) make words like *writer* and *rider* phonetically indistinguishable.

Phonology can also help explain spelling errors such as the failure to include the final *d* in phrases like *used to* and *supposed to*. Some writers who do not hear or pronounce both the /d/ and the /t/, but instead hear and pronounce only the /t/, will omit the *d* when they write. Other writers, no more likely to pronounce both sounds, are conscious of the orthographic and grammatical conventions dictating the inclusion of the *d*. The phrases in question involve the use of the past participle, which is formed by the /d/ allomorph of the morpheme PastPart (cf. (18–21) and the discussion following in chapter 6). The letter *d* denoting that allomorph must appear when the words are written, even if it is not pronounced by most speakers.

Thus far we have been considering spelling problems that result from the difference between sounds and their orthographic representations. But there are some cases in which spelling is consistently used to represent a pronunciation difference, and in these cases writers who know certain spelling rules can be guided by pronunciation when they spell. For example, although the double spelling of consonants signifies a single consonant sound (there being no long consonants in English—see chapter 5, section 2.2), the double consonant does serve the purpose of indicating pronunciation. Specifically, double consonants provide the cue that the immediately preceding vowel has a short sound, as is the case in the words *specifically* and *immediately* in this sentence. In the first case, the *a* preceding the *ll* has the schwa sound rather than /e/; in the second, the initial *i* is pronounced /I/ rather than /i/. This pronunciation-imitating print-code convention becomes especially helpful when we wish to represent two words that differ only in the vowel pronunciation, such as *later* and *latter*. The double consonant in *latter* is pronounced no differently from the single *t* in *later*; it serves only to signal that this word is pronounced with the /æ/ sound rather than with the /e/ sound of *later*. As suggested above, familiarity with this convention can prevent some spelling errors, but writers who do not know this rule often commit errors, particularly when the derivation or inflection of the word changes (see chapter 6, section 4). For example, ignorance of the relationship between vowel sound and the double consonant leads many writers to misspell *writing* as *writting*. This error may be explained by the faulty application of the convention to double the final consonant before adding a suffix that begins with a vowel, a convention that works when the vowel sound does change, as it does in the case of *write:written,* but that does not apply when the initial vowel sound does not change. The word *dine* offers a similar example: the *n* is not doubled if the vowel sound remains /ay/, as in *dining* or *diner,* but if the pronunciation changes, as it does with the derivation *dinner,* the consonant doubles to indicate that change. These examples suggest a hierarchy of conventions for doubling consonants:

(8) (i) Double consonants indicate that the preceding vowel has a short sound.
(ii) Therefore, in cases of doubt (as in *later* and *latter*), pronunciation offers a legitimate guide to spelling.
(iii) The pronunciation convention (i) has precedence over the convention of doubling the final consonant before adding a suffix beginning with a vowel (*write:writing:written*).

This hierarchy suggests not only the limits of the convention that guides the doubling of consonants before certain suffixes, but also reminds us that few print-code conventions are without exceptions since a convention tends to be more logical and regular than the language. Further, the spelling errors that occur as a result of the failure to apply convention (8.iii) demonstrate a point made earlier (in the context of diction errors—see chapter 1, section 1), that most errors are the result of imperfect knowledge of the print code. In other words, errors occur when knowledge of the print code does not equal language competence (see chapter 2, section 1.1, where the same point is made about sentence-boundary errors). It seems likely, for example, that certain kinds of misspellings do not occur simply because native speakers of a language are aware of the distribution limits of various sounds. The distribution of /s/ in English (see (14.ii–iv) and (15.i–iii) in chapter 5) rules out an English word *s*. Native speakers know that consonants do not occur in the initial-final position and thus do not attempt to spell words containing only a consonant. Similarly, except when they are deliberately trying to create an odd or onomatopoeic word, writers do not attempt such spellings as **wprd*. Misspellings occur only when writers try to spell an unfamiliar word and neither pronunciation nor their knowledge of the print-code offers them sufficient guidance. There is no English word pronounced **wprd,* so there would be no reason for a writer to try to approximate that pronunciation in print. Even misspellings are guided by pronunciation, even though most native speakers are aware that spelling often deviates from pronunciation. Furthermore, no misspellings occur where pronunciation provides an accurate guide to spelling and there are no options in the way a sound is pronounced. No native speaker, for example, is likely to misspell words like *rat, that,* or *dad,* in part because the words are simple and common and the speaker has probably memorized their spelling, but also because the pronunciation of each word is an accurate guide to the spelling. Such words, in fact, are among the first ones young children learn to spell and read if they are taught to read phonetically.

As we have suggested in the discussion of double consonants, sometimes the spelling of a word does provide cues to (or is an attempt to represent) its pronunciation. Spelling also enables writers to indicate differences among identically pronounced but semantically different words. This is the case of homophones such as *two, to,* and *too; there, their,* and *they're;* and so on. In this case, different spellings indicate different lexical morphs. Spelling can also indicate grammatical morphemes. For example, (14) in chapter 6, reproduced here as (9), represents the four forms of the same word, *boy*.

(9) boy boys

boy's boys'

In speech, context and syntax combine to allow listeners to distinguish among the three identically pronounced forms in (9) and to determine whether plural, singular possessive, or plural possessive is being used. In writing, context and syntax might allow readers to distinguish between plural and possessive. For example, in (10.i), the noun *hats* indicates syntactically that the possessive is being used. The absence of a second noun following *boys* in (10.ii) indicates that the plural noun is intended by the writer. However, the apostrophe is necessary in (10.i) if readers are to be absolutely certain whether the writer means singular possessive or plural possessive. Here, spelling is used to emphasize differences in meaning.

(10) (i) The boys' hats are on the shelf.
(ii) The boys were in the kitchen.

Obviously, the similarity of the plural and possessive forms of many nouns is a source of confusion and error for many writers. The situation is made more complex by the fact that the same set of allomorphs that characterizes the morphemes Pl and Poss, {/-s/ /-z/ /-əz/}, also characterizes the morpheme PresThirSg—the third-person singular form of the present tense of many verbs (see (9)–(11) in Chapter 6). Subject-verb agreement in English depends on the use of singular verbs with singular nouns and plural verbs with plural nouns. For language learners, the fact that the plural of nouns and the singular of most third-person present-tense verbs are represented identically is a frequent source of error. Children and nonnative speakers often use the singular form of the verb with a plural noun, speaking or writing sentences like *The boys runs as fast as they can*. This error, also a feature of some dialects such as Black American English, can be explained as an effort to be consistent by adding the same suffix to the verb as that added to the noun in order to indicate plurals. In other words, efforts to follow the agreement rule of singular with singular and plural with plural can be thwarted if a language user does not recognize that the same allomorph can represent several morphemes. And in the case of subject-verb agreement, efforts to be consistent can, ironically, result in the very error one is trying to avoid.

For most nouns and verbs, plural and singular are indicated by grammatical morphs, and subject-verb agreement can be, as it has been above, explained in terms of confusion over the multiple and opposite grammatical functions of the same allomorph. The other category of agreement error mentioned in chapter 1, section 2.1, pronoun-antecedent agreement, can be explained by the fact that pronouns are lexical morphs that contain within them features of person, number, and, in some cases, gender and case (but see chapter 6, section 3, for a suggestion that pronouns are "borderline"—having qualities of both lexical and grammatical morphs). The features for personal pronouns are charted in (11).

The chart makes clear the complexity of the personal pronoun system in English, especially its inconsistency. For example, most pronouns have two forms of the possessive, but third-person singular masculine does not, nor does the gender-free third-person singular pronoun *its*. Of those pronouns that do have two possessive forms, only the first-person singular has two different lexical allomorphs (*my:mine*) to represent the two forms of the morpheme; the others (*your:yours; her:hers; our:ours;* and *their:theirs*) differentiate the two forms by seemingly—but not in fact—adding a grammatical morph.

According to (11), and as (12.i–ii) illustrate, the first of these possessive forms is used when the word identifying the possessed object or quality

(11) Features of Personal Pronouns

Pronoun	Person	Number	Gender	Case	Followed by noun
I	first	sg	x[a]	nom.	no
me	first	sg	x	obj.	no
my	first	sg	x	poss.	yes
mine	first	sg	x	poss.	no
you	second	sg or pl	x	nom. & obj.	no
your	second	sg or pl	x	poss.	yes
yours	second	sg or pl	x	poss.	no
he	third	sg	m	nom.	no
him	third	sg	m	obj.	no
his	third	sg	m	poss.	yes
she	third	sg	f	nom.	no
her	third	sg	f	obj.	no
her	third	sg	f	poss.	yes
hers	third	sg	f	poss.	no
it	third	sg	x	nom. & obj.	no
its	third	sg	x	poss.	yes
we	first	pl	x	nom.	no
us	first	pl	x	obj.	no
our	first	pl	x	poss.	yes
ours	first	pl	x	poss.	no
they	third	pl	x	nom.	no
them	third	pl	x	obj.	no
their	third	pl	x	poss.	yes
theirs	third	pl	x	poss.	no

[a]The "x" in the gender column indicates that the pronoun can be used without regard to gender, or, in the case of *it* and *its*, to refer to genderless nouns.

immediately follows the possessive pronoun; the second form is used in other situations.

(12) (i) Her hat is on the shelf.
(ii) The hat on the shelf is hers.

It is worth noting that (12.i–ii) are semantically identical but their syntactic structure differs because the syntactical rules governing the use of each form of the possessive pronoun differ.

When the gender, number, and person of the antecedent are obvious, as in (13.i), pronoun-antecedent agreement errors are infrequent. But if the gender and number are not immediately discernible or if, as in the case of indefinite pronouns, the number is not always obvious to native speakers (13.ii–iii), errors occur.

(13) (i) A man who wishes to succeed should realize that he will have to work hard.

(ii) *A person who wishes to succeed should realize that they will have to work hard.
(iii) *Everybody who wishes to succeed should realize that they will have to work hard.

(13.iii) is a fairly common error, and one which is understandable given the misleadingly apparent collective—and thus plural—nature of the word *everybody*. To avoid or correct it, one must be aware not only that pronouns must agree with their antecedents, but also that the word *everybody*, comprised by two lexical morphs which are each singular, is itself singular and can be paraphrased as 'each individual person,' but not as 'all of the people.' Such an error emphasizes the complexity of the morphological, syntactic, and semantic relationships underlying correct usage. (13.ii) is somewhat less common because, while used equally impersonally and collectively, a *person* has a much more clearly expressed number.

SECTION 3. SENTENCE ERRORS

It is important to note that in the following discussion of sentence errors, our focus remains, as it has in the previous section of this chapter and throughout the book, on errors as phenomena perceived as incorrect by native speakers. That is, linguistics as a discipline is not responsible for labeling a particular usage or syntactic structure as an error; instead, linguistics provides rules that match and thus formalize native speakers' ability to distinguish between correct and incorrect language use and the resulting judgment they make about the appropriateness of a particular usage. As explained in chapter 7, section 4, Chomsky referred to the kind of syntactic correctness we are interested in as grammaticality. Because linguistics does not attempt to judge what is correct versus what is incorrect, but only to provide descriptive rules for generating correct sentences, we cannot expect it to "solve" errors in any way. And as we will discuss later, linguistics, or specifically transformational grammar, is no more successful as a tool for teaching error-avoidance than any previous grammars have been. Part of the reason for this has been suggested in chapter 9: Linguistics is concerned with **casual** language, with idiolects and dialects, whereas composition studies and pedagogy are interested in **noncasual** langusge—**SAE** or, in Hirsch's (1977) terms, the **grapholect.** The latter, as we have previously noted (see chapter 1, section 3.3, and chapter 9, section 1), is in a sense a foreign dialect for all native speakers, some of whom speak dialects that resemble it more closely than do others, but none of whom speak a dialect that duplicates it exactly. While transformational grammar may not be an effective method for teaching error-avoidance, it is, as the analyses which follow demonstrate, useful to the teacher of composition because it provides insights into the aspect of linguistic structure and the linguistic rule involved in the error.

The linguistic analysis of sentence errors begins with the categorial rules of Chomsky's standard grammar listed in (25.i–v) in chapter 7, and repeated here:

(14) (i) S → NP⁀VP
(ii) VP → Aux⁀V⁀NP
(iii) NP → (Det)N
(iv) Det → {*the*}
(v) Aux → M

(14.i) identifies fundamental parts of most English sentences, and (14.ii–v) describe their constituents. Groups of words that violate these (descriptive, not prescriptive) rules are not sentences. Thus, fragments such as those cited in chapter 2, section 1.1—repeated below as (15.i–iii)—occur when the minimum requirements of (14.i) are not met.

(15) (i) Starts every time
(ii) Exhausted by his efforts
(iii) A low, steady, mechanical hum

Specifically, (15.i) is simply a VP without the necessary NP; (15.ii) contains a V, but contains neither the Aux necessary for it to function with a following PP nor the preceding NP itself; (15.iii) is an NP which, without either a subsequent VP or a preceding NP and V, is incomplete. Possible corrections for each fragment are suggested in (16.i–iv).

(16) (i) The car starts every time.
(ii) He was exhausted by his efforts.
(iii) A low, steady, mechanical hum could be heard in the room.
(iv) She heard a low, steady, mechanical hum.

Other fragments can be explained as a writer's failure to recognize the requirements of embedding sentences within one another. Relative clause transformations, for example, allow one clause to be embedded into another, as in (17.i), which is composed of (17.ii) and (17.iii).

(17) (i) He bought the car which he looked at yesterday.
(ii) He bought the car.
(iii) He looked at the car yesterday.

The effect of the relative clause transformation is to allow the repeated coreferential element (*the car*) in the second sentence to be replaced by the relative pronoun (*which,* in this case), but the transformation also requires that the second clause be joined to the first. Writers who punctuate (17.i) as

(18) may have failed to recognize this requirement of the transformation. However, as was suggested in both chapter 1, section 3.1, and chapter 10, writers who have failed to learn a print-code convention for punctuation may also make this error. Teachers must be aware of both potential sources of this and other errors which may have print-code as well as linguistic explanations. Students who recognize that isolated relative clauses are fragments but who still produce the error in (18) need instruction and practice in punctuation; students who fail to recognize that such clauses are fragments need to be taught how clauses can be combined and embedded within one another and to practice such embeddings (see chapter 12, section 1).

(18) He bought the car. Which he looked at yesterday.

Again, it is worth noting that the failure to recognize a requirement of a formal rule is simply a linguistic analysis of this error. (18) is incorrect not because linguistics has a rule that says it is, but because most native speakers continue to agree that it is incorrect. And as we have noted in chapters 9–10, matters of correctness and incorrectness are subject to change over time, on the basis of whether native speakers recognize a particular structure or usage as correct or not.

A writer's unfamiliarity with embedding transformations may lead to other kinds of sentence errors, such as the consolidation errors mentioned in chapter 2, section 1.2. (19.i), for example, occurs when a writer deletes not only the common subject of (19.ii–iii) before combining them, but also the unshared verbs.

(19) (i) He paid for the car in cash and a better deal.
(ii) He paid for the car in cash.
(iii) He got a better deal.

Sentence-combining exercises (see chapter 12, section 1) provide students with practice in embedding transformations, thus enabling them to add to their competence in SAE.

CHAPTER 12

Style

Although style per se is not a linguistic phenomenon (see chapter 10, section 2.3), linguistics has proved a valuable source of concepts which have been applied to specific problems of syntactic variation (including emphasis), clarity, and conciseness, all of which are frequently categorized as stylistic matters.

SECTION 1. SYNTACTIC VARIATION

Because transformational grammar so successfully describes syntactic relationships, allowing for the kind of analysis of sentence boundary errors presented in the previous chapter, some composition researchers also believed that it might prove to be a useful tool for teaching students to avoid errors and to write more effective sentences. In one regard, this belief seems naive, since research has consistently demonstrated that formal grammar instruction has neither effect (for a summary of numerous studies, see Braddock, et al. 1963; Meckel 1963; and Mellon 1969). Nevertheless, Chomsky's theories provided the impetus for new research into the relationship between instruction in grammar and the teaching of writing, research which if nothing else confirms that English teachers have blind faith that grammar of one kind or another will eventually play an important role in composition instruction.

One such study, that of Bateman and Zidonis (1964), reported that students instructed in transformational grammar did reduce the number of errors in their writing and, in addition, wrote sentences that contained a larger number of transformations than did students who did not receive such instruction. The apparently positive results of the Bateman and Zidonis study stimulated other research designed to identify more accurately the specific causes for the improvement Bateman and Zidonis reported. In particular, Mellon (1969) and O'Hare (1973) questioned the extent to which the growth reported by Bateman and Zidonis could be attributed to formal instruction in transformational grammar versus the extent to which such growth should be attributed to actual practice in applying transformations.

The distinction between formal instruction and practice has ties to

Chomsky's distinction between competence and performance, discussed previously. Following Chomsky, Hunt (1965) and subsequently Mellon and O'Hare argued that students possess the competence, that is, the intuitive linguistic knowledge, that allows them to recognize as grammatical and in most cases to use most of the transformations that Bateman and Zidonis claimed to have taught. According to Hunt, what distinguished the syntax of mature writers from that of younger writers was that the former used a greater number of sentence-embedding transformations, not that mature writers have a significantly larger repertoire of transformations to call on. The efforts of Mellon, O'Hare, and others whose research followed theirs has thus been focused on developing pedagogical strategies for providing students with practice in embedding sentences in order to increase their linguistic performance. Mellon's research included instruction in transformational grammar with embedding exercises while O'Hare, interested in demonstrating the competence of his subjects, eliminated grammar instruction and developed cued, or signaled, embedding exercises, as represented in (1), designed to elicit specific transformations.

(1) (i) The quarterback threw the ball well. (NEG)
(ii) The quarterback didn't throw the ball well.
(iii) Someone has been copying my homework. (WHO-QUES)
(iv) Who has been copying my homework?
(v) Peter noticed SOMETHING.
(vi) There were nine golf balls in the river. (THAT)
(vii) Peter noticed that there were nine golf balls in the river.

The parenthetical cues in (1.i, iii, and vi) are modeled on the negative, interrogative, and noun phrase embedding transformations identified in transformational grammar. (NEG) cues the student to transform the original sentence from affirmative to negative (1.ii); (WHO-QUES) is a cue to change the sentence from declarative to interrogative. The capitalized word SOMETHING in (1.v) indicates an open nominal position, that is, the location at which a word, phrase, or clause is to be embedded, and (THAT) provides the student with the word to be used for the embedding.

Subsequent research has demonstrated that students can successfully complete uncued exercises, particularly if they are not expected to produce a specific target sentence structure. Indeed, O'Hare's use of transformational cues such as (NEG) and (QUES) is of little practical value since there is no evidence that writers consciously think of negative or interrogative sentences as being transformations of affirmative or declarative sentences. Writers simply do not need practice transforming affirmative sentences to negative or declarative to interrogative since the ability to form all four types as the communicative situation demands is part of all native speakers' competence. Embedding cues are more useful if the goal of the exercise is for students to practice a specific sentence type.

The embedding exercises—commonly called sentence-combining exercises—developed by Mellon, O'Hare, and others are based on a simplified notion of the relationship between deep structure and surface structure. As was explained earlier (chapter 7, section 3.2), Chomsky used the term **deep structure** to refer to the underlying pretransformational structure which exists as an abstract concept in the mind of the language user. The deep structure can be represented by simple sentences called **kernel sentences** in the early version of transformational grammar. **Surface structure** refers to the actual sentence that is spoken or written after the transformations have taken place. The deep-structure/surface-structure relationship is represented in (2.i–iii).

(2) (i) An idea is valuable.
(ii) An idea is new.
(iii) A new idea is valuable.

(2.iii) represents the surface structure product of the transformation that embeds (2.ii) into (2.i), a simple embedding of the nonrepetitious information in (2.ii) into (2.i).

Taken alone, (2) is a simple uncued sentence-combining exercise. Without any formal grammatical instruction, native speakers, even young children, can be asked to combine the ideas in (2.i–ii) into one sentence that is not as choppy or as repetitious as the original, and will come up with (2.iii). Their ability to do so is an indication that the competence for embedding sentences is intuitive for native speakers.

Transformational grammar provides descriptions for a number of sentence-embedding transformations, all of which can be incorporated into sentence-combining exercises. Whereas (2) illustrates the embedding of a single adjective into another sentence, (3) demonstrates that an entire sentence can be embedded into another.

(3) (i) The fact angered me.
(ii) John was late.
(iii) The fact that John was late angered me.

The rewriting rule that describes this embedding is **NP → (DET) + N + S.** A similar rule, **NP → NP + S,** accounts for relative clause embeddings:

(4) (i) The boy was John.
(ii) I saw a boy.
(iii) The boy whom I saw was John.

The difference between (3.iii) and (4.iii) lies in the fact that in (3.iii) the complete sentence (3.ii) is embedded, whereas in (4.iii) the relative pronoun *whom* replaces the noun phrase *a boy* from (4.ii).

Both (3) and (4) illustrate embedding into the NP, but sentences can also be embedded into the VP, as (5) illustrates.

(5) (i) The children refuse.
(ii) The children eat.
(iii) The children refuse to eat.

This embedding is described by the rewriting rule **VP → V + S.** The recursive nature of the rewriting rules accounts for these embeddings as well as much more elaborate ones of the "This is the house that Jack built" type, as in (6).

(6) Jim said that Mary told him that her father was angry that she had been late.

Such sentences are grammatical, but they do not appear frequently because they are hard to understand.

Sentence-combining exercises can be written to allow students to practice a variety of syntactic structures that might not be part of their ordinary repertoire but that are, nevertheless, part of their competence. For example, (7) illustrates an exercise which results in the use of participle phrases.

(7) (i) He stumbled down the stairs.
(ii) He gasped for air.
(iii) He was horrified by the sight.
(iv) Gasping for air, he stumbled down the stairs, horrified by the sight.

Similar exercises have been devised for appositives, absolutes, prepositional phrases, and other syntactic structures.

Sentence combining is valuable as a means for encouraging stylistic variation for several reasons. First, sentence combining provides students with practice in a variety of syntactic patterns that, though part of their competence, they might not otherwise attempt to use. Such practice opens their eyes to ways of expressing themselves that they might not otherwise have considered. Second, sentence-combining exercises emphasize the syntactic choices available to writers. Students who practice sentence combining quickly realize that there are numerous ways to convey the same idea. For most students, this is a revelation: They assume that the first linguistic structures—words, phrases, sentences—they use to express themselves are the only structures available and thus have a difficult time discovering how they might revise sentences or restate ideas differently. A four-sentence exercise such as (8) can quickly demonstrate the flexibility of English syntax, as students discover for themselves the large number of ways these sentences can be combined (9).

(8) (i) The cheese melts.
(ii) The cheese is creamy.
(iii) The cheese is stringy.
(iv) The cheese is on top of the pizza.

(9) (i) The creamy, stringy cheese melts on top of the pizza.
(ii) The melting cheese on top of the pizza is stringy and creamy.
(iii) The cheese which is on top of the pizza is stringy and creamy.
(iv) As it melts on top of the pizza, the cheese becomes stringy and creamy.
(v) Melting cheese on top of the pizza is creamy and stringy.
(vi) When the cheese melts on top of the pizza, it becomes creamy and stringy.

Of course, (9) does not exhaust the number of possible combinations of the sentences in (8). Nor would one necessarily argue that all of the sentences in (9) have exactly the same meaning. In fact, one benefit of sentence-combining exercises is that they provide a context for discussing the effectiveness of various combinations. Similarly, the options for combining encourage discussion of how meaning and emphasis may vary depending on how one chooses to structure sentences (see Weiser 1979). (10) illustrates how sentence combining can demonstrate why writers should be conscious of which clauses they embed and which they embed others into.

(10) (i) The old train station was once the hub of the city.
(ii) The old train station is now the dilapidated refuge of rats.
(iii) The old train station, which was once the hub of the city, is now the dilapidated refuge of rats.
(iv) The old train station, which is now the dilapidated refuge of rats, was once the hub of the city.

(10.iii–iv) show that writers can choose to emphasize one idea by leaving it in the main clause while embedding a less important one as a relative clause. This is a fairly simple point, and one which is made in many traditional discussions of style. Sentence-combining exercises such as (10.i–ii) force students to be conscious of the effects of their decisions about embedding since the exercise allows them correctly to arrive at either solution, (10.iii) or (10.iv). In fact, while the previously cited research indicates that sentence-combining practice may help students reduce errors, especially those resulting from improper embedding (see chapter 2, section 1.2, for examples), the main value of such exercises goes beyond simple correctness: Because the exercises provide students with experience in manipulating sentence structure, they increase students' awareness of the syntactic options available to them and allow them to make stylistic and rhetorical decisions based on their familiarity with a variety of syntactic structures.

SECTION 2. SYNTACTIC CLARITY

Linguistics cannot identify a sentence as clear or unclear, or as concise or wordy. These are matters of judgment, concerned with effectiveness, not with grammaticality, meaningfulness, or even appropriateness. But linguistics can enable us to understand the syntactic and semantic bases on which such judgments are made, as (19) in chapter 11 illustrates. For example, it is commonly assumed that passive sentences are less effective than active sentences. Linguistics cannot in any way prove this assumption to be true or false because effectiveness is not a linguistic entity, but transformational grammar does provide an explanation for the native speaker's sense that active and passive versions of the same sentence, as in (11) (cf. (15.i–ii) in chapter 7), mean roughly the same in most cases.

(11) (i) The boy kissed the girl.
(ii) The girl was kissed by the boy.

The explanation is contained in the simplified passive transformation ((18.i) in chapter 7), reidentified here as (12).

(12) $NP_1 + V + NP_2 \Rightarrow NP_2 + be^* + V^* + by + NP_1$

(12) indicates that (11.i–ii)—and for that matter the active and passive versions of any sentence—are different representations of the same idea. In terms of transformational grammar, (11.i–ii) have almost the same deep structure—the only difference being the presence or absence of a formal element triggering the passive transformation, but different surface structures.

Similar transformations also underlie the syntactic manipulations, mentioned in chapter 2, section 3.3, for creating emphasis by moving actors away from the subject position of a sentence. The **cleft sentence transformation** describes the difference between (13.i) and (13.ii).

(13) (i) This country needs a good ten-cent cigar.
(ii) What this country needs is a good ten-cent cigar.

There are also transformational rules for the **it inversion,** which describes the differences in the sentences in (14).

(14) (i) Bill met Tom at the airport yesterday.
(ii) It was *Bill* who met Tom at the airport yesterday.
(iii) It was *Tom* whom Bill met at the airport yesterday.
(iv) It was *yesterday* that Bill met Tom at the airport.
(v) It was *at the airport* that Bill met Tom yesterday.

In (14.ii–v), whole-sentence emphasis is shifted away from the subject and verb by the use of *It was* and a relative clause-embedding transformation. However, specific elements within each sentence are emphasized by being placed immediately after the verb, as the italics in (14.ii–v) suggest.

While transformations such as those described above can enable a writer to be more clear or to shift emphasis from one part of a sentence to another, they can also lead to ambiguity, as (15) illustrates.

(15) (i) The dog barked loudly.
(ii) The barking of the dog was loud.
(iii) The hunters shot terribly.
(vi) The shooting of the hunters was terrible.
(v) Somebody shot the hunters and that was terrible.

The NP that serves as the subject of (15.ii) is a nominalized and embedded version of *The dog barked,* derived from (15.i). (15.iii) has a structure identical to (15.i), but if the same nominalization and embedding occur, the resulting sentence (15.iv) is ambiguous: It could mean the same as (15.iii), but, because the verb *shoot* is transitive, it could also mean the same as (15.v). As was pointed out in chapter 8, section 4.1, (15.iv) can be disambiguated only by the context in which it is used.

As we suggested in chapter 7, section 3.2, the number of standard transformations that have been identified surpasses 300, and it is certainly beyond our intention here to demonstrate how each describes specific syntactic manipulations. The point is simply that transformations do describe and thus allow for the analysis of a variety of syntactic structures. An understanding of the concept of transformations may therefore be valuable for the writing teacher trying to analyze students' syntactic problems or to develop pedagogical techniques for teaching students to revise syntax.

SECTION 3. CONCISENESS

We expect each word in a sentence to contribute to the interpretability of the sentence by providing the listener/reader with specific information about the speaker/writer's message. As we have already suggested in our discussion of redundancy (chapter 1, section 1.1, and chapter 11, section 1), it is possible for words to duplicate semantic information and thus interfere with interpretation. Such duplication of semantic information is also the source of the wordiness of the phrases in (16).

(16) (i) each and every
(ii) due to the fact that
(iii) concerning the matter of

In (16.i) the duplication is based on the synonymy of *each* and *every;* indeed, the dictionary definition of *every* begins with *each.* And in most cases, the two words can be used interchangeably. Their difference, however, can be illustrated by the **diagnostic construction** (see chapter 8, section 2.2) in (17).

(17) each other : every other

Here, both phrases are meaningful, but their meaning is not synonymous. The phrase *each other* is an idiom meaning *one to another,* as in (18).

(18) They gave presents to each other.

Every can not be substituted for *each* in (18). The phrase *every other* has a different idiomatic meaning; in fact, it has two possible meanings, as illustrated in (19), both different from the meaning of *each other*.

(19) (i) They gave presents to every other person.
(ii) They gave presents to everyone else there, but not to some unnamed person or people to whom they did not give presents.
(iii) They gave presents to each alternate person, so that half of the people received presents and half did not.

(19.i) is ambiguous in ways suggested by (19.ii–iii) and in a way that (18) is not. Further, both (19.ii–iii) exclude the possibility of a mutual exchange of presents, which is exactly what (18) means. The fact that (20.i–ii) are ungrammatical, while (18) and (20.iii) are not, suggests another way that *each* and *every* are nonsynonymous: *each* can be used to modify another adjective whereas *every* must modify, at least indirectly, a noun or pronoun.

(20) (i) *They gave presents to every other.
(ii) *There were many gifts, every different from the other.
(iii) There were many gifts, each different from the other.

Thus far, we have illustrated that *each* and *every* are not totally synonymous (few words are), but the fact that to do so we had to rely on idioms is evidence of their similarity. In their unidiomatic usage, they mean essentially the same thing, and thus a phrase like (16.i) is redundant. It can be used legitimately to create emphasis (21.i), but it is often used in ordinary discourse in which emphasis is unnecessary (21.ii).

(21) (i) Each and every citizen has the obligation to vote in the upcoming election.
(ii) Each and every puppy in the box is for sale.

Whereas (21.i) might be appropriate in the context of a patriotic message, (21.ii), because the selling of puppies rarely demands the emphasis *each and every* provides, seems like deliberate exaggeration at best, a kind of huckster's sales pitch.

In the cases of (16.ii–iii), the wordiness comes not from duplication of semantic information within the phrases, but from the fact that the same semantic information can be expressed more concisely, in a single word. As was pointed out in chapter 2, section 3.2, *because* or *since* can substitute for *due to the fact that,* and *about* can substitute for *concerning the matter of*. The explanations for such substitutions are complex and illustrate why overgeneralizing or misunderstanding them can lead to error. (22) serves as the basis for the explanation that follows.

(22) (i) Due to the fact that he was late, he missed the bus.
(ii) Because of the fact that he was late, he missed the bus.

(iii) Because he was late, he missed the bus.
(iv) *Due he was late, he missed the bus.

(22.i–ii) demonstrate that *due to* and *because of* are, in this use, synonymous, sharing both function, as conjunctions, and meaning—they indicate a causal relationship. (22.iii), a correct, concise paraphrase of both (22.i) and (22.ii), seems to indicate that *of the fact that* is a syntactic unit that can be deleted without affecting the meaning of the sentence. A faulty extension of that logic could lead to the production of (22.iv), an ungrammatical sentence. *Due to* functions idiomatically as a semantic unit, similar in meaning to *because of,* but *due* alone does not share meaning with *because*. (22.iii) is a paraphrase of (22.ii) because *because* is synonymous with *because of the fact that* and contains within its meaning the same feature contained by the relative pronoun *that*. An intuitive test is our recognition of (23) as ungrammatical.

(23) *Because that he was late, he missed the bus.

The wordiness that occurs when modifiers with functional but imprecise meanings are used can also be explained by reference to semantics. In (24.i–ii), the italicized modifiers are intended to intensify and emphasize the meaning of the words they precede, but the degree to which they intensify and emphasize meaning is not precise.

(24) (i) I read a very good book.
(ii) I read a really good book.

The potential for wordiness in these cases lies not so much in the modifiers themselves, although the information they convey about the book is ambiguous. Instead, these modifiers have lost their emphatic force through overuse.

The concept of inference can be useful in explaining wordiness that is the result of a sentence or, as we shall discuss in more detail in the following chapter, a discourse containing more information than is necessary or information the reader may be assumed to know. Williams's (1985) sentence (chapter 2, section 3.2, reproduced here in (25)) illustrates such overdetailization.

(25) Imagine a mental picture of someone engaged in the intellectual activity of trying to learn what the rules are for how to play the game of chess.

Inference, as was explained in chapter 8, section 5.2.5, refers to whatever the reader/hearer can derive from the writer/speaker's utterance and the context of that utterance. Native speakers would be able to infer that a person who is imagining is creating a mental picture, that trying to learn rules is an intellectual activity, and that chess is a game. Therefore, (25) contains more information than is necessary for the reader/hearer to understand the message; it contains details that can be easily inferred by anyone familiar with the meaning of words like *imagine* and *learn* and *chess*.

Scripts (see chapter 8, section 4.2, and chapter 10, section 3.3) account for the contextual meaning of such inference-carrying words. A partial script for the word *chess* would include not only the information that chess is a game played on a checkered board by two people, each using 16 playing pieces, and having as its goal the checkmating of one player's king by the other, but also such less factual information as chess being a game of complex strategy, requiring skill, practice, and knowledge of the rules on the part of players. In addition, the script would include such notions as chess often being associated with highly intelligent people. Because the scripts of words carry information that readers who know the word can infer, the meaning of sentences such as (25) can be conveyed much more concisely, as in Williams's revised version ((28.ii) in Chapter 2). In other words, scripts account for the fact that words carry connotations which often go far beyond their denotations. When writers are not aware of the scripts, or connotations, of the words they use, they may write sentences that are unnecessarily wordy.

In a sentence like (25), the excessive use of details is fairly obvious because it is possible to see that phrases are used that mean essentially the same thing as single words that also appear in the sentence. Thus this kind of overcompleteness, as van Dijk (1977) calls it, is based on redundancy. Because it is based on the repetition of semantic features within the words of the discourse, it is fairly easy to recognize and to teach students to eliminate as they revise their writing. But overcompleteness is not always so readily identifiable since what a reader is capable of inferring from a sentence depends on the reader's knowledge of the actual words used, the context in which they are used, and the context of the discourse—not simply on the script or definition of the words—and writers cannot always predict what their readers will know. Thus while most of what we have identified as unnecessary in (25) could be inferred by nearly any reader familiar with the words *imagine, learn,* and *chess,* such is not the case with sentences like (26).

(26) The concepts of linguistic competence, or the native speaker's intuitive, internalized knowledge of his or her language, and linguistic performance, the speech or discourse produced by a speaker, have important implications for the researcher interested in error analysis.

It is not possible to assume that the definitions of competence and performance in (26) would be inferred by all readers, but it is certainly possible that for many readers that information could be inferred. Readers familiar with linguistic theory and terminology would find the definition-containing appositives unnecessary and might judge (26) to be wordy, while readers who do not know what competence and performance mean in the context of linguistic discourse would find the definitions essential, despite the fact that the scripts for those words would contain information about their linguistic meanings. Writers can make decisions about the amount of information to include in a sentence only to the extent they can accurately determine who their readers will be and how much they will know about the subject of the discourse. Thus the assessment of (26) as overcomplete or effective is rhetorical, not linguistic.

Thus far, the kinds of wordiness discussed in this section have been semantic, but wordiness can also be attributed to similarities that are essentially syntactic. In (11.i–ii) and (12), we illustrated the deep-structure similarity between passive and active sentences that convey essentially the same meaning. As chapter 2, section 3.2 points out, passive versions of sentences are longer than the active versions. In the case of (11.i–ii), the passive version is seven words long, while the active version is only five; that is, the passive is 40% longer than the active. Over the course of a long text, consistent use of the passive voice can add substantial length without usually adding substantial meaning.

The same is true of the use of nominalizations. (27.i–ii) present nominalized and verbal sentences which are essentially the same in terms of deep structure and which are semantically the same—they share the same semantic features. But the nominalized version is 75% longer than the version in which the action is conveyed by the verb *investigated.*

(27) (i) We made an investigation of the complaint.
(ii) We investigated the complaint.

For reasons that are often rhetorical or stylistic (one sound linguistic reason may be the appropriate **empathy** (see Kuno 1975, especially Kuno and Kaburaki 1975, and Reinhart 1975), writers may deliberately choose to use passive voice or nominalizations. That they may do so without changing meaning significantly can be explained linguistically since passives and nominalizations are surface-structure expressions of meanings that can be expressed by a number of different syntactic structures.

CHAPTER 13

Linguistic Applications to Discourse

SECTION 1. LINGUISTICS BEYOND THE SENTENCE

Rhetoricians since Aristotle have concerned themselves with how language is used in actual communications, either written or spoken, and thus have been interested not simply in individual sounds, words, or sentences, but instead in whole discourses. Writing teachers have distinguished their task from that of grammar teachers by identifying their goal as helping students learn to apply rhetorical principles to written communication. They do not limit their instruction to teaching vocabulary, grammatical and mechanical conventions, syntax, or style, but instead include these topics in their broader instruction of how writers create effective discourses—paragraphs, essays, reports, and so on.

Linguistics has until recently (see chapter 4) limited itself to sounds, words, sentences, and much more recently meaning as conveyed by words and sentences. But as we have pointed out (chapter 8, section 3–4), semanticists had argued that accounting for the meaning of a sentence in any context was an unattainable upper bound of semantic theory. Katz and Fodor (1963) made the **sentence in isolation** the object of semantic theory, and for some linguists the sentence remains the largest language element that linguistics can say anything about.

The problem with such a view is that it is contrary to the overall goal of linguistics identified by Chomsky in the 1960s and accepted by linguists for the past two decades: that the goal of a linguistic theory is to model the native speaker's intuitive knowledge of language. Native speakers' intuitive knowledge of language is obviously not limited to their ability to interpret sentences in isolation; indeed, sentences in isolation may be more difficult to interpret than sentences in context since isolated sentences may be ambiguous in ways they are not in a specific context, as (35) in chapter 8 illustrates. But while it is clear that native speakers do possess linguistic competence that goes beyond the sentence in isolation, it is less clear to what extent linguistics can presently account for or model that competence. The interpretation and analysis of whole discourses incorporates both linguistic and encyclopedic knowledge, and linguists have not yet agreed on where to place the boundary between the two. Thus, while the goal of a linguistic theory of discourse is clear—to model the native speaker's linguistic knowledge about whole discourses, something we might call "discourse competence"—there is currently no agreement about what **linguistic knowledge of discourse** includes or excludes. Van Dijk (1977:4), for example, suggests that "in a LINGUISTIC THEORY OF DISCOURSE we are only concerned with the general conditions, morpho-syntactic, semantic, and pragmatic, determining the well-formedness, interpretability, and appropriateness, respectively, of any discourse of a particular language." But Green and Morgan (1981:167) suggest that "most of the work of accounting for discourse comprehension is to be done not by a linguistic theory of discourse, but by a general theory of common-sense inference, plus certain kinds of language-related knowledge distinct from linguistic competence as presently conceived," and they are specifically critical of van Dijk's "attempt to construct 'linguistic' theories of discourse" (171). In part, this disagreement can be explained by a point made earlier (see chapter 8, section 5), that those who perceive of semantics as noncontextual view pragmatics as a separate discipline from linguistics. Clearly, van Dijk's definition of a linguistic theory of discourse explicitly includes pragmatics as a legitimate part of linguistics. Green and Morgan, on the other hand, suggest that there are "kinds of language-related knowledge distinct from linguistic competence," kinds of knowledge they would classify as pragmatic. Often, the distinction drawn is between knowledge of language—of phonology, morphology, syntax, and semantics—and knowledge **about the use** of language, the former linguistic and the latter pragmatic. Even here, we find the boundaries unclear: Is it knowledge of language or about the use of language that enables native speakers to recognize that (1) (previously cited in chapter 3, section 3) is not coherent?

(1) The quarterback threw the ball toward the tight end. Balls are used in many sports. Most balls are spheres, but a football is an ellipsoid. The tight end leaped to catch the ball.

As the incorporation of pragmatic phenomena into semantics in chapter 8 suggests, it is neither our intention nor our hope to resolve here once and for all the debate over the existence or placement of a boundary between semantics and pragmatics or linguistics and pragmatics. The applications of contextual semantics and pragmatics which follow in the next sections of this chapter will be limited as much as possible to phenomena we feel are part of linguistic knowledge rather than encyclopedic knowledge, but we recognize that we will be dealing with notions that are unresolved, still very much the source of hypothesizing, and often interdisciplinary. There are certainly no commonly accepted rules to parallel those in phonology, morphology, and syntax, nor a common methodology for analyzing discourse beyond the isolated sentence. Our approach will be first to discuss cohesion, which seems to us very clearly open to linguistic analysis, and then to turn our attention to coherence, where textual and extratextual boundaries are less clearly defined.

SECTION 2. COHESION

In chapter 3, section, 3, we distinguished cohesion from coherence by pointing out that the former is a textual quality whereas the latter is both textual and contextual (or extratextual). More specifically, cohesion is attained through the use of grammatical and lexical elements that enable readers to perceive semantic relationships within and between sentences. Cohesion contributes to the flow or continuity of a text, to the sense that the ideas expressed in the text are connected to one another, and to the overall unity of the text. It is cohesion that writing teachers seek when they instruct students to link sentences with transitions such as those listed in (10) in chapter 10, but while cohesion is indeed attained through the use of such connectives, there are many other means of making a text cohesive.

2.1. Grammatical Cohesion

Grammatical cohesion is attained through the use of cohesive devices, or **ties,** which link sentences but do not necessarily add new semantic information. Halliday and Hasan (1976) have identified three types of grammatical cohesive ties—reference, substitution, and ellipsis—each of which allows a writer to link ideas within and between sentences.

Reference ties create cohesion by replacing or referring back to previously used words. The most common reference ties—pronouns, comparatives, demonstratives, and definite articles—are illustrated in (2).

(2) (i) The boy loved cars. *He* dreamed about *them* day and night.
 (ii) Unfortunately, he was never satisfied with a car for long. *This* meant he was always in debt.
 (iii) The first car he owned was an old sedan. It was not in good condition, but he said to himself that it was *better* than no car at all.
 (iv) Each car he bought cost more than the last. *The* car he owns now cost over $20,000.
 (v) A car is parked outside. Inside *the* car sit two people.

The italicized words in the second sentence of each pair (2.i–iv) can be interpreted only by referring to the first sentence. In (2.i), the pronouns *he* and *them* refer to *boy* and *car,* respectively. The word *this* in (2.ii) refers to the whole clause preceding it, in effect replacing an understood embedded subject *that he was never satisfied with a car for long* in the second sentence. In these first two examples, the cohesive ties do not add to the information contained in the previous sentence, but instead simply replace specific words or clauses that have already been used. In effect, personal pronouns and demonstratives fill a syntactic slot that could have been filled by what they refer to. Such is not the case in (2.iii–iv), where the cohesive ties also contain semantic information. In (2.iii), the interpretation of the comparative *better* depends on the information contained in the previous sentence, specifically that *he* owned an old car. Comparatives can be interpreted only in relationship to some previously identified object or concept: There must be something to be compared. But the comparative does not simply replace a previously used word; it adds meaning by defining one thing in relationship to another. In (2.iii), *better* tells us that the boy considers owning an old car to be a preferable condition to owning no car at all. Finally, *the* in the second sentence of (2.iv), like all definite articles, precedes a noun that we assume to be interpretable on the basis of already known information, in this case that *he* has bought cars. The definite article indicates that the car identified is among those mentioned in the previous sentence. Definite articles thus convey semantic information that communicates that the noun they precede is one which is specific and identifiable, as (3) demonstrates.

(3) (i) A car is parked outside.
(ii) The car is parked outside.

(3.i) must be interpreted to mean that some car, perhaps and probably unknown to the speaker of the sentence, is parked outside. (3.ii), different only in the use of the definite article, can be interpreted to mean that some specific car, known to the speaker and, in all likelihood to the hearer, is parked outside. The use of the definite article implies a context, textual or contextual. Often, as in (2.iv), a noun preceded by the definite article is one that has been referred to before in the text. And, as (2.v) illustrates, the definite article can serve as a cohesive tie without introducing new semantic information, since the car referred to in the second sentence is identical to the one referred to in the first.

Substitution involves the replacement of one item with another, again with the restriction that no new semantic information is added. Halliday and Hasan explain that "a substitute is a sort of counter which is used in place of the repetition of a particular item" (1976:89). Thus, since the substitute, like a personal pronoun, is used instead of repetition, it must be semantically neutral—that is, it must be able to fill the same grammatical slot in the sentence without adding to or subtracting from the meaning of the item for which it substitutes. In (4.i), *one* substitutes for *car* in the previous sentence.

(4) (i) He decided to buy a new car. His old *one* was too unreliable.
(ii) "I know what kind he will buy. *Do* you?"
(iii) "Do you think he wants an import?" "I think *so*."

Most of the cohesive ties we have discussed thus far involve reference to or the replacement of nouns, but (4.ii–iii) illustrate that cohesion can be attained with verb and clausal substitutes. In (4.ii), *do* substitutes for *know,* or more accurately, for the predicate of the first sentence. In (4.iii), *so* substitutes for the clause *he wants an import.*

Ellipsis is similar to substitution. In fact, Halliday and Hasan refer to ellipsis as "substitution by zero" (1976:142), suggesting, as we shall demonstrate, that ellipsis involves the deletion of a word, phrase, or clause without the replacement of the deleted structure by another. Witte and Faigley, in their discussion of Halliday and Hasan's work, point out that substitution and ellipsis create cohesion by "extend[ing] the textual or semantic domain of one sentence to a subsequent sentence" (1981:190). That is, cohesion occurs because the meaning of the first sentence in a pair in which substitution or ellipsis is used determines the interpretation of the second. As in substitution, there can be nominal, verbal, or clausal ellipsis. We will allow one illustration (5) to serve for all.

(5) Is he really going to buy another car? He owns three now.

The ellipsis is obvious: The word *car,* rather than being repeated (in plural form, as this example would require), is simply deleted. The hearer or reader of these sentences would understand, however, that *three* refers to *cars.*

2.2. Lexical Cohesion

Lexical cohesion differs from grammatical cohesion in several ways. In the first place, lexical cohesion depends on the semantic relationship of one lexical item with another, while grammatical cohesion does not. For example, pronouns such as *it,* comparatives such as *better,* and demonstratives such as *this* serve as cues to readers to look for a referent in the text. Thus, their appearance in a text indicates a cohesive relationship, and if one is not found, as in (6), we judge the text to be flawed.

(6) John bought a new car. It was a two-story colonial.

The pronoun *it* tells readers to expect cohesion between the two sentences in (6). But (6) is not cohesive precisely because there is no lexical cohesion. *It* can only refer to *car* in the preceding sentence, and the syntax of the second sentence in (6) identifies two-story colonial as descriptive of *it.* Since cars do not fit the description *two-story colonial,* that is, since there is no semantic relationship between these lexical items, (6) is not cohesive.

A second difference between lexical and grammatical cohesion is implied in what we have said above: Grammatical cohesion is often created by cohesive ties that are interpreted on the basis of the words to which they refer or which they replace. Lexical cohesion, as we shall see, results from the co-occurrence of semantically similar words that do not independently indicate cohesion. Witte and Faigley point out that "every lexical item is potentially cohesive and . . . nothing in the occurrence of a given lexical item necessarily makes it cohesive" (1981:192). Thus, in (7.i), we would not identify *car* as contributing to the cohesiveness of the text, but in (7.ii), *car* contributes to cohesion because it co-occurs with a similar word, *coupes*.

(7) (i) The car he bought is expensive. He had to take out a large loan.
(ii) The car he bought is expensive. Coupes usually are.

Lexical cohesion, therefore, is the result of the co-occurrence of words, not of the presence of individual lexical items.

Halliday and Hasan distinguish between two types of lexical cohesion, **reiteration** and **collocation.** The former involves the repetition of an item, either exactly, or through the use of synonyms, near synonyms, superordinates, or general words. Collocation refers to the co-occurrence of words that we recognize as sharing lexical and semantic features; that is, words that "go together," such as *night* and *day, school* and *teacher,* and so on. Halliday and Hasan say that such pairs "share the same lexical environment" (1976:286). We will illustrate both types of lexical cohesion in the following pages.

The simplest form of **reiteration** is the exact repetition of a word. In (8), the repetition of the word *car* creates cohesion between the two sentences.

(8) John's **car** gets twenty-two miles per gallon. That's almost as much as my **car** gets.

(8) illustrates another feature of reiteration, one that helps distinguish it from reference, and which Halliday and Hasan explain as follows: "It is not necessary for two lexical occurrences to have the same referent . . . in order for them to be cohesive" (1976:282). Thus, while a pronoun such as *it* refers to the identical item it replaces, *car* in the second sentence of (8) does not mean the same car referred to in the first sentence. It is simply the co-occurrence of the words that brings about cohesion.

Synonyms and near synonyms create cohesion in the same way exact repetition does. In (9.i), *automobile* and *car* are cohesive.

(9) (i) The *automobile* has had a profound impact on our society. The *car* has changed the way we live, work, and play.

(ii) *Cars* enable us to go where we want when we want. These *vehicles* have added to our personal freedom.

(iii) But the freedom *cars* have brought has not been without its costs. Many people resent the way the *things* have polluted our air and destroyed our quiet.

(9.ii) illustrates the cohesive effects of hyponyms, terms that include the word they refer to, such as *vehicle* for *car*. In (9.iii), the universal hyponym *things* in the second sentence is used to denote *cars* in the first sentence, thus bringing about cohesion in a way resembling reference since the interpretation of *things* depends on the presence of its referent earlier in the discourse.

Collocation is a term borrowed by Halliday and Hasan (1976:287) from Firth's semantics (see Firth 1957) and used to account for "all lexical cohesion that is not covered by what we have called 'reiteration.'" It is, in other words, a catchall category which accounts for the fact that there are words in English that tend to appear together in texts and are semantically associated with one another. Collocation thus includes antonyms of various kinds (10.i) and (10.ii), and, generally, words from the same semantic field (10.iii) and (10.iv).

(10) (i) The *boys* wanted to play baseball. The *girls* wanted to play soccer.

(ii) Jane *loves* hiking in the winter. John *hates* to be outdoors when it is cold.

(iii) On *Tuesday* the report must be finished. We need it for the meeting on *Wednesday*.

(iv) I am feeling *ill*. I think I will call the *doctor*.

In some of these examples, it is easy to discover the semantic features that account for the cohesion. For example, in (10.i), *boys* and *girls* share features (listed in (4) in chapter 8) (+Physical object) (+Animate) (+Human) (−Adult), and differ only in the feature (Male). The relationship in (10.ii) could be similarly described. The semantic analysis of the collocated elements in (10.iii) and (10.iv) requires more sophistication. Thus, for instance, scripts (see chapter 8, section 4.2, and chapter 10, section 5.3) can be used for this purpose. The scripts for *Tuesday* and *Wednesday* both contain information about days of the week, and this common information is what contributes to the cohesiveness of (10.iii). The fact that the script for *doctor* includes the notion of 'treats disease' provides the semantic link with the word *ill*. Indeed, scripts offer a precise explanation for the cohesiveness created by lexical co-occurrence, especially when the shared semantic features of the lexical items are not obvious.

2.3. Conjunction

Although Halliday and Hasan include **conjunction** as an essentially grammatical means of creating cohesion, they acknowledge that it also has a lexical component (1976:6). Grammatically and lexically, conjunctive cohesion differs significantly enough from the previous types of cohesion discussed in that it warrants separate treatment. Unlike reference, substitution, and ellipsis, conjunction does not refer to or replace a specific grammatical element in a previous sentence. Nor does conjunction provide a new lexical item that echoes or otherwise connects with a word used previously. Instead, conjunctives create cohesion by relating successive sentences that otherwise have no links. (11.i), for example, contains two sentences that have no obvious semantic or grammatical relationship between them. (11.ii), however, is cohesive because the conjunction *afterwards* provides a semantic link which creates a relationship between the proposition in the first sentence and the proposition in the second.

(11) (i) The boys played soccer. It rained.
(ii) The boys played soccer. Afterwards, it rained.

We do not mean to imply that (11.i) is not interpretable. It is, but not because of any cohesion-creating or other textual clues. The interpretability of (11.i) depends on the willingness of anyone hearing or reading it to assume that it is a meaningful text and to impose meaning on it, very much in accordance with Grice's (1975) cooperative principle and—more specifically—his maxim of relation (See chapter 8, section 5.2.4) The presence of the conjunction not only makes the text more obviously cohesive, but also makes the relationship between the two sentences (in this case temporal) more explicit.

As (11.ii) suggests, conjunction refers to cohesion achieved by connectives (see chapter 10, section 2.1.1.2), also called transitions. Like others (Fahnestock, 1983; Winterowd, 1970), Halliday and Hasan have classified these transitions according to the semantic relationships they suggest. Their categories, illustrated in (12.i–iv), are **additive, adversative, causal, temporal,** and **continuative,** respectively (for more expanded and updated lists of such discursive links, emerging from computer-based natural language processing, see Reichman 1985 and Tucker, Nirenburg, and Raskin 1985).

(12) (i) He thought the car was too expensive. *And* he had borrowed more than he could afford already.
(ii) He thought the car was too expensive. *However,* he was determined to own it.
(iii) He thought the car was too expensive. *Consequently,* he decided not to buy it.

(iv) At first, he thought the car was too expensive. *Then* he compared its price with those of other cars and it no longer seemed too much.
(v) He thought the car was too expensive. *Well,* he couldn't expect prices to have stayed the same since he bought his last car ten years before.

Additive conjunctions constitute the most general category. *And* produces cohesion simply by signaling that there is more to say about the topic of the previous sentence or, even more generally, that the two sentences linked by *and* are intended to be seen as related. This conjunctive use of *and* differs somewhat from its use as a coordinating conjunction in which *and* joins two parallel or semantically equivalent words, phrases, or clauses. The **adversative** conjunctive ties indicate a contrastive relationship. The second sentence in the linked pair presents a proposition that contradicts or is contrary to the proposition expressed in the first. **Causal** ties indicate that the second sentence will present a reason or result—as in (12.iii)—derived from the information in the preceding sentence; and **temporal** ties, it is fairly obvious, suggest relationships in time. Adversative, causal, and temporal ties are alike in that the lexical items by which they are expressed contain the semantic features indicating the purpose of the tie. *However* and *but* indicate contrast; *consequently* and *as a result* signal a causal relationship; *then, next,* and *after* provide information about sequences of events. **Continuatives,** on the other hand, like additives, are less semantically specific and, therefore, good candidates for a wastebasket category. Words like *well* and phrases like *of course* indicate a speaker's or writer's intention to offer an explanation or elaboration of what has previously been said or written, but they do not imply a specific relationship between the two sentences, only a general "relatedness." Even such a general link, however, produces cohesion.

It must be pointed out that the use of conjunctives does not create cohesion if no lexical or semantic relationship exists. Despite the conjunctives, (13) is neither a cohesive nor a coherent text.

(13) The boy loved cars. However, many people enjoyed the movie. After work, she went to visit her mother. But dogs are better pets for people who live alone. Consequently, no one supported the decision.

2.4. Cohesion and Pragmatics

The cohesive ties presented in the previous sections of this chapter can be understood in terms of two topics included in the discussion of pragmatics, **presupposition** and **semantic recursion** (chapter 8, sections 5.2.1 and 5.2.2). Both presupposition and semantic recursion are concerned with the conditions that have to be met for a sentence to be understood correctly. Certainly, in the examples of cohesion we have presented, the interpretation of the second sentence in each pair depends on the presence of the first sentence. More specifically, cohesion occurs between two sentences when words that refer to something outside the sentence in which they appear can be interpreted by reference to another sentence. Usually, the sentence that allows for the interpretation precedes the sentence that includes the external reference. Such a relationship, illustrated in most of the examples in this chapter so far and in (14.i), is called **anaphoric.** But the cohesive relationship can occur when the interpretation of the first sentence in a pair depends on information in the next, a relationship called **cataphoric** (14.ii).

(14) (i) John bought a new *car. It* was a sports coupe.
(ii) *This* is what you should do. Go to the library and look for recent articles on semantics.

In (14.i), interpretation of *it* depends on the presence of the word *car* in the preceding sentence. In (14.ii), interpretation of the word *this* depends on the information in the sentence which follows. In each case, we can explain the cohesion by saying that the sentence containing the cohesive tie presupposes information that does not appear in that sentence but which is retrievable from the adjacent sentence.

Neither presupposition nor semantic recursion is limited specifically to information appearing in the preceding or succeeding text. The second sentence of (14.ii) contains a number of presuppositions, some listed in (15), based on knowledge of the language and knowledge of the world.

(15) (i) One can find information in libraries.
(ii) Semantics is one topic one can find information about in libraries.
(iii) Information can be found in articles.
(iv) Articles are found in journals.
(v) Journals may be found in libraries.
(vi) Recent articles are the most useful sources of current information.

Many of these presuppositions can be described through an analysis of **scripts,** but the analysis of these presuppositions is not what is pertinent here. Although interpretability of sentences often depends on both what is in the text and what the reader brings to the text, only the textual elements produce cohesion. Cohesion is produced by specific grammatical and lexical elements within a text which bind sentences together, not by reference to general contextual or extratextual knowledge. Thus cohesion is concerned with only the first two operations of semantic recursion presented in (51) in chapter 8: distinguishing all the non-self-sufficient elements of the sentence (i.e., the semantic recursion triggers or cohesive ties) and relating the sentence to the previous (or following, in the case of cataphora) sentence in the discourse. The third operation, relating the sentence to pertinent information not contained in the discourse, addresses coherence rather than cohesion.

2.5. Cohesion in Larger Texts

Thus far, we have limited our discussion of cohesion to pairs of sentences, but the cohesive ties we have identified operate within larger texts as well. In fact, cohesion contributes to our recognition of textual boundaries since it provides grammatical and semantic links between individual sentences. The absence of cohesion between two sentences may therefore be an indication that one text is ending and another beginning. More pertinent for the writing teacher, the failure of students to use cohesive strategies may be one reason that their texts often seem unfocused and fragmented.

In this section, we will discuss cohesion within paragraphs, but we do not wish to imply that the upper limit of cohesion is the paragraph or that cohesion is a feature of textual structure. Cohesion is a feature of most effective texts, regardless of their length, and, as we suggested in the previous paragraph, may be a text-defining feature. But cohesion cannot be studied as a structural feature of texts, at least not in the same way that syntax is the study of sentence structure, contrary to the notions of early adherents of text linguistics (see, for instance, van Dijk 1972) who believed that a successful linguistics of the sentence can be simply extended and extrapolated to account for the paragraph and discourse. In sentences, it is possible to identify specific **syntactic slots** (see chapter 10, section 2) such as the subject, the predicate, and the object. Further, despite the fact that the potential number of correct, or grammatical, sentences is infinite, the syntactic relationships that form sentences are finite. Thus any sentence, regardless of its complexity, can be analyzed according to a manageable number of linguistic rules that describe syntactic relationships.

Analogous structural rules for discourse beyond the sentence have not been discovered, though, as we shall discuss in the section on coherence, linguists are making efforts to discover them. Presently, however, it is not possible to say that a paragraph that begins with a particular sentence or a particular idea must therefore be structured in a definite way or that any paragraph (or longer discourse) with a particular communicative function must be structured according to specific rules or must fit a particular pattern (though some such formatting constraints do exist for certain types of texts). Texts are definitely semantic entities; they are not, apparently, structural entities in the same constrained sense sentences are (see chapter 8, section 1). Although native speakers seem to have the ability to recognize whether something is or is not a text, it is not clear that their ability to do so is based on meaning or on both meaning and structure.

The same kinds of cohesive ties that produce cohesion between two sentences produce cohesion within larger texts. And the function of these ties is the same: to signal or produce continuity. (16) illustrates how cohesive ties function within a paragraph.

(16) (i) The boy loved cars. (ii) He dreamed about them day and night. (iii) Unfortunately, he was never satisfied with a car for long. (iv) This meant that he was always in debt. (v) The first car he owned was an old sedan. (vi) It was not in good condition, but he told himself that it was better than no car at all. (vii) He didn't own it long before he traded it for a newer, more expensive model. (viii) Each car he bought cost more than the last. (ix) The one he owns now cost over $20,000. (x) And his car payments are more than $500 per month.

We have already identified the cohesive ties for most of these sentences when we introduced them in (2). Now we will discuss how the ties work to link not only paired sentences but the discourse as a whole.

The cohesion in (16) is based on the continuity of two concepts introduced in sentence (16.i), *boy* and *cars,* and a concept introduced in sentence (16.iv) by the word *debt*: the concept of expense. The chart in (17) summarizes the cohesive ties that link these through the paragraph.

(16.i) does not actually contribute to the cohesiveness of the paragraph since it does not depend on the presence of any of the other sentences or of any preceding sentences for its interpretation. Instead, it establishes the basis for the cohesion-producing presuppositions which follow. The noun *boy* in (16.i) is presupposed by the pronouns *he, himself,* and *his,* one or more of which appear in all of the other sentences in the paragraph. These pronouns make up a cohesive chain which, through reference, links every sentence to those preceding it. The word *cars* in (16.i) similarly provides the basis for a cohesive chain, this one more complex because of the variety of cohesive ties involved. The pronouns *them* and *it* and the comparatives *first* and *better* are reference ties; the repeated word *car* and the word *sedan,* for which *car* is a hyponym, are examples of reiteration; the word *model* exemplifies collocation; the words *last* and *one* provide cohesion through the related techniques of ellipsis and substitution, respectively. (16.iv) introduces a new concept, expense, with the word *debt,* which is the basis of the cohesive chain formed by the comparatives *more* in (16.vii) and (16.viii) and the collocations *expensive, cost, $20,000, payments,* and *$500*.

In addition to the cohesive ties described in (17), there are at least three other cohesion-producing strategies used in (16). In (16.iv), the demonstrative *this* refers to all of (16.iii), which could have served as the embedded subject of (16.iv): *That he was never satisfied with a car for long meant that he was always in debt. Now* in (16.ix) is a temporal conjunctive, and *and* in (16.x) is an additive conjunctive.

(17) Sentence	Boy Concept	Car Concept	Expense Concept
(i)	boy	cars	
(ii)	He	them	
(iii)	he	car	
(iv)	he		debt
(v)	he	first	
		car	
		sedan	
(vi)	he	It	
	himself	it	
		better	
		car	
(vii)	He	it	
	he	it	more
		model	expensive
(viii)	he	car	cost
		last	more
(ix)	he	one	cost
			$20,000
(x)	his	car	payments
			$500

The importance of these cohesive ties can be demonstrated by examining a text that does not contain them (18).

(18) The boy loved cars. The boy dreamed about cars day and night. Unfortunately, the boy was never satisfied with a car for long. That the boy was never satisfied with a car for long meant that the boy was always in debt. The first car the boy owned was an old car. The car was not in good condition, but the boy told *the boy that the car was better than no car at all.

It is not necessary to repeat the entire passage to show that cohesive ties enable writers to avoid unsophisticated repetition. In addition, as the last sentence in (18) illustrates, the ties are often grammatically necessary: *the boy told *the boy* is at best ambiguous, suggesting the possibility of two boys involved in a conversation, and at worst ungrammatical. Cohesive ties also help establish a sense of what ideas are dominant in a discourse. In (16) the first appearance of the words *boy, cars,* and *debt* are not, as we have said, cohesive. But because these three words—or more precisely, the concepts they represent—are succeeded by cohesive ties that depend upon them for interpretation, readers understand the paragraph to be based on these topics. In (18), the reappearance of *boy* and *car* seem to signal that no dominant topic has been established for the paragraph, that the reader should not interpret *boy* and *car* as presupposed information. Finally, certain kinds of cohesive ties allow for elaboration on concepts that have already been introduced. In (16.v), the word *sedan* presents new semantic information about the major topic *car,* thus increasing the specificity of the discourse while contributing to its cohesiveness.

SECTION 3. COHERENCE

In chapter 3, section 3, we distinguished coherence from cohesion by stating that the former refers to the overall consistency of a discourse—its purpose, voice, content, style, form, and so on—while the latter is a textual quality which contributes to coherence through verbal cues. Further, we asserted that coherence is in part determined by readers' perceptions of texts, dependent not only on what the texts say but also on readers' ability to draw upon encyclopedic knowledge as they interpret what they read. As we have emphasized throughout the earlier chapters of this book (see chapter 8, section 4; chapter 10, section 3; and chapter 13, section 1), the contributions of linguistics to the study of coherence are limited to the textual and contextual aspects of coherence and exclude the extratextual, encyclopedic aspects. But within those limits, linguistics offers concepts that suggest some of the ways language enables native speakers to understand what a text is about and to distinguish between coherent and incoherent texts. These concepts, introduced in chapter 8 as contextual semantics and pragmatics, will be discussed and illustrated in this section.

It will be useful to begin by referring to (19), a short text we have discussed before as cohesive but not coherent.

(19) The quarterback threw the ball toward the tight end. Balls are used in many sports. Most balls are spheres, but a football is an ellipsoid. The tight end leaped to catch the ball.

As we mentioned in section 1 of this chapter, some linguists have proposed methods for analyzing the structure of texts beyond the sentence. The most promising of this work involves the concept variously referred to as **topic/comment, given/new, theme/rheme,** or **old/new** structure (see chapter 10, section 3.2). Proponents of these structural explanations of coherence (and cohesion) suggest that certain sequences of syntactic patterns create coherence. What these structural views have in common is their claim that the subject of a sentence establishes a topic for that sentence and that the rest of the sentence provides a comment or elaboration on that topic. Coherent discourses are those in which one topic dominates over a sequence of sentences, as in (20), or in which the comment of one sentence becomes the topic of the next, as in (21) (cf. Witte 1983).

(20) *Dogs* make excellent pets for people who live alone. *Dogs* provide companionship. *They* are loyal and eager to please, ready to come when called and to obey their owners' commands. *Dogs* are intelligent, too. *They* can learn tricks and seem to understand the routines of their environment. Finally, *dogs* are territorial, and so they provide security for their owners because they are willing to protect their owners' property.

(21) The *quarterback* threw the ball to the *tight end*. The *tight end* was closely defended by a *linebacker* who grabbed the ball just before it reached the tight end. The *linebacker* had an open field in front of him and ran in for a *touchdown*. That *touchdown* turned out to be the winning score.

As (20) suggests, the cohesion created by the repeated topic *dogs* and the pronouns that refer to it is the major contributor to the coherence of the paragraph. Discourses dominated by one topic will avoid the incoherence of (19), in which the topic shifts between the first and second sentence, remains the same between the second and third, but then shifts again between the third and fourth.

In (21), each sentence has a different topic from the one preceding, but the passage is coherent because the topic for each sentence is derived from the comment of the previous sentence. *Tight end* from the first sentence becomes the topic for the second, *linebacker* from the second sentence becomes the topic for the third, and so on. This pattern suggests why (22) is coherent.

(22) The quarterback threw the ball toward the tight end. The tight end leaped to catch the ball.

There are several problems with this kind of structural analysis of discourse. In the first place, it is easy to follow either of the patterns illustrated in (20) and (21) and still come up with incoherent discourse, as (23 and (24) demonstrate.

(23) *Dogs* make excellent pets for people who live alone. *Dogs* bark at all hours of the day and night. *Dogs* have been domesticated for centuries. *Dogs* are often categorized as sporting or working, according to their original relationship with their owners. Purebred *dogs* are often very expensive. *Dogs* quickly learn to respond to their names.

(24) The quarterback threw the ball to the *tight end*. The *tight end* had played for *Purdue* when he was in college. *Purdue* is well known for its *engineering school*. *Engineers* are demanding very high starting salaries these days.

Thus patterns of topical structure are not themselves indicative of coherence. It is not sufficient for the topics of sentences to be derived from or semantically related to information which appears in the preceding discourse. The semantic connection must include the meaning of whole sentences. That is one reason that scripts, which account for meaning in each word of the sentence and thus the sentence as a whole, are more satisfactory indicators of coherence.

Another problem of the analysis of texts according to topical structure is that many texts, such as (25), do not fit either of the patterns illustrated in (20) and (21).

(25) She turned the wheel hard to the right, then sharply back to the left. The tires squealed, then slid through the gravel on the apron, then squealed again as they returned to the pavement. She brought the car to a stop and sat shaking and crying for a full three minutes before she could go on.

While it is likely that the preceding or succeeding discourse would provide the context for (25), most readers would be able to identify the topic of the passage to be something like "the actions she took to avoid an accident and her reaction to her narrow escape." In such passages, the topics of individual sentences are not related to one another or to the comments of preceding sentences, and thus do not establish the topic of the discourse explicitly. Instead, the sentences which make up this portion of discourse imply the topic of the whole discourse through inference or presupposition. Readers know what the discourse is about not because the topics of individual sentences follow a particular pattern which establishes emphasis and coherence but because the discourse as a whole implies its topic. In such cases, the whole is more than the sum of its parts, and the structure of the whole is not restricted to any particular pattern. As Witte (1983) points out, in such passages the topic of discourse is derived not from the text alone, but from the interaction of the reader's understanding of the text and his or her world knowledge. In other words, the coherence of such texts depends heavily on extratextual knowledge and thus is only partially attributable to linguistic features.

For any purely linguistic-based structural approach to the analysis of discourse to be successful, it must parallel what syntactic analysis can do: reduce to a finite number of rules the infinite sentence-producing ability of native speakers. As we have suggested in the previous paragraph, topical structure analysis fails to provide this parallel because it cannot account linguistically for the coherence of passages in which the discourse topic must be inferred by the reader. It is not clear that the structural analysis of discourse is a dead-end, but it seems likely that such an analysis will yield structures appropriate to specific types of discourse rather than to discourse as a whole. It may be that there are certain structures for narrative, others for persuasion, and still others for presenting factual information, and it may be that such structures are linguistic structures rather than cognitive or logical structures, but such structures have yet to be proposed.

From a linguistic perspective then, discourse coherence can best be described semantically, through scripts, and through the related concepts of inference and presupposition. How can linguistics help explain why we recognize (19) as incoherent? One answer can be drawn from script-based semantics (Raskin 1981, 1984). The script for a word includes not only typical dictionary information about that word's meaning, but also contextual information (see chapter 8, section 4.2, and chapter 10, section 3.3). While the script for the word *ball* contains contextual information concerning the shapes (spherical, ellipsoid) and uses (in sports, in machinery, and so on), that contextual information is presupposed in (19). The words *quarterback* and *tight end* include within their scripts the concepts *player, game,* and *football,* in addition to more specific information about the roles of each player in the game. Consequently, the much more general information about the uses and shapes of balls, as well as the identification of a football as ellipsoid, is presupposed by (or, from a different perspective, can be inferred from) the first sentence. Thus part of the reason that the second and third sentences interfere with the coherence of (19) is that they present information that is already available to the reader. But the repetition of information is not the sole cause of incoherence (nor is repetition necessarily a cause of incoherence, as should be clear from the use of reiteration as a cohesive tie). It seems likely that the incoherence of (19) is also a result of the fact that the information conveyed in the second and third sentences is incompatible with the football-playing script established in the first sentence. The appropriate script is determined early in the discourse, and deviations from that script, particularly deviations that introduce general and inferrable information, produce incoherence. If we remove the offending sentences from (19), we have a coherent text (22) because the football-playing script established in the first sentence is continued in the second.

The incoherence of (19) can thus be attributed in part to the fact that it contains irrelevant information in terms of the script of the passage as a whole and unnecessary information in terms of what can be inferred from the scripts of specific words. Incoherence also results from texts that contain either insufficient or unnecessarily detailed information, as in (26) and (27) (from Raskin 1986a:34), respectively.

(26) Next winter I am going to Florida. I hate shoveling snow.

(27) Winters bring much snow here. In order to make the pavements and driveways passable one has to shovel snow all the time. I hate doing it, so I am going to spend next winter in Florida instead of here. The climate is warmer in Florida,

and one does not expect snow at all there, or least as much as is here, in winter. Therefore, it is likely that I will be able to avoid shoveling snow in Florida and thus save myself from doing something I don't like doing.

As we indicated in chapter 8, section 5.2.4, the cooperative principle suggests that readers make the effort to interpret texts, even if those texts are not clear or if the writer violates one of Grice's (1975) maxims of bona fide communication. (26), although interpretable through effort on the part of the reader, requires the reader to make a number of inferences about the writer's intention. The first inference the reader must make is that the writer intends the two sentences to be part of a single discourse and that therefore some relationship exists between the writer's hatred of shoveling snow and his going to Florida next winter. From that point, the reader must infer several things: that it snows in the winter where the writer resides, that the writer must shovel the snow, that in Florida it is not necessary to shovel snow in winter; essentially the reader must infer everything that is spelled out in great detail in (27). Readers can infer all of this because the scripts for the words *winter, Florida, shoveling,* and *snow* contain the necessary information. But readers may not be willing to do this much work to interpret a passage, especially if the passage has little to do with the reader's well-being. For effective communication to take place, the writer must not place too much of the interpretive burden on the reader by forcing the reader to make all of the inferences necessary to understand the discourse.

On the other hand, discourse such as (27) provides information that the reader could easily infer. The second sentence, for example, is probably unnecessary for any reader familiar with tasks related to snow, and the fourth and fifth sentences contain information easily inferrable from the third sentence. Even the phrase *instead of here* at the end of the third sentence can be inferred from what precedes, because if the writer did not mean that Florida was a place other than where he already was, he would not have named it. Instead, he would have written: "I am going to spend next winter *here*." To say *Florida* if he were already in Florida would be a violation of the maxims of quantity and manner. Readers would be able to understand (27) easily, but would probably, unless they were children, find it to be overly detailed and not as coherent as it might be because readers expect to make some inferences as they read.

Obviously, if (26) is underdetailed and (27) is overdetailed, there must be some happy medium. (28) is a text that provides a reasonable amount of information while not overwhelming the reader in easily inferrable information.

(28) There has been so much snow here lately. I have been shoveling it all the time, and I don't like doing that. Next winter I am going to Florida.

(28) begins with an essential piece of information missing from (26): that there is a lot of snow where the writer resides. But unlike (27), (28) does not bother to explain that the snow occurs in winter, since that can be inferred from the script for the word *snow*. Nor does (28) include the obvious information that a great amount of snow demands (usually) that pavements be shoveled. All three passages explain that the writer dislikes shoveling snow, but (26) fails to make explicit the fact that the writer has been required to do so, largely because one cannot easily infer from (26) that the writer lives where there is snow. All three passages also explain that the writer intends to spend the following winter in Florida, but (28) avoids the unnecessary details of (27) by allowing the reader to infer the information in the last two sentences about the climate of Florida and the writer's expectations that he will be able to avoid shoveling snow in Florida. Thus (28) is a more coherent text than either (26) or (27) because it provides readers with enough information to be able to interpret the text completely without providing so much detail that the text seems childishly simply or unemphatic.

CHAPTER 14

Linguistics and the Composing Process

SECTION 1. A PROCESS MODEL OF COMPOSING

Thus far, we have discussed specific language-based problems in rhetoric and composition which are in many cases receptive to linguistic analysis and explanation. But over the past two decades, composition theorists and researchers have begun to view composing not in terms of isolated problems to be solved or single components that can simply be combined to produce a written text. Instead, writing has come to be understood as a complex, recursive **process** involving planning, drafting, and revising. In this chapter, we will shift our view from the contribution linguistics can make in the analysis of specific problems in a text to the way linguistic concepts correlate to a process approach to composing.

Although writing-as-a-process is becoming more and more widely accepted by teachers and a process approach to teaching is beginning to be reflected in writing texts, terminology used to discuss the composing process varies. For that reason, we will begin by presenting and explaining the terms we will be using to discuss the activities involved in composing. As we indicated above, the composing process can be divided into three phases which, while not discrete, identify three kinds of activities that occur when one writes. **Planning,** also called **invention** or **prewriting,** is concerned with the mental and written activities (listed in (1)) which usually take place before a writer attempts a first draft of a text.

(1) **Planning Activities**

- (i) Analyzing the purpose or goal of the writing task (whether self-assigned or assigned by another person, such as an employer or instructor)
- (ii) Determining the characteristics of the audience or potential audiences and the writer's relationship to them
- (iii) Gathering information necessary to complete the writing task, either through introspection or through formal or informal heuristic procedures
- (iv) Selecting an organizational pattern or format for the text

(1.i) includes identifying both the **topic** of the text—what the text is about—and the purpose or **aim** of the text (see chapter 3, section 2). (1.ii) requires that the writer assess the pertinent knowledge, attitudes, and values of those who will be reading the text in order to determine how best to attain the purpose for which he is writing. (1.ii) may require the writer to choose the most appropriate audience from among a number of potential audiences, particularly if the writing task is one that the writer has selected himself, as might be the case for a free-lance writer or a scholar pursuing a topic that interests him. Often, however, the audience is determined by the rhetorical situation so that the writer knows that he is writing for an employer, a client, a subordinate, an instructor, a close friend, and so on. In either case, the relationship between the writer and the audience governs a number of linguistic choices the writer must make (we will elaborate on these in section 2.2). (1.iii) is concerned with the identification and discovery of the content of the text. In the case of a personal reminiscence, the writer may simply need to spend time searching his memory for details of the events he wishes to recount. Some essays in which the writer offers a personal opinion or states a personal belief may require introspection and thought, but not formal research or study (although such essays may be the product of previous research, reading, or study). Other writing tasks demand extensive original research or study before the writer can begin to do more than make notes about what the text might include. (1.iv) involves decisions about genre and arrangement, decisions which influence linguistic choices since the diction and syntax of informal discourse differ from those of formal discourse, just as the diction and syntax of poetry differ from those of prose, and literature in general from nonliterary texts.

Drafting is the act of writing the text itself. Traditionally, writing instruction has concentrated on drafting as the central, if not the only, thing meant by writing. Though writing texts and many instructors emphasize the need to plan before one writes, until recently there has been little in the way of practical advice about how one goes about planning a written text. For decades, writers have been instructed to choose a topic, narrow it down, find several (usually three) things to say about it, and write the paper, checking for errors before submitting it. Such one-draft writing tasks emphasize quickly produced, error-free writing, especially when writing assignments are expected to be completed within the limits of a one-hour class period, as is often the case in introductory composition classes.

Such an approach ignores the importance and complexity of **revising,** elements of which are listed in (2).

(2) **Revising Activities**

- (i) Assessing the success with which the draft meets the goals set during planning; doing further planning as necessary
- (ii) Evaluating the text for unity and coherence; rearranging, adding, and deleting as necessary

(iii) Evaluating the text, with particular attention to individual paragraphs, for cohesion
(iv) Evaluating diction for appropriateness
(v) Evaluating syntax for clarity, effectiveness, and correctness
(vi) Identifying and correcting print-code and non-print-code errors
(vii) Preparing a final version of the text
(viii) Proofreading the final version for scribal or typographical errors

Thus revision encompasses assessing and changing the whole text (2.i–iii), as well as activities that might be called **editing** (2.iv–vi) and **proofreading** (2.viii). The order in which these activities are presented in (2) suggests a hierarchy which emphasizes the importance of examining the rhetorical or communicative effectiveness of a text before focusing on errors in usage and mechanics, an order which makes sense not only since correcting errors in an early draft may prove to be a waste of time if parts of the text will be deleted or rewritten dramatically, but also because the absence of errors does not assure that a text will be an effective communication. Further, this order acknowledges, especially in (2.i), that writers may discover something new about their topic or may change their minds about their purpose or thesis as they write. The process of planning, drafting, planning again, and redrafting encourages writers to postpone closure and to prolong the opportunity to gain further insights about their topic.

Of course, writers usually do not follow the order of (2.i–viii) mechanically, nor is the planning, drafting, revising order meant to be a linear model either of how all writers or even good writers behave or of how all students should be taught to write. It seems clear that writing is truly recursive, that writers mix planning, drafting, and revising by stopping to think and plan as they draft, to change sentences and words, to make corrections as they detect them. The value of the process model of composing is that it identifies the various activities in which most writers engage, thus providing a cognitive model useful for the teaching of writing and for the analysis of problems individual writers may have. Writers who have never had the opportunity to learn planning strategies or to revise but have instead been encouraged to think of writing as the act of correctly putting information on paper benefit from becoming aware of the complex, multilayered activity writing is. Familiarity with the composing-process model enables writing teachers to suggest that students spend more time on specific activities such as analyzing the characteristics of their audience or revising for cohesion in order to solve problems with a particular text.

In the sections which follow, linguistic concepts will be discussed in terms of their relationship to planning, drafting, and revising, thus both synthesizing and extending the applications of linguistics presented in chapters 10–13.

SECTION 2. LINGUISTICS AND PLANNING

2.1. Goal Analysis

Linguistics does not have a lot to say about what the goal or purpose of a text should be. Such a determination is concerned more with the real-world situation that produces the need to write, whether that need be one perceived by the writer independent of anyone else or whether it be a need imposed on the writer by someone else—that is, a task assigned to the writer. For writers (and writing teachers), what linguistics has to offer in the second situation is a description of how language conveys meaning. Thus writers faced with a task imposed by someone else must be able to act first as readers (or listeners). As such, writers rely on semantic knowledge to interpret the assignment, but in doing so they are not performing specially because they are writers; they are using the same ability to detect inferences and presuppositions, speech acts, scripts, and so on that people rely on to interpret language in any situation. And as is the case in any communication, a failure to understand such linguistic phenomena may have undesirable consequences. In the special case of a writer misinterpreting a task or assignment, the undesirable consequence is a text that fails to achieve its goal. For example, a student asked to analyze a specific portion of a literary text who does not recognize that such an assignment presupposes the writer's familiarity with techniques of literary analyses—strategies such as citing and quoting from the text—will be likely to write an inadequate analysis. Thus a text written as the response to an assignment may go wrong because the writer has failed to interpret the task correctly. For writing teachers, the implication is twofold. First, writing assignments must be made carefully, with attention given to what they presuppose, the potential for ambiguity, and what kind of text they are designed to elicit. Second, teachers should consider that student writing that goes wrong may be the result of the writer's failure to make the proper inferences about the assignment.

2.2. Audience Analysis

Audience analysis requires that writers consider how much linguistic and encyclopedic knowledge their readers possess, in other words, what scripts they have at their disposal. Characteristics of the audience such as age, educational background, religion, social values, economic status, and so on affect a writer's linguistic choices. Writers choose diction and syntactic patterns and are guided in determining how much inference is appropriate according to their knowledge of such characteristics and their perceptions of their own relationship to their readers. In a persuasive text, for example, what writers presuppose to be shared values or beliefs is reflected in the text they produce. They do not attempt to persuade their readers to accept what they assume the readers already believe, but instead concentrate on those matters upon which they perceive disagreement. Failure to analyze the readers accurately may result in texts that are overcomplete or undercomplete for the particular audience (see the discussion of (26) in chapter 12, section 3, and (26–28) in chapter 13). Undercompleteness is a particular problem for inexperienced writers, many of whom are extremely egocentric and thus unable to recognize that what seems clear to them may not be clear at all to their readers. Their writing often assumes that readers are familiar with information that cannot be inferred from the text, as the following excerpt from a college freshman's paper suggests:

(3) Much like *Teenage Radiation Band* with Steve Doll and Gary Meyer, *Johnnie and the Leisure Suits* make fun of people, but in a more mature way. This type of humor is from the same egg as the city of Chicago. They are one in the same. This style is shown in "We're All Crazy in Chicago" which was written by Johnnie and his band. The type of humor in this song and others on the Loop's morning show is what so many of us miss, and are missing out on.

The initial three paragraphs of this paper provide some information essential for understanding this paragraph: The author is a student at a university approximately 130 miles from her home in Chicago, *Johnnie* is a morning radio personality for a Chicago station, the signal for this station cannot be received at the university because of the distance from Chicago, the music on Johnnie's shows often consists of comic songs written and performed by Johnnie and a band he leads. But there is much in (3) that demands special knowledge that the writer does not provide. The reference to the *Teenage Radiation Band* is meant to offer readers a basis of comparison for *Johnnie and the Leisure Suits,* but such a comparison presupposes readers familiar with the first group. Such a presupposition, given the fact that the author is writing about Chicago radio to readers at a large university who cannot be assumed to be familiar with those stations, is unwarranted. Indeed, if the writer *were* to assume that her audience was familiar with Chicago radio, her detailed description of this program would be unnecessary. One must infer from her paper that her intended audience is unfamiliar with this program specifically and with Chicago radio stations generally. That choice of audience also makes the writer's reference to *The Loop's morning show* ambiguous. Most readers would be familiar with the use of the phrase *The Loop* as a reference to the central business district of Chicago. The phrase *The Loop's morning show* would thus be understood by those readers as an indication by the author that this program has been embraced by a large number of Chicago radio listeners, that it is, in effect, the most popular show in Chicago. It is not until the end of the next paragraph that the author indicates that such an interpretation is incorrect and that *The Loop* is a nickname for the particular station. The author's failure to consider what her audience cannot infer is also demonstrated throughout the passage by her use of the demonstrative *this* (*this type of humor, this style*) and the definite article *the* (*the type of humor in this song*). Since the writer is not explicit about the humorous style of Johnnie's songs—she does not, for example, quote from any of them—readers cannot be expected to understand what the specific nature of the humor is.

2.3. Gathering Information

Information gathering or the discovery of content is not a linguistic matter.

2.4. Selecting an Organizational Pattern

As we pointed out in chapter 13, section 3, text linguists, rhetoricians, and discourse analysts have proposed linguistic approaches to arrangement or text structure. The notion of topic/comment is one such approach, as is the concept of **macrostructure** (van Dijk 1977), which suggests that a language user's ability to perceive the semantic relationship between two (or more) sentences that are not obviously related to one another may be accounted for by the language user's recognition of a larger discourse topic which encompasses the concepts of both sentences. Those interested in the relationship between linguistics and text structure often point out that there are conventional structural patterns for various kinds of discourse—narratives, arguments, and so on—but they have not been able to demonstrate that those patterns are essentially linguistic as opposed to psychological or rhetorical or simply conventional. Certainly the linguistic features that enable readers to perceive that a text is cohesive and coherent contribute to the structural integrity of that text, but no strictly linguistic rules, syntactic or semantic, describing the appropriate structure for particular kinds of texts have yet been discovered.

SECTION 3. LINGUISTICS AND DRAFTING

From a linguistic perspective, drafting is perhaps the most obvious and at the same time most slippery component of the writing process to discuss. If one perceives of drafting to be the act of composing the initial version of the text, as we have described it in section 1, then drafting requires the total application of a writer's linguistic knowledge. As people write, they concentrate on the goal established in planning and the plan formulated for attaining that goal, but they turn their attention away from the discovery of their goal to the attainment of it in their text. When they draft, writers select words and syntax that they believe will help them communicate their message clearly. Regardless of how deliberate or spontaneous this selection process may be, writers make use of both their intuitive and their learned knowledge about phonology, morphology, syntax, and semantics as they transfer their ideas into language. The choice of a word, the spelling of that word, the structure of the sentence in which the word appears, and the syntax and meaning of the sentences preceding and following the sentence in which the word appears all reflect a writer's linguistic knowledge.

SECTION 4. LINGUISTICS AND REVISING

The success of the initial draft of a text depends on how well the writer has planned as well as how well he or she has carried out that plan. Revision, whether it is carried out at some time following the writing of the initial draft or whether, as for some writers, it is simultaneous with the writing of the initial draft, allows the writer to assess both the linguistic and nonlinguistic elements of the text-in-progress. The more familiar the writer is with the conventions of Standard American English, the less effort he or she will have to put in the parts of revision identified in (2.vi) and in the part of (2.v) that is concerned with syntactic **correctness** or **grammaticality.** But most writers will—or should be taught to—recognize that the initial draft of a text is rarely as well developed, well worded, cohesive, and coherent as it might be, and thus the other elements of revision identified in (2) deserve their attention.

Because revision involves a thorough reexamination of a whole text, nearly all of the linguistic concepts we have discussed are potentially relevant to the revision tasks listed in (2). No single text is likely to call upon all of the linguistic knowledge of the writer trying to revise it or the instructor offering suggestions for revision, but (4), a text written by a college freshman, illustrates a variety of typical first-draft problems that can be explained linguistically.

(4) (i) When people go to buy a used car they usually do not spend as much time or put as much effort into it as they should. (ii) You should consider carefully what you are going to invest your money in. (iii) There are a lot of aspects that can be over looked which can make a big difference in whether or not you get your money's worth.

(iv) The first things you should decide are: what kind of car you want; how much money you want to spend, and who sells that type of car. (v) Dealers are more dependable, and they will know more about the background of the car than a used car salesman would. (vi) A dealer also has his new car reputation to keep up so he is going to carry quality used cars. (vii) You should ask for any

previous maintenance records, and any previous owner's names. (viii) Give them a call and ask them how the car performed when they owned it.
(ix) The next step is to check the car over thoroughly. (x) Look over the exterior to see if there are any signs of damage, abuse, or if the car looks like it was well taken care of or not. (xi) Then look over the inside checking again for damage, abuse, or something that does not work properly. (xii) Check the lights, blinkers, windshield wipers, to make sure everything is in proper working order.
(xiii) Once you feel that you have thoroughly checked the car inside and out, open the hood and look the engine over. (xiv) Check the oils, fluids, and waterlevels. (xv) Also check to see if they have been changed recently or if they look pretty used. (xvi) Look to see if anything shows signs of abuse or wear like the hoses, wires, or battery connections. (xvii) Take the air cleaner cover off, and check the filter. (xviii) Also look in the carburetor to see if it is clean or not. (xix) While the hood is up, check the frame to see if the car has been wrecked. (xx) Once the car has been wrecked, it will never be the same. (xxi) Check the trunk too. (xxii) Look for any signs of rust, and make sure there is a spare, jack, and a lug wrench. (xxiii) Make sure that the trunk closes easily and locks properly.
(xxiv) To insure that the car is right for you, take it for a drive. (xxv) Make sure the ignition, brakes, transmission, steering, and acceleration all work properly. (xxvi) Drive the car at highway speeds to see if there is any vibration in the front end. (xxvii) If the car does vibrate, the car is out of allignment, and the tires have probably worn funny. (xxviii) Do you feel comfortable driving the car? (xxix) Are the pedals and steering wheel in awkward positions? (xxx) Is this car going to be right for you?
(xxxi) Once you think you have checked everything, do not be to quick to buy. (xxxii) Look around to see if someone else is selling the same type of car. (xxxiii) If you are looking at a small dealer, it would be a good idea to give some of the bigger dealers a call. (xxxiv) Bigger dealers buy in larger quantities and usually have lower prices because of this. (xxxv) Driving a few extra miles to a larger dealer could save you a few thousand dollars. (xxxvi) Do not be in a big rush because you do not want to invest in something you will regret later.

For the purpose of analysis, we will assume that the writer has prepared this draft as carefully as possible (2.vii) and that any errors or problems in it reflect his difficulties with composing rather than proofreading errors (2.viii). Our discussion therefore will be limited to those linguistic features of the text that apply to the revision tasks listed in (2.i–vi).

4.1. Goal Attainment

The success with which writers attain their goals is determined by all of the features of their texts. Readers are influenced not only by the content of the text, but also by the linguistic and nonlinguistic elements identified in (2.ii–vi). It is possible, however, to determine the apparent goal of a text and to identify any major problems that prevent that goal from being attained. The goal of (4) is to inform readers, to provide them with advice about how to select a used car. The author asserts the value of this goal in (4.i) by stating that most people do not make this selection properly. He emphasizes it in (4.ii) by saying that readers should consider their investment in a used car carefully and in (4.iii) by asserting that people overlook things that affect their satisfaction with their investment in a car. This theme of making a satisfactory choice is made explicit toward the end of the paper as well, in (4.xxiv) and (4.xxx), where the author uses the phrase *right for you,* and in (4.xxxvi) reminds readers to be cautious before making an investment in a used car. These sentences, appearing at the beginning, near the end, and at the end of the text, create a cohesive chain which dominates the text as a whole. Semantically, the chain is composed of the concepts of caution, investment, and satisfaction, which together establish the major theme or goal of the text.

Once the apparent goal of a text has been identified, one can examine the text for problems that prevent the goal from being attained. A key consideration is the success with which the text is addressed to an appropriate audience. The obvious audience for (4) is potential used car buyers. The assertion in (4.i) that *people usually* do not make such a purchase wisely demonstrates that the writer presupposes the existence of a large audience. Since he does not modify *people* with limiting adjectives such as *some,* or even more inclusive adjectives like *many* or *most,* the implication is that all people who buy used cars are included in his audience. *Usually* presupposes that what the author describes is customary behavior for all of the forementioned people. Thus the audience for this paper can be inferred to be people who may at some time purchase a used car but who are unlikely to make this purchase wisely. Although the author states that the problem for used car buyers is that they *do not spend as much time or put as much effort* into the purchase as is necessary, (4.iii) suggests that it is lack of knowledge about *aspects that can be over looked,* rather than simply lack of time and effort, that is the real danger to the reader. The audience, therefore, can be further identified as people who lack the knowledge to make a prudent decision about buying a used car—and as we indicated earlier, the author perceives this audience to be a large one.

At this point it becomes possible to identify, on the basis of linguistic knowledge, a major obstacle to the success of this paper. Throughout the paper, the author presupposes that his readers possess knowledge about cars that is inconsistent with the audience he has identified. In (4.x) he advises readers to check the exterior of the car for *signs of damage, abuse,* but he does not elaborate on what these signs might be. In (4.xi), he offers the same advice about the interior of the car, and while (4.xii) might be inferred to elaborate on (4.xi), it presupposes that readers will not limit their interior inspection to controls for exterior devices. If the author means only to remind readers to look for obvious indications of abuse or damage such as dents, broken lights, and ripped upholstery, then these sentences may not presuppose more knowledge on the part of readers than is appropriate. But the same kinds of presuppositions appear in (4.xiv–xix), where following the author's advice requires more technical knowledge. For example, (4.xiv) does not include, nor is it followed by, any information about how to check the fluids or what to look for when checking them (it may be that the ambiguity of the sentence is caused by a print-code error, the writing of *water levels* as one word—we shall return to this error later). Nor is there any elaboration on what the author means by *fluids*. Apparently, he is referring to fluids other than the oil and water, but it is unlikely that the unskilled car buyer will know what they are or how to check them. In most cases, the author simply tells readers to look for signs of wear without indicating what those signs are or to check an item, such as the air filter in (4.xvii), without explaining how to perform that check or what to check for. Even when the text does provide information about what to look for, the information is unlikely to be sufficient for the audience. In (4.xviii), the reader is told to *look in the carburetor to see if it is clean,* advice which assumes familiarity with engine parts and with how carburetors are supposed to look when they are clean. After reading (4.xix), the reader can only infer that frame damage occurs exclusively to the front of a car, on a part of the frame visible from above while the hood is open.

Another problem that prevents this paper from attaining its goal is conceptual rather than linguistic in origin, but it may be that linguistics can provide the basis for an explanation which would make the problem clear for the writer. The problem involves the implications of (4.iv) and (4.xxxiii). In (4.iv), the ambiguous phrase *what kind of car you want* can be interpreted to mean either (5.i) or (5.ii).

(5) (i) the specific make and/or model of car you want
(ii) the general category of car you want (large, small, sedan, van, station wagon, economy, luxury, and so on)

The ambiguity here is semantic, based on the various meanings of the word *kind*. Readers inferring the former meaning would also interpret the phrase *type of car* later in the sentence to mean a particular make and/or model, while those inferring the latter meaning would understand *type of car* more generally. The author does not indicate which of the two meanings he intends, either explicitly or implicitly, in sentences (4.vii–xxx). These sentences concentrate on how the reader should go about evaluating a specific car in which he is interested, but the information provided in them would apply to either interpretation of (4.iv) because it presupposes that the reader has made a decision about a particular car, regardless of his initial criteria for selection. Sentence (4.xxxii), however, undercuts all of the preceding advice that makes up the bulk of this text. The advice to see if *the same type of car* is for sale elsewhere suggests that the phrases *kind of car* and *type of car* in (4.iv) are to be understood to mean (5.i), a specific make and/or model of car. In (4.xxxii), the author presupposes that all 1983 Ford sedans, for example, will be in the same condition as the particular 1983 Ford sedan that the reader has checked so carefully. This presupposition renders meaningless all of the advice about expending the time and effort to check a specific car since finding a satisfactory car is now presented as a matter of selecting the right make and/or model in the first place. In (4.xxxiv–xxxvi), the author explains that the reason for seeking the same *type of car* elsewhere is a matter of saving money, as much as *a few thousand dollars*. Thus (4.xxxii–xxxvi) imply that the major criterion for selecting a used car is the price. Such an implication throws into the background the apparent intention of this paper by reducing the advice about how to buy a used car to a single point which has nothing to do with the information presented throughout most of the text.

The preceding discussion is based on a number of semantic concepts discussed in chapter 8: **semantic ambiguity** (section 3), **contextual semantics** and **scripts** (section 4.2), **presupposition** (section 5.2.1), and **inference** (section 5.2.5), but it is not a discussion of the semantics of (4). Rather, it is an explanation of why this paper fails to attain its goal, and is thus relevant to the first of the revision tasks in (2).

4.2. Unity and Coherence

Bamberg's (1983) criteria for coherence (see chapter 3, section 3) include **unity,** which can be considered as the adherence of each sentence of a text to the topic of the text as a whole. The incoherence of our oft-quoted paragraph about football, analyzed in detail in chapter 13, section 3, would be identified as a lack of unity in most composition texts. (4) is free from incoherence caused by the presence of such blatantly irrelevant sentences; every sentence in the text has some direct bearing on the topic of buying a used car.

But lack of coherence is a major problem in this text for other reasons. The underdetailization, the numerous presuppositions, and the faulty implications discussed in the previous section contribute to the incoherence of the paper. The lack of cohesiveness of the second and fourth paragraphs, which will be discussed in the following section, is also a source of incoherence. Another source of incoherence is the contradiction between sentences (4.v) and (4.xxxvi), a contradiction made apparent by an analysis of the inferences of these two sentences. Since (4.v) distinguishes between *dealers* and *a used car salesman,* one inference of (4.v) is that *dealers* refers to new-car dealers whose stock of used cars comes from trade-ins. A related inference is that the used-car salesmen the author refers to are not employees of new-car dealerships, but are engaged exclusively in the sales and (again by inference) purchase of used cars. (4.v) states that new-car dealers *will know more about the background of the car,* an unsupported assertion which implies one or more of the ideas in (6).

(6) (i) New-car dealers are more careful about accepting trade-ins than used-car dealers.
(ii) New-car dealers keep for sale only the best of the cars they accept as trade-ins.
(iii) New-car dealers accept only models they are familiar with as trade-ins.

Each of these interpretations is based on possible meanings of the phrase *know about* in (4.v). Readers with world knowledge about the automobile business might feel confident about rejecting (6.i) and (6.iii) as reasonable interpretations, but linguistic knowledge allows for each of these interpretations, and thus potential ambiguity.

Given the inferences of (4.v), (4.xxxiv) is a contradictory statement which affects the coherence of the text. All of the inferences of (4.v) indicate that (new-car) dealers get used cars as trade-ins, but (4.xxxiv) uses the word *buy* to describe how dealers acquire cars. There is no linguistic reconciliation of this contradiction since the scripts for the words *buy* and *trade* differ in that the former indicates acquisition through the exchange of money for goods and/or services and the latter indicates acquisition through the exchange of goods and/or services for other goods and/or services. If we specify the use of the words to a *car-buying* script, the issue is still unclear since car buying and trading often involve the exchange of both money and goods **from the buyer** to the dealer, so that *buy* remains inconsistent with the subject *dealers*. The most appropriate context for (4.xxxiv) is a description of how new-car dealers acquire new cars, including the point that larger dealers buy (and sell) more cars than smaller dealers and can thus sell cars for less because they can accept a smaller profit on each sale. But this interpretation, based more on world knowledge than linguistic knowledge, is not consistent with the used-car topic of the text as a whole. For it to contribute to the coherence of the text, (4.xxxiv) would have to be elaborated upon by the author in his next draft.

4.3. Cohesion

The author of (4) demonstrates some understanding of cohesive ties, but certainly not mastery. He apparently has learned to use transitions to indicate continuity between paragraphs, as evidenced by the use of *first* in (4.iv), *next* in (4.ix), and *once* in (4.xiii) and (4.xxxi). These words are links in a cohesive chain which begins with the phrase *a lot of aspects* in (4.iii). Each of these paragraph-opening cohesive ties reminds readers that this text is enumerating the *aspects* that a prospective used-car buyer should consider before making a purchase. Sentence (4.xiii) illustrates another kind of cohesion, reiteration. The words *thoroughly, check(ed),* and *car* are repeated from (4.ix), the word *inside* is repeated from (4.xi), and the word *out* reiterates "exterior" from (4.x). Cohesion is created in the three paragraphs composed of (4.ix–xxx) through the use of words like *check, look, make sure,* and *see,* all of which emphasize the theme of caution mentioned in section 4.1.

There are, despite these and other cohesion-creating words, problems with the cohesiveness of this text. Individual paragraphs, with the exception of the third, are not cohesive, even though the author sometimes uses cohesive ties to try to reinforce cohesion. In (4.v), the author lists three items the used-car buyer should consider first. For the paragraph to be cohesive, it should address each of these items. But the third item, *who sells that type of car,* begins a new cohesive chain made up of *dealers* in (4.v) and *dealer* in (4.vi), and the first two items of the series in (4.iv) are not referred to again. Further, the *dealer* chain itself ends after two sentences, and the advice in (4.vii–viii) about consulting previous owners begins without any cohesive tie linking it to what precedes. Cooperative readers would probably infer from (4.vii) that the omitted object of the verb *ask* is *the dealer,* but this elliptical reference fails to create cohesion since the advice in (4.vii–viii) has nothing to do with reasons to buy a used car from a dealer, the point being made in (4.v–vi). Similarly, cohesion breaks down at (4.xxi). In (4.xiii), the author begins a paragraph which advises the reader to look at the engine. The collocation of terms referring to engine parts in (4.xiv–xviii) creates cohesion for much of this paragraph, and though the author changes focus slightly in (4.xix–xx) when he tells readers to examine the frame for damage, the temporal conjunctive *while* and the repeated word *hood* in (4.xix) allow readers to perceive the conceptual continuity of the text. Less clearly a cohesive part of the paragraph, however, is the chain composed of (4.xxi–xxiii), which is about the trunk of the car. The author uses *too,* an additive conjunction, as a lexical link between (4.xx) and (4.xxi), and the words *hood* and *trunk* might be perceived as collocations since they share semantic features. But these cohesive devices connect separate cohesive chains instead of extending a single chain.

It is important to recognize the relationship between the analysis of cohesion and decisions about text structures, including paragraph boundaries. As we indicated in chapter 12, section 1, cohesion is a phenomenon which can be analyzed linguistically, particularly by applying semantic concepts. But the analysis of cohesion (or lack thereof) in a text or a part of a text does not necessarily provide information about how successfully the text is structured or about how to improve the structure of the text. The analyses of (4.iv–viii) and (4.xiii–xxii) indicate breakdowns in cohesion that the writer and/or instructor must address, but the decisions about how to address these problems are rhetorical rather than linguistic. While linguistics can enable one to reach the conclusion that a new cohesive chain begins at (4.xxi), linguistics cannot provide advice about whether a separate short paragraph composed of (4.xxi–xxiii) is preferable to the paragraph as it is structured now. From a rhetorical perspective, the introduction of a new concept or topic in a text is often a signal for a new paragraph to begin, but the decision to separate (4.xxi–xxiii) from what precedes it would also be influenced by the effect such a short paragraph would have on the readability of the text as a whole, including such nonlinguistic matters as paragraph development and length.

4.4. Diction

One problem with the diction of (4), the repetition of words, is only tangentially linguistic. Although repetition is one method of creating cohesion, extensive repetition, such as the frequent use of *look, check,* and *make sure,* is stylistically undesirable. As we pointed out in chapter 1, section 1, vocabulary study may enable a writer to increase his or her store of words, and of course any study of vocabulary that goes beyond mere memorization of definitions involves morphology and semantics.

(4) contains only a few of what we have called (in chapter 1, section 1.1, and chapter 11, section 1) **diction errors,** redundancy being the most common. In (4.x), the phrase *or not* is redundant. *If,* which introduces a clause describing what the prospective buyer should look for, implies that alternatives could exist: There either will or will not be signs of damage. Because the concept *alternative* is implicit in *if,* it need not be made explicit by *or not,* so that last phrase is unnecessary. In (4.xi), the phrase *or something that does not work properly* is redundant because it repeats semantic information present in the words *damage* and *abuse* which appear earlier in the sentence: Something that does not work properly is, necessarily, damaged (though damage is not necessarily a sign of abuse).

Diction **errors** are not as serious an impediment to communication in (4) as is the semantic ambiguity caused by the writer's reliance on words whose specific meanings cannot be derived from the text. One reason that the essay as a whole is not coherent lies in the fact that (4.iii) fails to establish a context for the advice which follows. Instead, the writer uses *a lot* and *aspects,* neither of which conveys precise meaning or limits the context of what the text will be about. Throughout the text, the author uses words (like *a lot*) whose meanings depend on and are relative to the contexts in which they appear. In (4.xv), the word *pretty* modifies *used* and describes the appearance of engine fluids. The degree of being *used* that *pretty* is meant to indicate cannot be retrieved from the text because the script for *pretty* has no semantic information to enable readers to interpret how it is used in reference to automobile fluids. We can easily eliminate the script for *pretty* that has to do with physical beauty and identify that in this sentence the word means *more than a little,* but beyond that there is nothing in the meaning of the word or the context of the sentence in which it appears to help the reader interpret it. Instead, the reader is forced to rely on world knowledge to understand the advice which is being given. Similarly, the word *funny* in (4.xxvii) describes how tires wear if a car is out of alignment. *Funny* has no specific script relating to tire wear; the script that applies here simply indicates that *funny* means *in an atypical, unusual, or undesirable manner.* In light of the presupposition that the readers are not knowledgeable about cars (see section 4.1), *pretty* and *funny* are vague and/or ambiguous. The phrase *right for you* in (4.xxiv) and (4.xxx) and the word *comfortable* refer to specific features of a car, but appear without textual clues to clarify their meanings. Finally, in (4.xxxiii–xxxv), the writer uses *small, bigger,* and *larger,* words which rely upon shared world knowledge for their complete interpretation and which are therefore at least potentially ambiguous if the reader's perception of relative size differs from the writer's.

Semantics offers an insight into each of the examples of ambiguity cited above. In each case, the interpretation of the word or phrase depends on both world knowledge and linguistic knowledge. Script analysis explains why most readers understand (7.i) to mean (7.ii), for example, and also enables us to see the boundary between linguistic and world knowledge which explains why only some readers understand (7.iii) as an inference of (7.i). Scripts, as was pointed out in chapter 8, section 4.2, and chapter 10, section 3.3), contain only linguistic information. (7.ii) can be understood on the basis of the linguistic information contained in the script for the word *funny.* (7.iii), on the other hand, implies knowledge about the effects of misalignment on the tires of a car that goes beyond the linguistic information contained in the scripts for *funny* or *alignment.*

(7) (i) If the car is out of alignment, the tires have probably worn funny.
(ii) If the car is out of alignment, the tires have probably worn unusually.
(iii) If the car is out of alignment, the tires have probably lost tread unevenly.

4.5. Syntax

(4) contains few errors in syntax. Those few that appear fall into two categories, errors in punctuation and errors in consolidation. The punctuation errors, as we indicated in chapter 1, section 3.1, are print-code rather than

linguistic in origin and will thus be discussed in the following section. Sentences (4.x) and (4.xxii) illustrate two kinds of consolidation errors. In (4.x), the author attempts to consolidate two clauses, *if there are any signs of damage, abuse* and *if the car looks like it was well taken car of or not,* by using the coordinate conjunction *or* between them. However, because the author has not used a conjunction between *damage* and *abuse,* the second clause appears to be the third element in a series (of which *damage* and *abuse* are the first two elements). It thus appears that the author has attempted to consolidate a clause with two nouns rather than with another clause. The error can be made clear by uncombining the sentence from the first clause:

(8) (i) if there are any signs of damage,
(ii) if there are any signs of abuse, or
(iii) *if there are any signs of if the car looks like it was well taken care of or not

Syntactically, coordinating conjunctions signal the end of a list of coordinated words. Thus (8.i) and (8.ii) must be combined with a conjunction in order to indicate that *damage* and *abuse* comprise a list or series. The absence of the conjunction indicates that more than two items are being coordinated, and the coordinating conjunction *or* signals, falsely, that the following clause is the final element of the series. In (4.xii), the absence of the coordinating conjunction in the series *the lights, blinkers, windshield wipers* indicates that the author has not internalized this structure completely, even though elsewhere in the text he uses conjunctions properly in series, in (4.xi), (4.xiv), and (4.xvi), for example.

A similar consolidation error appears in (4.xxii). Here, although the author correctly uses a coordinating conjunction in the series *a spare, jack, and a lug wrench,* the missing article before the word *jack* affects the clarity of the sentence. The surrounding commas are print-code indications that *jack* is a separate item in the series, but the missing article creates ambiguity, allowing readers to question whether the first comma or the missing article is an error. Does the author mean *a spare jack and a lug wrench* or *a spare, a jack, and a lug wrench?* Even readers who infer that the latter is intended make the inference not because the meaning is clear in the sentence but because the punctuation cues and world knowledge (about the contents of automobile trunks) allow them to do so.

Consolidation errors occur when a writer fails in his attempt to pack information into concise, dense sentences. Interestingly, although the author of (4) commits these errors, he also ignores opportunities for making his sentences more brief. For example, (4.i), repeated below as (9.i), begins with a long introductory clause which establishes the topic for this paper. In the main clause of (4.i), the author must refer to this topic again, so he uses the pronouns *they* and *it* in order to avoid repeating what he has already written. His sentence could be more concise if he had chosen to announce his topic in the main clause, as (9.ii) illustrates.

(9) (i) When people go to buy a used car they usually do not spend as much time or put as much effort into it as they should.
(ii) People usually do not spend as much time or put as much effort into buying a used car as they should.

The decision to write (9.ii) instead of (9.i)—or to revise (9.i) into (9.ii)—is based not on linguistics, but on readability. However, as most writing teachers would acknowledge, it is easier to rewrite (9.i) than to explain why (9.ii) has the same meaning. Linguistics offers several ways to discuss the similarities of the two sentences. *Buying a used car* can be substituted for *it* since the latter is a pronoun which replaces the former semantically and syntactically (see chapter 13, section 2.1). The same is true for *people* in (9.ii) and *they* used as a subject in (9.i). The adverb *when* in (9.i) suggests a specific time at which people fail to make the appropriate expenditure of time and effort, but the concept of time is presupposed by the script of *buying a used car,* and does not need to be explicit. Thus it is possible to eliminate the introductory clause by replacing the pronouns with what they refer to without changing the meaning of the sentence. (9.ii) is not linguistically superior to or more correct than (9.i), but it certainly can be defended as more desirable since it adheres to Grice's fourth maxim, "Be succinct" (see (63.iv) in chapter 8). The same kind of analysis could be applied to (4.xvi) to explain why it could be revised to be the more concise (10.ii) rather than the original (10.i).

(10) (i) Look to see if anything shows signs of abuse or wear like the hoses, wires, or battery connections.
(ii) Look to see if the hoses, wires, or battery connections show signs of wear.

Though the use of the word *like* suggests that the three specific items are examples of what the prospective buyer should examine under the hood, it is inappropriate and inconsistent that they be treated as such. Given the naive audience this text seems to be addressing, details rather than examples would be most helpful. The author seems to realize this, since throughout the text his references to specific parts are meant to be inclusive rather than exemplary. Here it seems likely that his syntax does not convey what he intends and that (10.ii) is a more accurate as well as more concise revision.

4.6. Identifying and Correcting Errors

Most of the errors in (4) are **print-code errors,** errors that can occur only in writing (see chapter 1, sections 3.1–2). In (4) these errors are of two types: punctuation errors and spelling errors. The inconsistency of the punctuation of this text suggests that most of the errors occur because the author's performance does not match his competence rather than because he does not understand the usage rule or the underlying syntactic pattern that dictates what the punctuation should be. For example, the author does not use a comma after the introductory clause in (4.i), but in (4.xiii), (4.xix), (4.xxiv), (4.xxvii), (4.xxxi), and (4.xxxiii), he punctuates similar sentences correctly. Even in (4.iv), it is impossible to say that the punctuation error occurs because the author is not sure about the syntax. If other samples of the student's writing demonstrated that he could use the colon correctly to introduce formal lists, then it might be possible to claim that this error occurred because he did not recognize *the first things you should decide are* is not a complete clause. Discovering the source of errors such as these is important for the writing teacher. If an error can be attributed to more than one source, in this case either an imperfectly learned rule about using the colon or a failure to recognize a complete clause, then it becomes possible to know how to help the writer learn to avoid it. Because punctuation is a print-code feature loosely tied to syntax, one must understand syntax to punctuate correctly and consistently. But it is certainly possible to understand syntax, to recognize that the clause cited above is not complete, and commit a punctuation error. In such cases, the writer must learn a print-code rule, not a syntactic pattern. And in such cases, linguistics does not provide a means of understanding the error.

Two of the spelling errors in (4) are types discussed in chapter 11, section 2. In (4.xxvii), the author incorrectly doubles the *l* in *alignment*. This error emphasizes what we pointed out in chapter 11, that the language is less regular than the rules we develop to try to explain it, since if the author were to apply the hierarchy presented in (8) in chapter 11, he would find his spelling justified. The error in (4.xxxi), the use of *to* for *too* (*do not be *to quick to buy*), like the previous error, emphasizes the arbitrary nature of spelling, which serves print-code rather than linguistic purposes.

The other two spelling errors in this paper, involving compound words, illustrate the complex effects that spelling errors can have on meaning and the role that knowledge of linguistics can play in analyzing the effects of such errors. In (4.xiv) the author erroneously writes *water levels* as *waterlevels*. We can speculate that this error occurs because the writer is more conscious of syntax than of spelling. We have pointed out in section 4.5 that the author has difficulty with consolidations which should create parallel structure. In (4.xiv), the author has used two plural nouns, *oils* and *fluids,* as the first elements of his series. It is possible that he felt he must use another plural noun as the final element of the series, rejected *waters* as ungrammatical, and combined *water* and *levels* in an effort to be correct. Such errors occur when competence outstrips performance. Writers recognize a problem but are uncertain about how to correct it. In this case, the ambiguity of this sentence mentioned in section 4.1 occurs, first, because although water and oil are both fluids, they are treated as syntactic and semantic equivalents to *fluids,* and second, because the word *levels,* which should identify what the prospective buyer should examine when checking all of these fluids, no longer seems to refer to all three of them. If we identify in (11) the sentences consolidated to form (4.xiv), this ambiguity becomes clear.

(11) (i) Check the oil level.
(ii) Check the fluid level.
(iii) Check the water level.
(iv) Check the oil, fluid, and water levels.

Correctly combined, (11.i–iii) would produce (11.iv), which, though still potentially ambiguous semantically, is at least clearer than the original version (12.iv), which is apparently the product of a different series of combinations, (12.i–iii).

(12) (i) Check the oils.
(ii) Check the fluids.
(iii) Check the waterlevels.
(iv) Check the oils, fluids, and waterlevels.

Here, the misspelled *waterlevels* creates ambiguity since, as we mentioned above, we do not know what we are to check about the oils and other fluids. *Levels* is tied to the word *water* and thus cannot be modified by *oils* and *fluids* as well. The context in which (4.xiv) appears further complicates the matter since (4.xv) advises readers to *Also check to see if they have been changed recently or if they look pretty used.* This specific information about what to check for prevents (4.xiv) from meaning *Check the oils and fluids for excessive use and check the water level.* Despite the likelihood that the author intended his sentence to mean (11.iv), the misspelling creates syntactic and semantic ambiguity.

The misspelling of *overlooked* as *over looked* in (4.iii) indicates that the author is unaware of the difference in meaning between the word *over* used as an independent morph and the prefix *over-,* a morph used in conjunction with others to form compound words. The author uses *over looked* in a verb phrase (13.i), where syntactically it fills a slot occupied by either a verb (13.ii) or an adverb (13.iii). But when *over* is used as an adverb, it follows the verb it modifies (13.iv). What the author intends is (13.v), in which *over* means something like *beyond* and the compound word *overlooked* means *to look beyond so as not to notice* or *to ignore.*

(13) (i) that can be over looked
(ii) that can be avoided
(iii) that can be easily explained

(iv) turn over, do over, come over
(v) that can be overlooked

In speech, (4.xiv) would still be ambiguous since it is not clear how oil and water are to be distinguished from other fluids or what those other fluids might be. But the ambiguity would be different from the syntactic ambiguity caused by the spelling error. If (4.xiv) were spoken, the spelling-based ambiguity would not occur. Nor would (4.iii) be unclear in speech. Spelling errors, like other print-code errors, appear in, and thus can affect, only written language.

A final print-code error in (4) is the author's incorrect placement of the apostrophe in (4.vii). He writes *owner's names,* which could be interpreted as either an incorrect plural possessive form or an incorrect plural noun, but because plural pronouns are used consistently in the next sentence to refer to *owners,* it is clear that the correct construction would be *owners' names,* not *owner's name*. Thus syntax provides the clue for the correct form, even though linguistics cannot explain why the print-code distinction exists.

Only one kind of **non-print-code error** appears in (4). Twice, in (4.iii) and (4.xxii), the author commits subject-verb agreement errors when he begins clauses with the *there are* and *there is* constructions. In (4.iii), repeated here as (14), the error is especially complex, reflecting a shifting sensibility on the part of the speakers with regard to two constructions (see chapter 9, section 5, and chapter 10, section 1.2.1). The use of the plural verb is consistent with the increasing tendency of speakers to treat *a lot* as plural, whereas the standard dialect considers it singular. Apparently, native speakers see *a lot* as analogous in meaning and use to *many,* and this interpretation is reinforced by the fact that *a lot* is usually followed by a plural noun. In fact, the singular aspect of the phrase is often overlooked by many people who write *alot,* thus merging the singular article with the noun and obliterating the print-code signal for singularity. Those who perceive *a lot* to be plural or who are influenced by the plural object of the prepositional phrase will thus incorrectly use the plural *are*:

(14) There are a lot of aspects

The second agreement error (15.i) reflects a similar difference between common usage and the standard dialect. Here the singular verb is used before a plural series which is the grammatical subject of the sentence. Interestingly, in this case the singular article and the singular noun seem to have led the writer to use the singular verb, whereas the same construction in the phrase *a lot* was interpreted as plural. Apparently semantics is a more powerful influence for this writer than syntax since his interpretation of *a lot* as plural caused him to use a plural verb. In (15.i), the author fails to recognize the plural nature of a coordinate series and bases his verb choice on the number of the first—or perhaps of each individual—item. The logic of this error can be demonstrated by examining the underlying clauses (15.ii–iv) which are consolidated to form (15.i). In each clause, the correct verb is singular, and it requires a fair degree of linguistic sophistication to recognize that, first, the nouns are the grammatical subjects of the clauses, and second, that consolidating them creates a plural subject which necessitates a change to a plural verb.

(15) (i) there is a spare, jack, and a lug wrench
(ii) there is a spare
(iii) there is (a) jack
(iv) there is a lug wrench

These errors emphasize the shifting nature of language. Acceptable usage changes more quickly in speech than in writing, and clauses like (14) and (15.i) are unlikely to be identified as incorrect in the more fluid, often less formal give-and-take of speech, though they violate conventions of the more fixed written language.

SECTION 5. APPROACHES TO TEACHING

The preceding analysis is far more thorough than the writing teacher faced with anywhere between 20 and 60 or more papers every few weeks should be prepared or be expected to do. Even if time constraints did not make such analyses of every paper impossible, such a detailed analysis, especially if it led to equally detailed and extensive annotations on the student's text, would be counterproductive to effective teaching. Students rarely understand that some of the more abstract aspects of writing, such as establishing an attaining a goal and writing coherently, cohesively, and clearly, are at least as important as surface correctness. But if students receive papers that have been analyzed and annotated as thoroughly as (4) has been, they are likely, first, to be confused about the variety and extent of the comments, and, second, to be drawn to the surface errors as the most readily correctable problems of the text. A more reasonable strategy for the writing instructor is to make comments about the most serious flaws in the text and to encourage the writer to continue to revise with a specific goal in mind, whether it be to improve the coherence of the text by adding or deleting information or to correct grammatical errors in an otherwise focused, well-written paper. For writers with numerous problems, such an approach has several obvious advantages. They will be able to concentrate on a single problem at a time and will not waste time by correcting errors or changing diction in a passage that needs to be more thoroughly rewritten or, perhaps, deleted. They will, guided by their teacher's instructions for revision, become familiar with the hierarchy suggested in section 1. And they will, by being asked to revise their texts at least once and often more than once, understand that writing, which they generally assume to be difficult, is difficult precisely because it is complex. They will understand that writers address that complexity by rewriting rather than by resigning themselves to producing inadequate single-draft texts. Thus a writing teacher should resolve the question about how much to analyze and annotate according to a holistic analysis of the most significant problems in a given text.

Still remaining is the question of how linguistics can be applied to **composition instruction.** We must emphasize that linguistically informed composition instruction is not instruction in linguistics. Students need not be taught phonology to gain insight into some types of spelling problems or morphology and semantics to improve their diction. They do not have to learn theories about inference and presupposition in order to make informed decisions about their intended readers or about how much information to include in a text, nor do they need to understand transformations to learn syntactic options. The sentence-combining research and techniques discussed in chapter 12 illustrate that instruction can be **informed by linguistics** without being **instruction about linguistics.**

The major role of linguistics in the teaching of writing is to provide writing teachers with analytical tools for understanding how language works and why some texts fail. The writing teacher is, of course, an instinctive user of linguistic rules, as is any native speaker. However, without the linguistic knowledge that makes these rules explicit, the teacher either would have to rediscover the rules in order to explain errors to students or would have to rely on prescriptive rules from a handbook. In the latter case, the teacher risks becoming an uncritical supporter of convention, asserting rules (such as "Avoid clichés," or "Never use the passive") which are ignored frequently in good writing. Linguistics assures teachers of immediate and routine access to rules and thus facilitates their understanding of language problems.

Thus, linguistically informed writing teachers are able to perform the kind of analysis presented in the previous section and use it as a basis for instruction. An instructor informed about semantics, for example, would recognize that throughout his text the writer of (4) presupposes his readers possess knowledge that is inconsistent with what can be inferred about them from the opening paragraph. One way to help the writer revise or to instruct the class as a whole about such problems would be to discuss the need to analyze one's audience and to present the students with, or help them determine, appropriate, generalizable criteria for such an analysis. Often student writers, caught up in the artificial environment of the writing class, are unable to imagine a reader beyond the instructor. They can be helped to imitate this important activity of real (i.e., noninstructional) writing situations by being required to answer specific audience-oriented questions as part of their planning. For instance, students might be asked to identify several potential audiences for a particular text, to explain how the general characteristics—age, educational background, economic status, and so on—and more specific characteristics such as previous knowledge about or attitude toward the subject might influence what information the author should include and what information the author can assume his audience already has. This kind of audience analysis exercise teaches students to think about the relationship between reader and content from the outset of the writing process and emphasizes the potential difference between what the writer knows and what the reader knows. Writers, working alone or with other students, can then study drafts of their papers, checking to see that what they have written is appropriate for the specific audience they have selected to write for. Instructors can use student texts such as (4) as models of what can go wrong if writers do not consider whether the kind and amount of information they have included in their texts is consistent with what their readers know before they read the paper or will learn as they read it. The instructor's familiarity with linguistic concepts of inference and presupposition, with script-based semantics and with semantics in general, will allow him to point out specific words that are sources of ambiguity or inconsistency without teaching those linguistic concepts directly.

Similarly, semantics offers the writing instructor information about cohesion-creating strategies that can be taught to students without teaching them either the specific semantic features of the words that create cohesion in a text or the categories of cohesive ties presented in chapter 13, section 2. Most college students, even the least experienced writers, are familiar with the use of temporal conjunctions, or can be introduced to them easily through a discussion of discourses that instruct, like recipes and other kinds of directions. By having students analyze and write such familiar kinds of temporally cohesive texts, instructors can introduce the role that transitional words play in enabling readers to understand the connection between separate sentences in a text. Other conventional transitional devices (see chapter 13, section 2.3) can be taught and practiced as well, and students can be shown that pronouns, which they use intuitively, also connect sentences since they usually refer to words already used in the text. Thus the more familiar kinds of cohesive ties can be taught before those which are more subtle, specifically the ties we have identified as lexical (chapter 13, section 2.2). Here, too, instructors can build on students' intuitive knowledge of language by having them identify words in a passage, such as (16), which "go together" (i.e., which illustrate reiteration and collocation) as the basis for a discussion of how such semantically related words unify a text.

(16) *Fashionable* college students today *dress* differently from those of a few years ago. No longer are *blue jeans* and *T-shirts* the standard *uniform*. Although most students still *wear them* for some occasions, more students are opting for

greater variety in their *wardrobes*. For casual *wear,* students have added *corduroy and cotton slacks* as well as *jeans* made in a wider variety of *fabrics and colors* than the old favorite *blue denim. Knit and oxford-cloth shirts* are popular, too. Students have not abandoned their traditional *fashion* favorites, but they have begun to *wear clothes* that are a little *dressier.*

The italicized words in (16) make up the dominant series of cohesive ties in the paragraph, the other consisting of *students* and related words. Although students may not be conscious that such lexical ties as those referring to clothing and fashion in (16) contribute to the unity of texts, this kind of practice allows them to discover it, and does so without depending on formal instruction in semantics.

Semantics and morphology not only enable instructors to analyze diction in students' texts, but also suggest instructional strategies for enabling students to be more sensitive to the denotations and connotations of the words they use. As we pointed out in chapter 6, section 1, *prefix* and *suffix* are traditional names for those grammatical morphs which occur, respectively, before and after lexical morphs designating roots. The lists of prefixes and suffixes appearing along with their definitions in most writing handbooks are an example of a conventional application of morphology to writing instruction. When they study or refer to such lists, students are familiarizing themselves with the general meaning of various morphs, and that familiarity enables them both to choose prefixes or suffixes according to the meaning they wish to convey and to learn distinctions between similar words such as *uninterested* and *disinterested.*

The concept of **semantic features** (chapter 8, section 2.1) can also play a part in diction instruction. As an instructional concept for composition teachers rather than as a linguistic concept, feature analysis can be simplified so that students are asked to identify shared and different features among similar words in order to distinguish between them. The kind of description of features in (3) in chapter 8 is clear-cut enough for any student to recognize and can serve as the basis for introducing the concept of 'meaning' features. Students can then be asked to analyze and discuss how other pairs or groups of words can be considered different and alike. Such discussions, especially of words like *domicile, house,* and *home,* or *associate, acquaintance,* and *friend,* force students to formalize their intuitions about connotations and can be particularly helpful to students who believe that a polysyllabic word is always preferable to a simpler word if they are writing in an academic or professional setting.

This informal feature analysis cannot, of course, be limited to the discussion of words in isolation, for the decision to use *house* rather than *home* or *acquaintance* rather than *friend* depends on the appropriateness of a given word for the context in which it appears. Thus, while diction study may begin acontextually, discussions of context will quickly become part of classroom work on diction since (as was pointed out in chapter 8, sections 4.1 and 4.2) native speakers can and do interpret words and sentences in context, not in isolation. Students may need to be taught to look for ambiguity, impreciseness, or inappropriateness in their diction, but they can be taught to do so and to analyze sentences such as those in (17).

(17) (i) The shooting of the hunters was terrible.
(ii) If the car is out of alignment, the tires have probably worn funny.
(iii) My mother always told me to come straight to my domicile after school.

The sentence-combining exercises presented in chapter 12 and the 'de-combining' analyses in section 4.5 in this chapter illustrate how syntactic concepts developed in linguistics have been applied to and can influence writing instruction. The positive influence of combining exercises has been demonstrated in research referred to in chapter 12, section 1. By practicing sentence combining, students can expand their active repertoire of syntactic patterns and can thus choose from a greater variety of syntactic structures when they write. In addition, combining practice forces students to consider the syntactic relationship between parts of sentences as they make decisions about what to eliminate from the kernel-like sentences they combine. As a result, students learn to avoid errors in syntax because they are familiar with correct ways to say what they wish. While sentence combining provides practice writing correct sentences, sentence decombining offers instructors a way to talk about sentences that need to be revised, as (8), (11), and (12) in section 4.5 demonstrate. Here, the kind of analysis the instructor conducts can also be used for instruction since the instructor can ask students to perform the decombining and recombining as a classroom activity, or, alternatively, can provide students with the 'decombined' sentences as a combining exercise. In the latter case, students will not have the original version as an incorrect, but nevertheless influential, model before them.

While linguistics lies behind the pedagogical approaches to audience analysis, cohesion, diction, and syntax described in the preceding paragraphs, linguistics does not offer the writing instructor any particular strategies for teaching students to correct or avoid print-code and non-print-code errors. Though this may seem a surprising claim, it is consistent with linguistic concepts discussed throughout the previous chapters. Linguistics is a **descriptive** science; its general goal, pointed out in chapter 4, section 1, is the scientific study of language, and its particular goal is to study language as it is used by native speakers who are members of the same speech community. Linguistics does **not,** on the other hand, attempt to provide **prescriptive** rules for language use. Instead, all linguistics can do is suggest criteria (see (13.i–ii) in chapter 9) for assessing ongoing changes in language as a way to evaluate the permanence of a linguistic change. Both print-code and non-print-code errors are designated as errors because they deviate from prescribed conventions for using language. In the case of print-code features such as spelling and punctuation, the conventions are nonlinguistic to begin with, conventions of graphology, not of language. Although, as we have pointed out in chapter 11, section 2, linguistics allows us to analyze some kinds of print-code errors, linguistics cannot tell us why they are errors. Non-print-code or usage errors, on the other hand, do fall within the province of linguistics; that is, linguists can formulate rules for particular conventions, such as subject-verb agreement, which describe native speakers' perceptions of grammaticality and ungrammaticality. But those linguistic rules are certainly too complex to be taught to most writing students who have failed to learn the conventions either through exposure to the language or through traditional instruction.

While linguistics does not offer specific pedagogical strategies for teaching students to avoid or correct usage errors, **linguists' approach to language** may at least help the writing instructor address the issue. Because linguists (and here we are deliberately excluding interdisciplinary work in sociolinguistics, psycholinguistics, and other linguistic areas) study language as it is used, they ignore, in their work at least, the social, economic, and cultural ramifications of various dialects and languages when they describe how those languages are used. Instead, they develop rules for describing the regularities of the specific language or dialect they are studying and do not consider one dialect or language as superior to another. Writing teachers can certainly adopt this attitude toward language, viewing various dialects as following their own conventions, possessing their own grammaticality. Errors in usage then appear as signs of inconsistency between the writer's dialect or idiolect and the essentially fictional standard dialect (see chapter 1, section 3.3, and chapter 9, section 6). Instructors familiar enough with the conventions of dialects that differ significantly and consistently from Standard American English, which is the target dialect of most college writing courses, may be able to point out usage differences between the two dialects. Thus instruction would be comparative, building on the knowledge the student has of a particular dialect in much the same way that instruction in a foreign language can be based on the knowledge the student has of his or her native language.

Linguistics also offers writing instructors the knowledge that languages change over time and that changes in actual use occur faster than changes in convention. Of course, this fact does not mean that the writing instructor or the writing student can dismiss errors in convention as reflections of language change with which no one can or should interfere. But an understanding of language change can affect both teachers' and students' attitudes toward error since language change, like dialect difference, provides a linguistic explanation for the reasons native speakers do not always conform to the conventions of Standard American English, particularly when they write. And for many writing students, being able to understand the complexity of language is an important antidote to their own explanation of their difficulties with language—that they somehow are not smart enough to use their native language properly. Many students reach college having failed to learn, or apply, rules that seem to them to bear no connection to the language they speak. They have become discouraged by the errors they commit when they write not only because they commit them, but because most of the time no one has pointed out to them that the English they are expected to write differs, often systematically, from the English they speak. Writing instructors whose approach to error is based on their knowledge of these differences can do much to improve students' attitude toward error in particular and writing in general. Thus while linguistics may not offer the writing teacher specific pedagogical strategies for addressing particular errors, it does offer information about language that can help both instructor and student address errors realistically, as deviations from a particular widely accepted way of using the language to communicate in writing, rather than as indications of stupidity or inferiority. Writing teachers may not be able to avoid the notion that Standard American English is a prestige dialect, and perhaps they should not, but they should confront the fact head-on, encouraging students to learn to master it for their own benefit.

CHAPTER 15

Limitations of Linguistic Applications to Rhetoric and Composition

This chapter will develop some general ideas on linguistic applications introduced in the preface. More specifically, it will identify the inherent limitations of linguistics as a source field which make it impossible or at least inconvenient to use in some areas of rhetoric and composition. It will also bring together and reiterate some remarks to this effect made throughout the book. The new concept of a legitimate metaphorical extension, as opposed to a regular application, will be explored here briefly for the first time in the literature. And finally, those areas of composition to which linguistics cannot be fruitfully applied will be commented on.

SECTION 1. APPLIED LINGUISTIC THEORY

This section deals with rules of correct application of one field to another, in general, and then—more specifically—with rules of linguistic application. The format of current linguistic theory and the ways it determines the format and function of applied linguistic theory are discussed.

1.1. Rules of Linguistic Application

The preceding parts of the book dealing with linguistic applications to rhetoric and composition may and should be perceived as a contribution to and partial realization of an **applied linguistic theory for rhetoric and composition.** Underlaid by such a theory, this and other linguistic applications follow some basic rules, which are also true for meaningful applications of other fields to their adjacent areas of research (see also Raskin 1984, chapter 2; 1986a).

When one field of study (the **source field**) is applied to another (the **target field**), a strict division of labor should be maintained. To simplify the situation, for the sake of argument, each field can be described as consisting of data, theories, methods, and problems, as shown in (1). (For further discussion see Raskin 1986a; for a discussion of this model in composition research see Weiser in press-c).

(1)

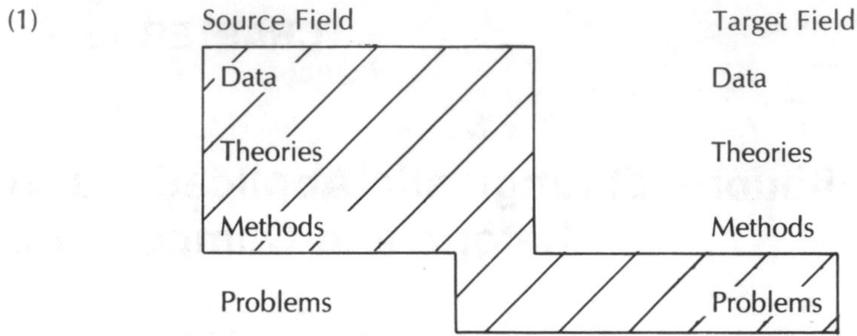

In a legitimate and meaningful application of the source field to the target field **the problems should come from the latter while the methods are supplied by the former.** The data and the theories may actually overlap but it is the source field that is primarily responsible for these as well. Any significant deviation from this normative situation of application represented schematically by the shaded area in (1) is likely to lead to largely irrelevant research.

1.2. Pseudoapplications

Thus, some two decades ago when the so-called mathematical linguistics came briefly into fashion, various statistical methods were applied to linguistic material. Statistics was then the source field and linguistics the target field. Statistics turned out to be rather easily applicable to linguistics since in most cases the linguistic entities constitute identifiable, discrete and countable objects, especially at such lower levels of linguistic structure as phonetics and morphology. The early applications led, for instance, to frequency tables of high reliability, generality, and validity, and there was nothing wrong with that. The only problem with many such applications was that there was no linguistic problem they were actually solving or, to put it differently, the statistical results could not be interpreted in a way that would yield any nontrivial conclusions about or insights into language. The fact that *the* tends to be the most frequent word in the English language, for instance, did not seem to signify much beyond itself, and in this and many similar cases, the statistical methods as applied to linguistic material at best corroborated what was well-known in linguistics anyway, and the heavy battery of statistics was usually redundant.

In this situation, the proud proprietor of a method was much more interested in applying it to some new material than the proprietor of the material was interested in having the method applied. On the other hand, when a linguist came up with a real problem and statistics proved to be useful in providing a (partial) answer to that problem, the result was valid research and a valid application to linguistics, that is, the problem of distance in semantic relations between words as researched statistically by Šajkevic (1963) or Garvin, Brewer, and Mathiot (1967).

Similarly, it would not really help poetics if the powerful apparatus of phonological theory were imposed on it and a detailed analysis of the phonemes making up a poem were made available, unless such an analysis addressed a valid issue in poetics itself or could be interpreted poetically in a nontrivial way. Thus, we do not perhaps want to know the distribution of all the distinctive phonological features in the quatrain if it does not contribute to our knowledge of rhyme or meter and does not help distinguish between good and bad poetry. On the other hand, if we ask ourselves what alliteration is and the answer comes phrased in terms of the recurrence of identical distinctive features of the phonemes in the line, then, again, it is a piece of useful research and an example of valid application in full accordance with the shaded area in (1).

The legitimate applications are, therefore, **problem-oriented**—they strive to solve a real problem of the target field using the available facts, techniques, and theories from the source field. The ill-advised applications are basically **method-oriented**—the interest is usually in extending the use of one's favorite method to some new material without much concern for the real need of the field to which this new material belongs. The result of a method-oriented application is not necessarily valueless—in fact, it can be quite interesting and informative as far as the method in question is concerned. However, it is highly unlikely to provide any fresh insights into the target field.

It follows then that if linguistics is to be applied to rhetoric and composition, that is, if **linguistics is the source field** and **rhetoric and composition is the target field,** then the problems, questions, and needs should come from rhetoric and composition as, indeed, has been the case throughout this book. What linguistics has to offer is a high-powered theory, complete with relevant concepts, fruitful ideas, and applicable methods. What linguistics cannot offer is what it does not have.

1.3. Format of Linguistic Theory

Modern linguistic theory was shaped by Chomsky in the mid-1960s (see Chomsky 1965). Given a set of primary linguistic data, linguistic theory must be able to perform the following tasks:

(2) (i) to provide complete and noncontradictory descriptions of the data and thus to distinguish any such description from a nondescription;
(ii) to provide a procedure and an evaluation measure for comparing two alternative descriptions of the data and for preferring one of them over the other;

(iii) to provide a procedure for the corroboration of the description by the native speaker.

(2.ii) and (2.iii) are closely connected with each other and with the crucial question of the **relation between a formal theory** and **the speaker's intuition.** Of the two competing descriptions, the theory is designed to prefer the one whose treatment of the data is more intuitively appealing to the speaker. The preferred description should assign a certain property to linguistic entities to which the speaker is intuitively sensitive and about which he is capable of passing judgments.

The cornerstone of Chomsky's linguistic theory was the property of **grammaticality** (see chapter 7, sections 1 and 4). His linguistic theory determined linguistic descriptions which assigned to each sentence one of the two values of the binary feature 'grammaticality,' namely 'grammatical' or 'ungrammatical.'

In practice, it meant that if his transformational grammar could generate a sentence by applying a certain sequence of rules to the initial symbol S, the sentence was grammatical. If the grammar barred a string of words from generation, that string was a non-sentence or an ungrammatical sentence. Thus, only (3.i) can be generated by a transformational grammar, while (3.ii–v) cannot:

(3) (i) I am reading a book
(ii) *I are reading a book
(iii) *A are book I reading
(iv) *I am read a book
(v) *I am reading book

Independently, the native speaker should be asked to rate the sentences in (3) in terms of whether they are "all right," "correct," "possible," and so on (obviously, an unsophisticated speaker cannot be asked whether the sentence is grammatical since the concept will be unfamiliar to him, and any explanation of the notion prior to his exposure to the sentences will "contaminate" his intuition). If the native speaker considers (3.i) grammatical and (3.ii–v) ungrammatical, his responses will coincide exactly with the output of the transformational grammar and, by virtue of this, will corroborate the grammar. If the native speaker's responses never deviate from the output of the transformational grammar, that is, if every sentence the grammar can generate is considered grammatical by the native speaker, and vice versa, and every sentence the grammar cannot generate is considered ungrammatical by the native speaker, and vice versa, then the grammar is a fully corroborated linguistic description. If we simplify and streamline Chomsky's own terminology, such a grammar is then a descriptively and explanatorily adequate linguistic description.

In other words, linguistic theory is designed to determine a formal object, usually a set of rules, which is applied to certain linguistic entities purely mechanically, according to a well-defined formal procedure. This formal object, treated as the most preferred description of the linguistic entities, assigns a certain feature to each of them. At the same time, the native speaker is asked to assign the same feature to the same entities on the basis of his linguistic intuition. If the same values of the feature are assigned by the description and by the speaker to each individual entity, the description can be said to simulate the speaker's intuition in one important respect, the one related to the feature in question.

Thus, in the case of the examples in (3), linguistic theory prefers a certain transformational grammar, which is a sequence of rules, as the linguistic description of English sentences. The grammar assigns to each English sentence the feature of grammaticality; in particular, it will characterize (3.i) as grammatical and (3.ii–v) as ungrammatical. Since the native speaker will pass the same judgments with regard to (3.i–v), the **grammar** is a good **model** of the native speaker's linguistic **competence** with regard to **grammaticality.** Thus, in (4), the theory should prefer Description 2 over Descriptions 1 and 3 since Description 2, as shown, is the only one that assigns to the data a feature matching the one assigned to the same data intuitively by the native speaker.

(4)

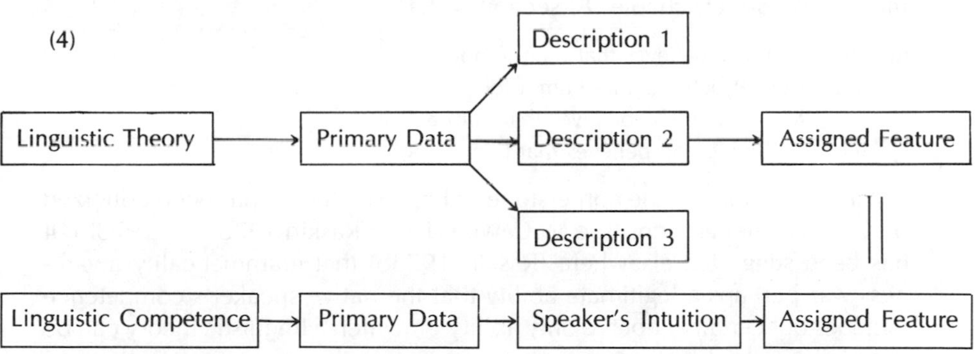

Good linguistic theory should be justified. It should be psychologically real to the speaker and not arbitrary in this sense; in principle, a descriptively adequate description of the primary data can be completely foreign and intuitively unappealing to the speaker. Naturally, the theory that describes the mental mechanisms underlying the native speaker's linguistic competence more adequately is preferable. However, these mental mechanisms are not accessible to direct observation and investigation, and our notion of them is based only on indirect and remote consequences of their functioning. The native speaker's ability to pass judgment as to the grammaticality or ungrammaticality of a sentence is one such remote consequence of the work of the mental mechanisms underlying language. In other words, the feature assigned to the linguistic entities by both the native speaker (intuitively) and the grammar (formally) constitutes the only basis of justification for the linguistic theory in question (cf. Raskin 1979b). Chomsky postulated grammaticality as such a basis and ignored completely all the other abilities provided by competence.

It is reasonable to suppose, however, that the ability to pass judgment as to the grammaticality or ungrammaticality of a sentence is not the only and perhaps not the most easily accessible component of linguistic competence. Chomsky himself had to expand the notion of grammaticality by including meaningfulness in it in his revised version of transformational grammar (1965), which no longer treated (5.i–iii) as grammatical:

(5) (i) *Colorless green ideas sleep furiously.
(ii) *Caesar is a prime number.
(iii) *The boy may frighten sincerity.
(iv) Sincerity may frighten the boy.

Lakoff (1971b) further complicated the matter by adding pragmatic considerations to the notion of grammaticality. According to him, the grammaticality of the sentences in (6) can be determined only on the basis of individual beliefs, assumptions, prejudices, and so on; in other words, if *you* believe that a frying pan is capable of believing, then (6.iv) is grammatical to *you* (cf. chapter 8, section 5.2.1).

(6) (i) My uncle believes that I am a fool.
(ii) ?My cat believes that I am a fool.
(iii) ?My pet amoeba believes that I am a fool.
(iv) ?My frying pan believes that I am a fool.

Grammaticality as the cornerstone of linguistic theory has been criticized on various other grounds (see McCawley 1976; Raskin 1976–77, 1978b). It has been suggested elsewhere (Raskin 1978b) that grammaticality awareness was perhaps a legitimate ability that the native speaker's competence includes but certainly not the only ability on which a linguistic theory can be based, listing truth-values awareness, presupposition awareness, coherency awareness, context awareness, and appropriateness awareness as examples of other abilities included in linguistic competence.

It is the existence of these other features about which the native speaker can intuitively pass judgment which provides a firm conceptual basis for meaningful linguistic applications and for applied linguistic theory.

1.4. Principles of Linguistic Application

If what linguistics can do is model formally an aspect of native competence, then the question of whether linguistics is applicable to an adjacent area can be answered by the flow chart in (7):

(7) (i) Is there an aspect of linguistic competence which is essential for the target area? If yes, go to (ii); otherwise, go to (v).
(ii) Is there an issue in the target area for which this aspect of linguistic competence is essential? If yes, go to (iii); otherwise, go to (v).
(iii) Will the modeling of this aspect of linguistic competence with linguistic methods yield an insight into that issue of the target area? If yes, go to (iv); otherwise, go to (v).
(iv) Linguistics is applicable to the target area. Go to (vi).
(v) Linguistics is not applicable to the target area. Go to (vi).
(vi) Stop.

In other words, linguistics is applicable to a target area if there is a property that correlates with a certain formal linguistic property or set of properties. Thus, in humor research, it has been established that the funniness of the text correlates with two contextually semantic properties of the text, whose presence can be formally discovered in the process of the regular semantic analysis of text (Raskin 1984). Linguistics always analyzes text and, therefore, still another way to formulate **the basic principle of a meaningful and correct linguistic application is that linguistics must be able to come up with the necessary and sufficient conditions for a text to possess a property, and whether a certain text possesses this property or not should be an essential issue in the target area.**

1.5. Function of Applied Linguistic Theory

The mechanism for bringing about a correct and meaningful application of linguistics to a certain target area on this principled basis should be provided by a special applied theory of linguistics for the target area in question. Such a theory brings together the linguistic expertise and the real issues of the target area and projects the knowledge about language that linguistics has onto the framework of the target area. In simpler terms, the function of an applied theory is to repair the frustrating universal situation in which the expert in a target area does not know enough linguistics to apply it correctly and meaningfully and the linguist does not know enough about the target area to be able to do anything for it on his own. The applied theory distills the language information the target area needs and sifts out the information that is of concern only to linguistics itself.

1.5.1. Fragment of an applied linguistic theory: an illustration. A fragment from the applied linguistic theory for natural language processing (NLP) will be used as an illustration. NLP deals with the development of computerized systems of text understanding for such purposes as machine translation, information retrieval, automatic abstracting, and so on. No further knowledge of NLP will be needed to appreciate the example. The simple connection with rhetoric and composition will be made right after the discussion of the example.

As an example of the relations between a fragment of linguistic theory and its projection onto applied linguistic theory, Postal's (1971) classic and sophisticated treatment of the English verb *remind* will be compared with what NLP is likely to need to know about it. Focusing on just one meaning of the verb as used in (8.i) and deliberately excluding the meaning in (8.ii) from consideration, Postal comes up with a number of sharp even if at times controversial observations about the verb, briefly summarized in (9). He then proceeds to propose a transformational treatment for the sentences containing the verb in the likeness meaning, again briefly summarized in (10). The sentences triggering and/or resulting from the transformational process are listed in (11).

(8) (i) Harry reminds me of Fred Astaire.
(ii) Lucille reminded me of a party I was supposed to attend.

(9) (i) The verb *remind* must be used with exactly 3 NPs in one particular syntactic structure, namely, NP_1 Verb NP_2 of NP_3.
(ii) *remind* differs syntactically from the other very few English verbs that can be used in this structure.
(iii) *remind* is unique in that no two of its three NPs can be coreferential.
(iv) sentences with *remind* in the likeness meaning are typically paraphrased as, for (8.i), (11.i).

(10) (i) The standard transformational generative processes are assumed to have generated a structure like that of (11.i).
(ii) A transformation called the 'psych movement' interchanges the subject and object of the higher sentence in the structure, yielding a structure like (11.ii).
(iii) A transformation called the 'remind formation' changes (11.ii) into (8.i).

(11) (i) I perceive that Harry is like Fred Astaire.
(ii) *Harry strike me like Fred Astaire.

(12) Harry is like Fred Astaire.

Typically for the best transformational work and very elegantly, the choice of transformations is determined primarily by the unique feature of *remind* (9.iii). It is demonstrated that each of the three non-coreferences involved is not unique and is, in fact, derived from one of the transformations applied to generate (8.i). One non-coreference follows from presenting the sentence as a two-clause structure with (12) as the lower clause, with similarly non-coreferential NPs. Another follows from the psych formation, motivated independently on other English material. And the last and most problematic non-coreference is shown to follow from the remind formation, which is, of course, postulated specially for the task and thus not independently motivated as a whole but, in its components, related to various other independently motivated rules.

The point of the description is that the verb *remind* is derived transformationally and therefore does not exist as a surface verb. That was supposed to prove that the claims of interpretive semantics concerning deep structure and lexical insertion were false (cf. chapter 8, section 3).

NLP will ignore both the theoretical point of the previous paragraph and the entire contents of the one before it. What NLP, or the applied theory catering to it, should extract from the entire description and discussion can be briefly summarized as (13).

(13) (i) *remind* has (at least) two distinct meanings illustrated in (8).
(ii) = (9i)
(iii) = (9iv), elaborated as (iv)
(iv) NP_1 reminds NP_2 of NP_3 = NP_2 perceive(s) that NP_1 is (are) like NP_3 = it strikes NP_2 that NP_1 is (are) like NP_3

The difference between what linguistics wants to know about the English verb *remind* and what NLP must know about it has a deep theoretical foundation. Linguistics and NLP have different goals, some of which are presented schematically—and necessarily simplistically—on the chart in (14).

(14)

Linguistics Wants:	NLP Needs:
(i) to know all there is to know about the complex structure mediating the pairings of sounds (spellings) and meanings in natural language	to use the shortest and most reliable way from the spellings to the meanings in the text(s) being processed
(ii) to structure linguistic meaning and relate it to context	to understand the text and make all the necessary inferences
(iii) to distinguish the various levels of linguistic structure, each with its own elements and relations	to use all the linguistic information needed for processing the text(s) without any concern for its source
(iv) to draw a boundary between linguistic and encyclopedic information to delimit the extent of linguistic competence and, therefore, the limits of the discipline	to use encyclopedic information on par with linguistic information, if necessary for processing the text(s)
(v) to present its findings formally, preferably as a set of rules in an axiomatic theory	to implement the available information in a practically accessible and convenient way.

Rhetoric and composition will have somewhat different needs but they will not need anything listed in the left column of (14) either (see section 2).

1.6. Format of Applied Linguistic Theory

While applied linguistic theory should be expected to "inherit" some of the formal properties of the parent linguistic theory, there will be a number of significant differences, all of them along the lines of adjustments to the specific target areas. The differences will include terminological compromises, the highlighting of different areas within linguistic theory which may be of more interest to one target area than to another, the degree of formalism, and so on. Most significant, however, applied linguistic theory will deviate from linguistic theory in its attitude to alternative approaches to language description.

Chomsky's thoughts on the relations between linguistic theory and linguistic description have not been in the center of linguistic concerns for the last two decades, nor have they been followed up by Chomsky himself. The unfortunate results of this neglect include the proliferation of proposals, which are dubbed theories but are in fact descriptions-cum-theories. As theories, such proposals suffer from the fact that they are also descriptions because they do not typically evaluate or even compare the theory to the alternatives on any theoretical or, in such a case, metatheoretical basis. As descriptions, they suffer because they are also theories, and this means that they are not specific or complete enough.

The theoretical inadequacy of much of contemporary linguistics may stem from what seems to be an erroneous concept of linguistic theory as it was described above. While very few linguists have given it much thought (and *Language,* the central journal of the Linguistic Society of America, has adopted a policy which unambiguously excludes work on linguistic theory from its pages unless theory comes on top of a particular description of a particular language—in other words, unless it is a description-cum-theory), they have apparently adopted Chomsky's view that there can be only one theory. As a result, much of linguistics has been dominated by heated debates about whose theory is better while, in fact, many different proposals are either notational variants of each other or perfectly viable alternatives. An alternative view of **theory as the exhaustive list of alternatives,** complete with the issues on which the alternatives differ and the consequences of each choice, is highly defensible from the point of view of the philosophy of science and—more important for us here—simply indispensable for applications. It appears then that linguistic theory as well will have to reconceptualize itself in terms of a calculus of choices, and the development of this format for applied linguistic theory is what will prompt this change.

SECTION 2. APPLIED LINGUISTIC THEORY FOR RHETORIC AND COMPOSITION

2.1. Applicability of Linguistics to Rhetoric and Composition

It is usually assumed that linguistics is automatically applicable to writing because linguistics deals with language and writing is in language as well. While the conclusion is correct, the reasoning is faulty. All human activity is conducted in natural language but that does not mean that linguistics is applicable to all forms of that activity. Moreover, linguistics is often delimited as the study of competence as opposed to performance (see chapter 4, section 1), and it can certainly be argued that writing is performance. But then again, is not performance a manifestation of competence? And can we not talk about writing competence? It is, and we can, but from that alone it does not follow at all that linguistics is applicable to rhetoric and composition.

The applicability of linguistics to rhetoric and composition can be established only by applying (7) as the criterion. Is there a basic issue of rhetoric and composition that linguistics can model? What is the basic issue of writing? Is it how to compose a well-written text? Formulated this way, it is not treatable by linguistics because, once again, linguistics analyzes text—it is, as it were, a post-text discipline. It can, therefore, relate to the question: Is a given text well-written? In other words, if a set of linguistic properties can be found, such that whenever a text is well-written it possesses these properties, and vice versa (see (15)), then linguistics is eminently applicable to rhetoric and composition.

(15)

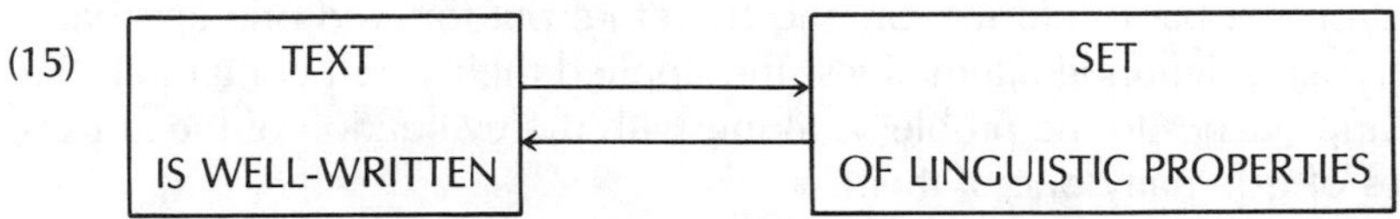

If (15) were indeed the case, not only would linguistics be applicable to rhetoric and composition but it would practically subsume it, and this is most clearly not the case. In other words, (15) is not accurate. What is it then that linguistics can do for writing? As is clear by now, what it can do very well is primarily to identify certain kinds of problems in the text. If a text is ridden with those language-use-related problems that fall within the realm of linguistics, it cannot be well-written. If, for the sake of convenience, we will loosely dub the linguistically treatable problems 'language-use problems,' then the basic issue in rhetoric and composition that linguistics can speak to is a subquestion of the one in (15), namely: Is the text free of language-use problems (16)?

(16)

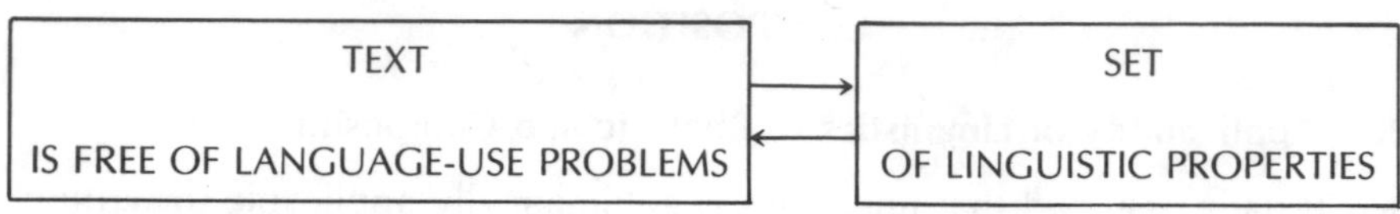

In practical terms, as this book has illustrated, one typically deals with a certain kind of language-use problem, such as misspellings, diction, fragments, and so on, and identifies subsets of linguistic properties that correlate with those kinds. **A rigorous linguistic application to rhetoric and composition is then the process of discovering the necessary and sufficient conditions for a certain trait of the well-written text to be present in a given text.**

2.2. Contents of Applied Linguistic Theory for Rhetoric and Composition

An applied linguistic theory for rhetoric and composition will go over the same material as chapters 4–9. One significant difference is that it will deemphasize—to the point of dropping—all those areas of linguistics that are not relevant to writing. Thus, very little of phonetics and just some basic elements of phonology will be part of the applied theory. There will be more morphology, still more syntax, and the whole structure will be enormously "top-heavy" because it is semantics and pragmatics that will matter the most. The applied theory should also be expected to be almost exclusively synchronical rather than historical.

The other significant difference is that, unlike chapters 4–9, which focused on the basic information and therefore put forward one approach for everything, ignoring alternatives, the applied theory will contain all the viable approaches to the problems along with the evaluation of the consequences of using any one of them.

The applied theory has to do systematically and completely what has been done sketchily and selectively in this book, namely to project all the parts of linguistics that are relevant to rhetoric and composition onto a level which is comprehensible and accessible to the experts in that area. What this involves is weeding out the elements speaking to exclusively linguistic concerns, such as the ones in the left part of (14), getting rid of the formalism unusable in rhetoric and composition, adapting, simplifying, and taking shortcuts whenever and wherever possible, while maintaining the same rigorous standards of adequacy which do, or should, characterize 'pure' linguistic theory. All of this adaptation is prompted not by condescension to those not "initiated" into linguistic wisdom but rather by the desire to cultivate and optimize the use of bona fide linguistic information within the field.

2.3. Pseudoapplications of Linguistics to Rhetoric and Composition

Unless such an applied linguistic theory is made available to the researchers and practitioners of rhetoric and composition, the currently experienced malaise with regard to linguistics will continue to exist in one of the four forms (17):

(17) (i) Linguistics is ignored where it should not be.
(ii) Lip service is paid to linguistics, typically by using a few linguistic or purportedly linguistic terms in vague and undefined meanings.
(iii) The whole study is presented as a linguistic application and made dependent on a misperceived and/or misrepresented linguistic concept, method, or approach.
(iv) A linguistic method is made to work on a typical rhetoric and composition corpus without gaining any insight into writing.

(17.i) is probably still the prevalent form of the malaise, its common-cold form. (17.ii) can be likened to a light skin rash and is generally of no consequence unless it is untreated, in which case it might lead to (17.iii). The latter, along with (17.iv), is quite serious because both create an illusion of an application without getting any significant results and at the same time creating the totally misleading role model for others interested in a genuine linguistic application. (17.ii–iii) may, however, be legitimate metaphorical extensions (see section 3).

SECTION 3. INHERENT LIMITATIONS OF LINGUISTIC APPLICATIONS TO RHETORIC AND COMPOSITION

The limitations of linguistic applications to the study of writing are of two basic kinds, those stemming from the nature of linguistics as a discipline and, therefore, affecting its application to any target area, including rhetoric and composition, and those caused by the extralinguistic dimensions in rhetoric and composition.

3.1. Limitations of Linguistic Applications in General

There are two basic limitations which pertain to all linguistic applications because of the nature of the discipline.

3.1.1. Linguistics needs text. As mentioned in the preceding section, linguistics analyzes text. It must, therefore, have a text before it is activated. It is not usable directly then for studying the composing process because it will have nothing to say before the very first draft is already composed. Linguistics can, however, contribute to the composing process less directly by discovering and commenting on the various problems with the text.

3.1.2. Linguistics does not evaluate. Modern linguistic theory is descriptive rather than prescriptive. In fact, unbeknownst to the general public, linguistics has shied away from any form of prescription for a few generations. It can be argued that it has been wrong of it to do so (cf. chapter 9, section 5), but it is a fact. As a result, linguistics is unable, if unextended, to examine two well-formed texts, such as (18.i–ii), and to rate one of them (18.ii) as written better than the other.

(18) (i) At this point in time, I would consider it timely to begin the consideration of the issue immediately at hand before us in terms of its relevance to our current problem.
(ii) I think we should discuss now whether this issue is relevant to our problem.

What this means is that linguistics is not applicable to various tasks involving quality judgments, such as (15). They can, however, be usually reduced in scope and freed from explicit evaluation along the lines of (16).

3.2. Extralinguistic Dimensions of Rhetoric and Composition

One difference between (15) and (16) is represented schematically in (19):

(19)
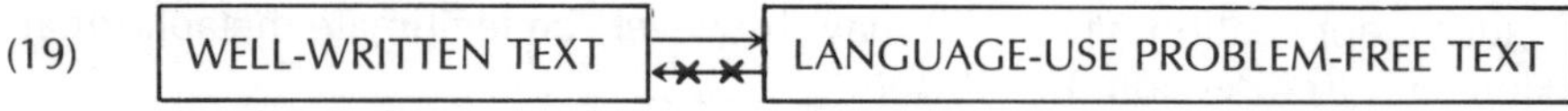

In other words, any well-written text should be free of those problems linguistics can detect and help correct, but a text which is merely free of those problems is not necessarily a well-written text. The other dimensions of well-writtenness include the parameters listed in (20):

(20) (i) appropriateness for the audience (length, complexity, scripts, etc.)
(ii) good and correct style
(iii) appropriateness for the purpose (persuasion, advertising, etc.)
(iv) conformity to the cultural rhetorical conventions
(v) conformity to format-related conventions

Many if not all of the factors in (20) are arbitrary from a linguistic point of view. In other words, a text may not satisfy some or any of them and still be a linguistically well-formed text. Linguistics can still be used to deal with those dimensions by way of a legitimate metaphorical extension.

3.3. Legitimate Metaphorical Extensions

A metaphorical extension occurs when the source area is taken beyond its legitimate boundaries. The term has been used primarily pejoratively since Chomsky's (1959) crushing critique of Skinner's behaviorist psychology. In his review article, Chomsky argued extremely convincingly that such terms as 'reflex' or 'reinforcement,' which are well-defined and used technically about rat behavior in tightly controlled experiments, lose their precise nature when extended to human behavior and are used loosely and largely without meaning. They are illegitimate metaphorical extensions.

It is claimed here, for the first time ever to our knowledge, that some metaphorical extensions are legitimate and even inevitable. To be good, a metaphorical extension should be tightly controlled as to its conformity to the following conditions (21).

(21) (i) A case should be made for the use of the term or concept beyond its legitimate domain in terms of potential insights into the target area, unachievable otherwise.

(ii) The extended concept or method should be reinterpreted and redefined for the source area and it should not be assumed that all of its parameters and dimensions in the source area automatically hold for the target area.

It can be demonstrated that many uses of such popular linguistic terms as 'meaning,' 'connotation,' 'deep structure,' or 'speech act,' do not qualify as legitimate metaphorical extensions in the sense defined above, and the more technical the term is in the source area, the more suspect it is when extended.

There are, obviously, concentric circles of metaphorical extensions, with some right outside the rigorous applications and others in the more remote periphery. The farther from the inner circle, the more the function of the metaphorical extension is limited to thought stimulation in the direction of emulating some things linguistics does rather than actually applying or even extending linguistics.

A careful exploration of legitimate metaphorical extensions—theoretically and practically—is of vital importance both to linguistics and to adjacent areas. Linguistics can broaden significantly the scope of its correct and fruitful applications. The adjacent areas can use the prescribed and "guaranteed" extensions of linguistics to gain insights into their subject matter. As this book demonstrates, rhetoric and composition would profit directly from legitimate and realistic metaphorical extensions by widening its areas of linguistic applicability well beyond those for which rigorous applications are available.

SECTION 4. NONLINGUISTIC CONCERNS IN RHETORIC AND COMPOSITION

In the previous section, (20), we have listed dimensions of **well-writtenness** which are arbitrary from a linguistic perspective. Each of the parameters listed in (20) can be detected in texts, but none, with the possible exception of that part of (20.ii) that concerns a **correct style,** is necessarily concerned with whether or not a **text is linguistically well-formed.** In this section, we will discuss concerns of rhetoric and composition which cannot be so easily detected in texts but which are, and have traditionally been, important considerations for speakers and writers.

4.1. Nonlinguistic Rhetorical Choices

As we suggested in chapter 14, sections 1–2, writers must make a number of nonlinguistic choices (identified here in (21)) before they actually begin to create their texts.

(21) (i) What to write about
(ii) Whom to write for
(iii) What to say
(iv) How to say it

Given the intricate and overlapping relationship of writer, reader, subject, and language in any communicative situation, it is impossible in practice to separate the choices writers make concerning (21.i–iv). What one chooses to write about influences and is influenced by whom one chooses to write for, what one chooses to say, and how one chooses to say it. Here, however, for explanatory purposes, we shall discuss each category separately.

4.1.1. What to write about. Obviously, a writer must have a **subject** about which to write. In some cases, when scholars write a book, for example, the subject is one the writers have chosen, perhaps from a number of interesting potential subjects they may have considered. Which subject they ultimately choose, the reasons for their choosing it, and the decisions they make about the scope of their discussion are vital. They are also entirely nonlinguistic. Indeed, such choices are greatly influenced by the writer's encyclopedic knowledge. Writers may choose a subject because they have knowledge of it, or because it is a subject about which little is known (and therefore they can contribute to knowledge generally), or because it is a subject about which they wish to know more.

In the case of writers who are totally free to select their own subject and in the case of writers who are provided with a subject about which they must write (students, people in business who write reports, letters, and so on), what the writer writes about is determined by his sense of exigency, that is, a sense that a particular subject is inherently worthy of writing about or must be written about because of external demands for information. For the scholars, this exigency may grow from, as suggested above, the writer's perception that he can make a contribution to knowledge or can address a pressing problem in his field. For the person engaged in business, the exigency may be the need to negotiate an agreement or make a contact. In both situations, other exigencies may be at play—the desire for promotion, recognition, increased remuneration, and so forth. In any case, the subject of a discourse, whether it is chosen exclusively by the writer or dictated to him by other people or by a specific situation or need, is not a linguistic matter.

4.1.2. Whom to write for. As was pointed out in chapter 14, section 2.2, the analysis of the characteristics of an audience requires writers to consider both the linguistic and encyclopedic knowledge of their potential readers. But the choice of an audience is not based on its members' linguistic knowledge. Instead, the audience may be determined by (and may help determine) the subject and purpose a writer has selected. Walzer (1985) demonstrates the fluid relationship among audience, purpose, and subject by analyzing the introductions of three articles by the same writers. The three articles describe results of the same research, but differ in purpose and focus according to the journals in which they appear. Interestingly, although one journal is popular, two are scholarly and, as Walzer points out, are likely to be read by the same people. While Walzer demonstrates that the authors' choice of audience (i.e., of journal) has textual ramifications, the initial choice of whom to write for cannot be attributed to linguistic considerations.

4.1.3. What to say. Once a writer decides what to write about, he must make decisions about the specific purpose, argument, and content of the discourse. We have suggested that the writer's purpose or exigency influences the choice of subject and audience. Purpose also influences (and once again is influenced by) the specific approach to a subject. The text about buying a used car in chapter 14 was intended to inform the prospective used-car buyer. Assuming the author had in mind the subject "used cars" or "buying a used car" when he started his project, he might, instead of writing to inform his readers about how to buy a used car, have chosen to inform them of the advantages and/or disadvantages of buying a used car. He might also have chosen to persuade rather than to inform—to persuade his readers to buy a particular kind of used car. Or he might have chosen to entertain his readers with an amusing story about his experiences with a particularly troublesome used car—or used-car salesman. Such decisions about purpose guide the writer's later linguistic choices, but the determination of purpose is not itself a linguistic matter.

Corbett (1971:36) asserts that "how to 'discover' something to say on some given topic . . . is the crucial problem for most students." The discovery of an argument or thesis and the appropriate content to develop that argument—what classical rhetoric calls *inventio* 'invention'—has become a central interest for many modern rhetoricians. They have developed formal and informal strategies for stimulating the discovery or elicitation of ideas and information, ranging from free-form association techniques such as brainstorming and free-writing to highly structured heuristics such as Kenneth Burke's dramatistic Pentad and the tagmemic matrix developed by Young, Becker, and Pike (1970). What these strategies share is the goal of helping the writer explore a topic in order to discover what he might choose to say about it—to discover as much about the topic as possible. This discovery of possible content must be followed by decisions concerning how to limit what one has discovered to what is appropriate and pertinent to one's audience and purpose. Traditionally, composition texts have spoken of selecting a thesis, a point one wishes to make about a topic. Recently, the notion of thesis has been enlarged to include the concepts of purpose and audience, so that the thesis a writer might hold in his mind (though not include in his text) would enable him to consider subject, purpose, audience, and point. Such a thesis for the used-car paper discussed in chapter 14 might be articulated as (22):

(22) This text is designed to inform people who do not know how to make a sound decision about buying a particular used car about how to check a car for specific defects and problems.

(23) identifies the four features of this thesis:

(23)		
	subject	buying a used car
	purpose	to inform
	audience	people who do not know how to make a sound decision about buying a particular used car
	topic	how to check a car for specific defects and problems

The only apparent application of a linguistic theory to the discovery of content is the tagmemic matrix mentioned earlier. This matrix is based on a metaphorical extension of the slot-and-filler grammar developed by Pike, and is not based on linguistic methods as much as it is on more general concepts of the theory. Thus it seems fair to say that the discovery of content and the development of a thesis are nonlinguistic rhetorical concerns.

4.1.4. How to say it. The writer who has decided what to write about, whom to write for, and what to say must still decide how to appeal to his readers, how to support his thesis, and how to structure his text. Rhetoricians since Aristotle have recognized the utility of his concepts of the **rational, emotional,** and **ethical** appeals and have extended them beyond their original application to persuasive discourse. Writers and speakers appeal to both the intellect and the emotions of their audiences, and they try, through their discourse, to establish themselves as speakers and writers who are worthy of the respect and consideration of those who hear or read their words. Of course, the effectiveness of these appeals depends on the writer's or speaker's linguistic skills, but the appeals themselves, though realized through language, are not linguistic entities and the writer's use of the appeals is governed by nonlinguistic decisions.

The same can be said of the selection and ordering of support. Once a writer has decided that the best way to support a point or to present information is through description or comparison or classification, he can draw on language that is appropriate for that particular strategy. But the decision to choose a particular strategy or combination of strategies for presenting information to readers is determined by the writer's knowledge of discourse conventions, of the particular audience, of the purpose of the text, and so on. A writer wishing to promote a particular point of view may choose to contrast it with another point of view that is either obviously less attractive or that the writer can demonstrate to be less attractive. A writer wishing to make a sophisticated, unfamiliar, or unusual point to an unsophisticated or uninformed audience may choose to tell a story that illustrates that point rather than present the point abstractly. Both rhetoric and composition are interested in the variety of methods of development and their role in communication, their appropriate use in particular rhetorical situations, the possibilities for using several methods complementarily in a single text, and so on. As was pointed out in chapter 3, section 2, Kinneavy (1971) emphasizes the subordinate role of these methods of development to purpose or aim. Writers make their decisions about how to develop their arguments by considering how they can best achieve their rhetorical goal.

A final issue related to *how to say it* is one we have discussed previously (see chapter 13, section 3, and chapter 14, section 2.4): the structure of the text. Obviously, a writer's choice of a particular method of development offers structural guidelines. Narrations are usually structured chronologically, as are descriptions of processes. Physical descriptions generally follow a particular spatial pattern—near to far, far to near, right to left, and so on. Though a writer may use linguistic cues in the text to guide the reader, the chronological, spatial, logical, or analytical structure is not itself dictated by linguistic rules.

In summary, linguistic applications are likely to be legitimate and useful to those areas of rhetoric and composition that involve the assessment of texts as free of language-use problems as we have defined them in chapters 1–3. Just as **linguistics does not prescribe well-writtenness** (see section 3.1.2), it cannot provide writers with prescriptions for making choices about the subject, purpose, audience, or structure of a text. Once writers make these choices and produce texts, linguistic applications of the kind we have presented in chapters 10–14 can help them assess whether **the language of the text contributes to or hinders its communicative goal.**

[illegible] worthy of [illegible] respect and consideration of those [illegible] word[illegible]. Of course, the effectiveness of these appeals depends on the writer's [illegible] skills, but the appeals themselves, although [illegible] through language, are not linguistic entities [illegible] governed by [illegible].

[illegible] the location and ordering of [illegible] within a text [illegible] composition classes [illegible] language [illegible] the decision to choose a particular strategy [illegible] for presenting information [illegible] is determined by the writer's knowledge of discourse conventions, of the particular audience, of the purpose of the text, and so on. A writer wishing to promote a particular point of view may choose to contrast it with another point of view that is either obviously less attractive or that the writer can demonstrate to be less attractive. A writer wishing to [illegible] to an [illegible] may choose to tell a story that illustrates that point [illegible] the [illegible] interested in the variety of methods of development and their role in communication [illegible] of the textual situations. It is possible [illegible] particularly in a single text, and [illegible] development to [illegible] develop their argument by considering how they can best achieve their rhetorical goal.

A third issue related to how [illegible] is one we have discussed previously [illegible] Chapter 3, and [illegible], section 4.4, the structure of the text. Obviously, a writer's choice of a particular method of development [illegible] structural [illegible]; narrations are usually organized chronologically [illegible] processes [illegible] generally [illegible] to [illegible] the [illegible].

[illegible] are [illegible] in these [illegible] and [illegible] to those [illegible] and composition that [illegible] role of language [illegible] as we have [illegible] them [illegible] does not [illegible] writers [illegible] with [illegible] choices [illegible] the subject, purpose, audience [illegible] of a text [illegible] writers [illegible] presenting [illegible] can [illegible] assess whether the language of the text contributes to achieving its communicative goal.

References

The Ann Arbor Case 1979. Washington, DC: Center for Applied Linguistics.

Austin, John L. 1962. *How to Do Things with Words*. New York: Oxford University Press.

Axelrod, Rise B., and Charles R. Cooper 1985. *The St. Martin's Guide to Writing*. New York: St. Martin's Press.

Bamberg, Betty 1983. "What Makes a Text Coherent?" *College Composition and Communication* 34:4, pp. 417–29.

Bar-Hillel, Yehoshua 1954. "Indexical Expressions," *Mind* 63, pp. 359–79.

Bateman, D. R., and F. J. Zidonis 1964. *The Effect of a Knowledge of Generative Grammar upon the Growth of Language Complexity*. Columbus: The Ohio State University. U.S. Office of Education Cooperative Research Project 1746.

Becker, Alton 1965. "A Tagmemic Approach to Paragraph Analysis," *College Composition and Communication* 16:4, pp. 237–42.

Braddock, Richard, et. al. 1963. *Research in Written Composition*. Urbana, IL: NCTE.

Britton, James 1970. "Talking and Writing." In: E. Evertts (ed.), *Explorations in Children's Writing*. Champaign, IL: NCTE, pp. 21–32.

Britton, James, et al. 1975. *The Development of Writing Abilities (11–18)*. School Council Research Series. London: Macmillan Education.

Chomsky, Noam 1957. *Syntactic Structures*. The Hague: Mouton.

Chomsky, Noam 1959. "Review of Skinner (1957)," *Language* 35:1, pp. 26–58.

Chomsky, Noam 1965. *Aspects of the Theory of Syntax*. Cambridge, MA: MIT Press.

Chomsky, Noam 1971. "Deep Structure, Surface Structure, and Semantic Interpretation." In: Steinberg and Jakobovits, pp. 183–216.

Christensen, Francis 1963. "A Generative Rhetoric of the Sentence," *College Composition and Communication* 14:3, pp. 155–61.

Christensen, Francis 1965. "A Generative Rhetoric of the Paragraph," *College Composition and Communication* 16:3, pp. 144–56.

Clark, Herbert H., and Eve V. Clark 1977. *Psychology and Language*. New York: Harcourt Brace Jovanovich.

Cole, Peter, and Jerry L. Morgan 1975. *Syntax and Semantics*, Vol. 3. *Speech Acts*. New York: Academic Press.

Corbett, Edward P. J. 1971. *Classical Rhetoric for the Modern Student*, 2nd. ed. New York: Oxford University Press.

Corbett, Edward P. J. 1976. "Approaches to the Study of Style." In: Gary Tate (ed.), *Teaching Composition: 10 Bibliographical Essays*. Fort Worth, TX: Texas Christian University Press, pp. 73–109.

D'Angelo, Frank J. 1975. *A Conceptual Theory of Rhetoric*. Cambridge, MA: Winthrop.

D'Angelo, Frank J. 1976. "Modes of Discourse." In: Gary Tate (ed.), *Teaching Composition: 10 Bibliographical Essays*. Fort Worth, TX: Texas Christian University Press, pp. 111–35.

D'Angelo, Frank J. 1985. *Process and Thought in Composition*. 3rd. ed. Boston: Little, Brown.

Emig, Janet 1977. "Writing as a Mode of Learning," *College Composition and Communication* 28:2, pp. 122–28.

Enkvist, Nils Erik 1964. "On Defining Style." In: John Spencer (ed.), *Linguistics and Style*. New York: Oxford University Press, pp. 3–56.

Epes, Mary 1985. "Tracing Errors to Their Sources: A Study of the Encoding Process of Adult Basic Writers," *Journal of Basic Writing* 4:1, pp. 4–33.

Fahnestock, Jeanne 1983. "Semantic and Lexical Coherence," *College Composition and Communication* 34:4, pp. 400–16.

Firth, John R. 1957. "Modes of Meaning." In his: *Papers in Linguistics 1934–51*. New York: Oxford University Press, pp. 190–215.

Flynn, James, and Joseph Glaser 1984. *Writer's Handbook*. New York: Macmillan.

Garvin, Paul L., J. Brewer, and M. Mathiot 1967. "Predication-Typing: A Pilot Study in Semantic Analysis," *Language* 43:2, Supplement, Pt. 2.

Giannasi, Jenefer M. 1976. "Dialects and Composition." In: Gary Tate (ed.), *Teaching Composition: 10 Bibliographical Essays*. Fort Worth, TX: Texas Christian University Press, pp. 275–304.

Gordon, David, and George Lakoff 1975. "Conversational Postulates." In: Cole and Morgan, pp. 83–106.

Green, Georgia M., and Jerry L. Morgan 1981. "Pragmatics, Grammar, and Discourse." In: P. Cole (ed.), *Radical Pragmatics*. New York: Academic Press, pp. 167–181.

Grice, H. Paul 1957. "Meaning," *Philosophical Review* 66, pp. 377–88.

Grice, H. Paul 1975. "Logic and Conversation." In: Cole and Morgan, pp. 41–58.

Halliday, M. A. K., and Ruqaiya Hasan 1976. *Cohesion in English*. London: Longman.

Hartwell, Patrick 1980. "Dialect Interference in Writing: A Critical View," *Research in the Teaching of English* 14:2, pp. 101–18.

Hartwell, Patrick 1985. "A Brief Reply to Daniel Hibbs Morrow," *Research in the Teaching of English* 19:2, pp. 181–82.

Haugen, Einar 1966. "Linguistics and Language Planning." In: W. Bright (ed.), *Sociolinguistics*. The Hague: Mouton, pp. 50–71.

Hirsch, E. D., Jr. 1977. *The Philosophy of Composition*. Chicago: University of Chicago Press.

Hunt, Kellogg W. 1965. *Grammatical Structures Written at Three Grade Levels*. Urbana, IL: NCTE.

Jakobson, Roman 1960. "Linguistics and Poetics." In: Thomas A. Sebeok (ed.), *Style in Language*. Cambridge, MA: MIT Press, pp. 350–77.

Kantor, Kenneth J., and Donald L. Rubin 1981. "Between Speaking and Writing: Processes of Differentiation." In: Barry M. Kroll and Roberta J. Vann (eds.),

Exploring Speaking-Writing Relationships: Connections and Contrasts. Urbana, IL: NCTE, pp. 55–81.

Katz, Jerrold J. 1971. "Generative Semantics Is Interpretive Semantics," *Linguistic Inquiry* 2, pp. 313–331.

Katz, Jerrold J., and Jerry A. Fodor 1963. "The Structure of a Semantic Theory," *Language* 39:1, pp. 170–210.

Kinneavy, James L. 1971. *A Theory of Discourse*. Englewood Cliffs, NJ: Prentice-Hall.

Kittredge, Richard, and John Lehrberger (eds.) 1982. *Sublanguage: Studies of Language in Restricted Semantic Domains*. Berlin: de Gruyter.

Kroll, Barry M. 1981. "Developmental Relationships Between Speaking and Writing." In: Barry M. Kroll and Roberta J. Vann (eds.), *Exploring Speaking-Writing Relationships: Connections and Contrasts*. Urbana, IL: NCTE, pp. 32–54.

Kuno, Susumo (ed.) 1975. *Harvard Studies in Syntax and Semantics*, Vol. 1. Cambridge, MA: Harvard University Press.

Kuno, Susumo, and E. Kaburaki 1975. "Empathy and Syntax," in: Kuno.

Lakoff, George 1971a. "On Generative Semantics." In: Steinberg and Jakobovits, pp. 232–96.

Lakoff, George 1971b. "Presupposition and Relative Well-Formedness." In: Steinberg and Jakobovits, pp. 329–40.

Lakoff, George 1972. "Linguistics and Natural Logic." In: Donald Davidson and Gilbert Harman (eds.), *Semantics of Natural Language*. Dordrecht: D. Reidel, pp. 545–665.

Lanham, Richard A. 1979. *Revising Prose*. New York: Scribner's.

Larson, Richard 1967. "Sentences in Action: A Technique for Analyzing Paragraphs," *College Composition and Communication* 18:1, pp. 16–22.

Lindemann, Erika 1982. *A Rhetoric for Writing Teachers*. New York: Oxford University Press.

Malinowski, Bronislaw (1923). "The Problem of Meaning in Primitive Languages." In: C. K. Ogden and I. A. Richards, *The Meaning of Meaning*. London: Kegan, Paul, Trench, Trubner, Appendix.

Mathesius, Vilem 1947. "O tak zvaném aktuálním clenení vetném" [On the So-called Functional Sentence Perspective]. In his *Cestina a obecný jazykopyt*. Prague, pp. 234–42.

McCawley, James D. 1972. "A Program for Logic." In Donald Davidson and Gilbert Harman (eds.), *Semantics of Natural Language*. Dordrecht: D. Reidel, pp. 498–544.

McCawley, James D. 1976. "Some Ideas Not to Live By," *Die Neuren Sprachen* 75, pp. 151–65.

Meckel, H. C. 1963. "Research on Teaching Composition and Literature. In N. L. Gage (ed.), *Handbook of Research on Teaching*. Chicago: Rand-McNally, pp. 966–1006.

Mellon, John C. 1969. *Transformational Sentence-Combining*. Urbana, IL: NCTE.

Moffett, James 1968. *Teaching the Universe of Discourse*. Boston: Houghton Mifflin.

Morrow, Daniel Hibbs 1985. "Dialect Interference in Writing: Another Critical View," *Research in the Teaching of Writing* 19:2, pp. 154–80.

O'Hare, Frank 1973. *Sentence-Combining: Improving Student Writing Without Formal Grammar Instruction*. Urbana, IL: NCTE.

Phelps, Louise Wetherbee 1985. "Dialectics of Coherence: Toward an Integrative Theory," *College English* 47:1, pp. 12–29.

Postal, Paul M. 1971. "On the Surface Verb 'Remind.'" In: Charles J. Fillmore and D. Terence Langendoen (eds.), *Studies in Linguistic Semantics*. New York: Holt, Rinehart, & Winston, pp. 181–270.

Prince, Ellen F. 1981. "Towards a Taxonomy of Given-New Information." In: Peter Cole (ed.), *Radical Pragmatics*. New York: Academic Press, pp. 223–55.

Quine, Willard V. O. 1960. *Word and Object*. Cambridge, MA: MIT Press.

Raskin, Victor 1968. "O semantičeskoj rekursii" [On Semantic Recursion]. In Vladimir A. Zvegincev (ed.), *Semantičeskie i fonologičeskie problemy prikladnoj lingvistiki*. Moscow: Moscow University Press, pp. 268–83.

Raskin, Victor 1971. *K teorii jazykovyx podsistem [Towards a Theory of Linguistic Subsystems]*. Moscow: Moscow University Press.

Raskin, Victor 1974. "A Restricted Sublanguage Approach to High Quality Translation," *American Journal of Computational Linguistics* 11:3, Microfiche 9.

Raskin, Victor 1976–77. "Dikdukiyut ve arakhey emet" [Grammaticality and Truth Values], *Iyun* 27, pp. 26–37.

Raskin, Victor 1977. "Literal Meaning and Speech Acts," *Theoretical Linguistics* 4:3, pp. 209–25.

Raskin, Victor 1978a. "Presuppositional Analysis of Russian, I: Six Essays on Aspects of Presupposition." In: Victor Raskin and Dmitry Segal (eds.), *Slavica Hierosolymitana*, Vol. 2. Jerusalem: Magness, pp. 51–92.

Raskin, Victor 1978b. "Problems of Justification in Semantic Theory." In: Wolfgang U. Dressler and W. Meid (eds.), *Proceedings of the 12th International Congress of Linguists*. Innsbruck: Institut für Sprachwissenschaft der Universität Innsbruck, pp. 224–26.

Raskin, Victor 1979a. "Is There Anything Non-Circumstantial?" In: Avishai Margalit (ed.), *Meaning and Use*. Dordrecht: D. Reidel, pp. 116–22.

Raskin, Victor 1979b. "Theory and Practice of Justification in Linguistics." In: P. R. Clyne et al. (eds.), *The Elements: A Parasession on Linguistic Units and Levels*. Chicago: Chicago Linguistic Society, pp. 152–62.

Raskin, Victor 1981. "Script-Based Lexicon," *Quaderni di semantica* 2:1, pp. 25:34.

Raskin, Victor 1984. *Semantic Mechanisms of Humor*. Dordrecht: Reidel.

Raskin, Victor 1985a. "Linguistic and Encyclopedic Knowledge in Text Processing," *Quaderni di semantica* 6:1, pp. 92–102.

Raskin, Victor 1985b. "Once Again on Linguistic and Encyclopedic Knowledge in Text Processing," *Quaderni di semantica* 6:2, pp. 377–83.

Raskin, Victor 1985c. "Script-Based Semantics: A Brief Outline," *Quaderni di semantica* 6:2, pp. 306–13.

Raskin, Victor 1986a. "On Possible Applications of Script-Based Semantics." In: Peter C. Bjarkman and Victor Raskin (eds.), *The Real-World Linguist: Linguistic Applications in the 1980s*. Norwood, NJ: Ablex, pp. 19–45.

Raskin Victor 1986b. "Script-Based Semantics." In: Donald G. Ellis and William A.

Donohue (eds.), *Contemporary Issues in Language and Discourse Processes.* Hillsdale, NJ: Erlbaum, pp. 3–61.

Reichman, Rachel 1985. *Getting Computers to Talk Like You and Me.* Cambridge, MA: MIT Press.

Reinhart, Tanya 1975. "Point of View in Sentences with Parentheticals." In: Kuno.

Riffaterre, Michael 1959. "Criteria for Style Analysis," *Word* 15:1, pp. 154–74.

Riffaterre, Michael 1960. "Stylistic Context," *Word* 16:2, pp. 207–16.

Šajkevic, Anatolij J. 1963. "Raspredelenie slov v tekste i vydelenie semantičeskix polej" [Word Distribution in Text and Distinguishing Semantic Fields in Language], *Inostrannye jazyki v škole* 2.

Schafer, John C. 1981. "The Linguistic Analysis of Spoken and Written Texts." In: Barry M. Kroll and Roberta J. Vann (eds.), *Exploring Speaking-Writing Relationships: Processes of Differentiation.* Urbana, IL: NCTE, pp. 1–31.

Searle, John R. 1969. *Speech Acts.* Cambridge, England: Cambridge University Press.

Searle, John R. 1975. "Indirect Speech Acts." In: Cole and Morgan, pp. 59–82.

Shaughnessy, Mina P. 1977. *Errors and Expectations.* New York: Oxford University Press.

Smitherman, Geneva 1975. *Black Language and Culture: Sounds of Soul.* New York: Harper & Row.

Steinberg, Danny D., and Leon A. Jakobovits (eds.) 1971. *Semantics: An Interdisciplinary Reader in Philosophy, Linguistics, and Psychology.* Cambridge, England: Cambridge University Press.

Tucker, Allen, Sergei Nirenburg, and Victor Raskin 1985. "Discourse, Cohesion and Semantics of Expository Text." In: Sergei Nirenburg and Allen Tucker (eds.), *The TRANSLATOR Project.* Hamilton, NY: Colgate University.

van Dijk, Teun A. 1972. *Some Aspects of Text Grammars.* The Hague: Mouton.

van Dijk, Teun A. 1977. *Text and Context: Explorations in the Semantics and Pragmatics of Discourse.* London: Longmans.

Vendryès, Joseph 1923. *Le Langage.* Paris: Albin Michel.

Walzer, Arthur E. 1985. "Articles from the 'California Divorce Project': A Case Study of the Concept of Audience," *College Composition and Communication* 36:2, pp. 150–59.

Weiser, Irwin 1979. "Sentence Combining for Diction and Detail Improvement," *Freshman English Resource Notes* 4:3, pp. 8–9, 12.

Weiser, I. (in press-a). "Better Writing Through Rhetorically Based Assignments," *Journal of Teaching Writing.*

Weiser, I. (in press-b). "The Communication Triangle, Rhetoric, and Writing Assignments," *The Writing Instructor.*

Weiser, Irwin (in press-c). "The Relationship Between Theory and Pedagogy," *College Composition and Communication.*

Williams, Joseph M. 1985. *Style: Ten Lessons in Clarity and Grace,* 2nd. ed. Glenview, IL: Scott, Foresman.

Winterowd, W. Ross 1970. "The Grammar of Coherence," *College English* 31:2, pp. 828–35.

Winterowd, W. Ross 1975. *Contemporary Rhetoric: A Conceptual Background with Readings.* New York: Harcourt Brace Jovanovich.

Winterowd, W. Ross 1985. "Response to Gary Sloan," *College Composition and Communication* 36:1, pp. 100–3.

Witte, Stephen P., and Lester Faigley 1981. "Coherence, Cohesion, and Writing Quality," *College Composition and Communication* 32:2, pp. 189–204.

Witte, Stephen P. 1983. "Topical Structure and Revision: An Exploratory Study," *College Composition and Communication* 34:3, pp. 313–41.

Woodman, Leonora, and Thomas P. Adler 1985. *The Writer's Choices*. Glenview, IL: Scott, Foresman.

Young, Richard, and Alton Becker 1965. "Toward a Modern Theory of Rhetoric: A Tagmemic Contribution," *Harvard Educational Review* 35:4, pp. 450–68.

Young, Richard E., Alton Becker, and Kenneth Pike 1970. *Rhetoric: Discovery and Change*. New York: Harcourt Brace Jovanovich.

Author Index

Subject Index

D

E

F

G

R

S

T

U

V

W